SIMI and Indian Mujahideen
Terror Approach

SIMI AND INDIAN MUJAHIDEEN

TERROR APPROACH

Brig. (Retd.) S. P. Lohia

NEHA PUBLISHERS & DISTRIBUTORS
DELHI

Publisher
NEHA PUBLISHERS & DISTRIBUTORS
4832/24,Prahlad Lane,S-207 Ansari
Road, Daryaganj, Delhi-110002
Ph.: 43570976, 23278261
Email: nehapubdistributors@gmail.com

Edition: 2015

ISBN: 978-93-80318-64-6

Laser Typesetting
JEE-VEE Graphics, Delhi

Price: 1195/-

Printed
Vikas Computers, Delhi

Preface

Established in 1977 and banned by the Government of India in 2001, the SIMI's vision of Islam derives from the voluminous writings of the Islamist ideologue, Sayyed Abul 'Ala Maududi, founder of the Jama'at-i Islami. For Maududi, as for the SIMI, the mission of the Prophet Muhammad is seen principally as having been the struggle to establish true monotheism or tauhid. This is taken to mean not just the worship of the one God but also, and equally importantly, the rule of the one God. Political power, in other words, is seen as central to the Islamic mission. All man-made systems of law are condemned as 'false', even Satanic, and Muslims are reminded that unless they actively struggle to be ruled in accordance with the shari'ah their commitment to and faith in Islam is not complete and remains suspect.

Although members of SIMI embraced militancy and began merging into what is now IM, IM as an organization did not appear formally until much later. In November 2007, IM claimed responsibility for several simultaneous blasts targeting lawyers in court premises in three cities in Uttar Pradesh (Varanasi, Ayodhya, and Lucknow). IM explained that these attacks were "Islamic raids," precipitated by the purported refusal of the lawyers to take on the cases of accused terrorists. In the wake of these attacks, Indian agencies increased pressure on the organization. At least six senior IM members reportedly fled to Pakistan, including Shahbandri.

SIMI was banned in September 2001, under the Unlawful Activities (Prevention) Act of 1967, due to alleged working relations with al Qaeda, the Taliban, and other Islamist terrorist groups. SIMI has unsuccessfully challenged the ban in the Supreme Court to seek its revocation.

This book maintains that the source of the terror that we condemn is definitely not from a divine religion, and that there is no room for terrorism.

—Editor

Contents

1

SIMI and the Indian Mujahideen

Given the potential biases in such reporting, some of the most extreme allegations about Pakistan merit further inquiry through other means. One of the most problematic issues inherent in such a study is that many—if not most—of the terrorism attacks that have taken place across India have been attributed by Indian media and official organizations as the work of Lashkar-e-Taiba (LeT).

This may be driven in part by a reluctance of Indian officials to recognize that India has a problem with domestic terrorism as well as by a political agenda to assert that India's internal security problem is due to Pakistan. Though it is possible that some of these attacks involved SIMI/IM operating in conjunction with LeT or supported by LeT (or other Pakistan-based organizations), it is difficult to discern the role of the IM or SIMI in these attacks due to the nature of the open-source reporting of these assaults.

Despite the importance of Islamist militant groups in India and the potentially volatile environment in which they operate, very little has been written about SIMI or IM, apart from journalistic accounts that often fail to provide adequate context or background for the various reports.

As such, there is a significant paucity of reliable and comprehensive information that can be obtained through open-source accounts of these organizations. This dearth of information renders it difficult to make assessments on such issues of interest as the potential impact of the recent terrorist events in India on the support base that SIMI/IM enjoys or the evidentiary bases of the various claims made about these groups and their ties to other militant or international organizations.

THE SIMI STORY

The identity of those behind the bomb blasts that shook Mumbai recently remains unclear. Some claim Hindutva terrorists were responsible, while others suspect the Pakistan-based terrorist outfit Lashkar-i Tayyeba or the banned Students Islamic Movement of India (SIM) or a combination of both. In the meanwhile, scores of suspected SIMI activists have been detained by the police.

Whether or not the SIMI was behind the blasts will be known only after a fair and impartial investigation. Yet, the fact remains that groups like the SIMI, although representing a tiny fringe of the varied landscape of Islam in India, do pose a grave threat not only to the country as a whole but, equally, to the Indian Muslims as well.

In a sense a response to growing Hindu fascism and deadly anti-Muslim pogroms, SIMI-style radical Islamism helps feed Hindutva forces, leading to further communal polarization, with all the consequences that this has for the country's welfare and that of the Muslims themslves, already a beleaguered and marginalized minority. In the wake of the Mumbai blasts and the allegations of SIMI involvement, many Indian Muslims are now wakening up to the need to denounce not just Hindutva chauvinism but similar Muslim groups, such as the SIMI, as well that speak the language of conflict, hatred, violence and revenge.

Established in 1977 and banned by the Government of India in 2001, the SIMI's vision of Islam derives from the voluminous writings of the Islamist ideologue, Sayyed Abul 'Ala Maududi, founder of the Jama'at-i Islami. For Maududi, as for the SIMI, the mission of the Prophet Muhammad is seen principally as having been the struggle to establish true monotheism or tauhid. This is taken to mean not just the worship of the one God but also, and equally importantly, the rule of the one God. Political power, in other words, is seen as central to the Islamic mission. All man-made systems of law are condemned as 'false', even Satanic, and Muslims are reminded that unless they actively struggle to be ruled in accordance with the shari'ah their commitment to and faith in Islam is not complete and remains suspect. Struggling to establish the Islamic state, the Caliphate or khilafah seen as a duty binding on all Muslims, and one that the Muslims of India, despite being in a minority, must abide by. Muslims who are 'comfortable living under an un-Islamic order' are warned that they shall be consigned, rather uncharitably, to Hell.

In the absence of the khilafah, the SIMI believes that Muslims cannot lead their lives fully in accordance with Islam. The khilafah is seen as a divinely ordained order and also as the only solution to the many problems of not just the Muslims alone but of all humankind.

It is envisaged as a pan-Islamic polity, for all Muslims are said to belong to the same nation (qaum, millat). Islam, in the SIMI's interpretation, does not recognize any national differences, and all Muslims are brothers to each other. Hence, they must be ruled by a single khalifa. Nationalism is seen as a false 'idol', and one devised by the non-Muslim 'enemies of the faith' to divide the Muslims and thereby weaken them. National, as well as racial, regional, linguistic and sectarian identities are seen as a sign of 'ignorance' (jahiliya), which is vehemently opposed to Islam, and represent major hurdles in the path of establishing the rule of a single khalifa over all Muslims.

In line with the general Islamist understanding, the SIMI sees Islam as a 'complete programme', providing detailed instructions on all matters, from the most intimately personal to collective affairs such as the state and international relations.

Thus, secularism, even in the form of state neutrality vis-a-vis religion or the separation of religion and state, is seen as inherently anti-Islamic, for to choose not to be ruled by God's laws is a sign of rebelliousness against Him. Likewise, democracy is also condemned, for to be ruled by man-made laws instead of the shari'ah is tantamount to the unforgivable sin of shirk or associating partners with God.

All ideologies and religions other than Islam are condemned as false and sinful (taghuti) and their adherents as 'rebels against God'. All non-Muslims are branded together as kafirs, and no distinction is made among them. Muslims are exhorted to give up the ways of the 'unbelievers' and to inculcate an unrelenting hostility to 'un-Islamic' culture and to fully abide by the path of the Prophet. Because the 'enemies of God' are expected to show stiff resistance to Islam, violent Jihad is to be waged, if need be, against those who put hurdles in the path of the struggle for establishing the khilafah. Islam thus comes to be seen as a militaristic political programme.

This understanding of Islam and the SIMI's methods of realizing its vision of the Islamic polity make no room for the particular context in which the SIMI operates, where Muslims are a relatively small and insecure minority. It is as if to contextualize the faith and that demands that it makes upon the faithful would be tantamount to cowardice, hypocrisy or deviation from Islam or even amount to apostasy.

The fact that to actively and openly struggle for the establishment of an Islamic polity in the Indian context would certainly invite stiff opposition from other communities is recognized, but the trials and tribulations that this would mean for Muslims are, it is insisted, to be welcomed as a true test of their faith and commitment and to have always been the lot of the true believers, from the Prophet's time onwards.

As Shahid Badr Falahi, President of the SIMI, once put it, 'The Qur'an itself says that the kafirs will naturally oppose the Muslims. If through any of our actions the kafirs are agitated this itself is a proof that what we are doing is right [.] We have deliberately adopted the policy of the Prophet in this regard. If this drives the enemies of Islam to anger we cannot help it'. An unflagging commitment to a combative and extreme understanding of the faith is thus seen as a sign of faithfulness to the Prophet, and for activists of the SIMI this is indeed a major source of the movement's appeal, faced as they are with a sense of being completely besieged.

The SIMI was floated by the Jama'at-i Islami Hind in the late 1970s. Although it was intended to work among Muslim students to create among them what it saw as 'Islamic consciousness' and to engage in peaceful missionary work among non-Muslim students, a succession of events occurred immediately after the founding of the organization that forced it to take an increasingly hard-line position.

The young SIMI activists seem to have relished controversy and sensationalism, seeing it as an opportunity to present their vision of Islam as the ideal 'solution'.

Being free of the control of the more moderate and experienced older leaders of the Jama'at, whom they saw as effete and too moderate, the young leaders of the SIMI drifted in the direction of a growing radicalism. In 1979, less than two years after the SIMI was established, the Soviet Union invaded Afghanistan, Ayatollah Khomeini toppled the Shah of Iran and in Pakistan, the military dictator Zia ul-Haq set about imposing Islamic criminal laws by force. The

SIMI voiced its opposition to the Soviet invasion, welcomed the Iranian revolution, seeing it as the first step in the eventual global revival of Islam, and wholeheartedly supported Zia's 'Islamization' policy. Gradually, as a result of events abroad and the consciousness of Muslims being an increasingly threatened community in India, the SIMI's rhetoric grew combative and vitriolic, insisting that Islam alone was the 'solution' to the problems of not just the Muslims of India but of all Indians as such and, indeed, of the whole world.

This growing radicalization of the SIMI was not looked upon favourably by top leaders of the Jama'at, who had been working to present a moderate image of their organization, seeking to dialogue with people of other faiths and to promote democracy and secularism in the face of the rapid growth of militantly anti-Muslim Hindu organizations.

Jama'at leaders demanded that the SIMI work under the Jama'at's over-all command, but the SIMI refused. Accordingly, in 1982, the SIMI separated from the Jama'at, which then revived its own students' wing, the Students Islamic Organisation. Yet, both the Jama'at as well as the SIMI continued to share a commitment to a common vision, as developed by Maududi, differing only on the question of the precise tactics and strategy needed in the Indian context to bring Maududi's vision to fruition.

Following its separation from the Jama'at, the SIMI expanded considerably, setting up branches in various parts of India. It published several periodicals in different languages and formed its own publishing company to propagate its message of 'Islamic Revolution'. By 2000, the SIMI had some 400 full-time workers or Ansars and 20,000 sypmathizers or Ikhwans, in addition to a cell for young children aged between 7 and 11, called the Shahin Force. It also established a special wing to work among madrasa students and 'ulama, the Tahrik Tulaba-i 'Arabia. Most of its activists and members belonged to lower-middle and middle-class families living in towns and cities.

It appealed to a class of Muslim students that saw themselves as, in some sense, deprived, for whom its message of the 'superiority' of Islam over the 'decadent' and 'immoral' West and 'polytheist' Hindus struck a welcome chord.

The SIMI's evolution from the 1980s onwards was dictated almost entirely by events taking place in India and in the wider world, these being interpreted as attacks directed against Islam and Muslims by the 'enemies' of the faith. Inevitably, then, the SIMI was driven to an increasing radicalism that won it support among a small number Muslims in India who saw themselves as increasingly beleaguered, victims of both Hindu chauvinism and the Indian state that was seen as representing essentially 'upper' caste Hindu interests.

The SIMI organized protest demonstrations against attacks on Muslims, both in India and elsewhere, which provided it publicity as well as possibilities for new recruits. It sought to intervene in and generate public support for its stand on other issues of major concern to the Indian Muslims, such as efforts to do away with the separate Muslim Personal Law, moves to dilute the Muslim character of the Aligarh Muslim University, and the Hinduisation of textbooks in government-run schools. Its activists were also involved in relief work among Muslims affected in anti-Muslim violence, which helped bolster the image of the organization as being seriously committed to the rights of the Muslims. It also provided other services such as libraries and free coaching classes for Muslim students from poor families.

The SIMI sought to propagate its message through mass contact programmes, lectures, seminars and rallies as well as through its abundant literature, mainly the writings of Maududi himself. A regular feature was its special week-long campaigns aimed at creating an awareness of the Islamic 'solution', in which, inevitably, the intention was to 'prove' that Islam alone had the solution to all problems afflicting humankind.

Thus, for instance, in 1982, the SIMI organized an 'Anti-Immorality' week, in the course of which 'social evils and general immorality' were condemned and 'immoral' literature was publicly burned. In 1983 the Kerala unit of the organization held a special 'Anti-Capitalism' week, in which it was sought to be stressed that the 'Islamic economic system' alone could provide genuine social justice.

In an effort to win the support of 'low' caste Dalits in its attacks on Hinduism, in 1994 the SIMI organized the 'Anti-Varna Vyavastha' week all over India, in the course of which, through public lectures and the distribution of leaflets and posters, it was stressed that the salvation of the Dalits lay in conversion to Islam, demanding, rather simplistically, for an 'immediate end to the caste system'.

Although a forceful champion of what it called 'Islamic Revolution' ever since its inception, the SIMI witnessed a further radicalization of its rhetoric from the 1990s, until, by 2000, the organization was proclaiming the need for Muslims to engage in armed Jihad in India. The radicalization of the SIMI since the 1990s must be seen in the context of, and as a response to, the growth of Hindu militancy, particularly in the north Indian states of Bihar and Uttar Pradesh where the SIMI also had a noticeable presence. The destruction of the Babri Mosque in 1992 and the subsequent massacres of Muslims in various parts of India proved to be a major watershed in the history of Hindu-Muslim relations in India. While some Muslims now insisted that the only way forward for the Muslims was to work together with Hindus to isolate both Hindu as well as Muslim militant groups, some fringe others, such as the SIMI, stressed that the time had now come for Muslims to wage Jihad against the Indian state or the Hindus, as, it argued, their lives and their faith were now under grave threat. As Shahid Badr Falahi, the President of the SIMI, asserted, the Muslims and Islam were now being targeted by Hindu militants in league with agencies of the state. Hence, he declared, 'It is high time that Muslims organize themselves and stand up to defend the community'.

By early 1991, the SIMI had begun mobilizing Muslims to struggle against Hindu militants, censuring Muslim leaders who advised restraint or dialogue. In February 1991 the SIMI organized the 'Babri Masjid' day all over India, holding demonstrations against the efforts of Hindu militants to destroy the disputed mosque in Ayodhya. SIMI leaders issued appeals to the Muslims to 'stop thinking in defensive terms' on the question of the mosque and the growing wave of attacks on Muslims.

Its rhetorical opposition to the campaign led by Hindu groups to destroy the mosque made for an increasing popularity of the SIMI, and indeed it was only after the SIMI took up the issue of the mosque, organizing meetings in various parts of the country to oppose the Hindu militants' campaign, that it really emerged as a significant force to be reckoned with, albeit in small pockets, having hitherto been restricted largely to a few towns of Uttar Pradesh.

Carrying on with its campaign to generate mass support for its position on the mosque, in September 2001 it organized a large conference at Mumbai, attended by some 25,000 students from various parts of India. At the conference it was stressed that the time had now come for Muslims to 'turn to Allah', to engage in 'missionary work' (da'wat) and to launch Jihad.

Following the destruction of the Babri mosque and the subsequent massacre of Muslims in large parts of India, the SIMI concluded that there was no hope for Muslims in seeking to dialogue with Hindus or the government because, in its view, both had turned irrevocably hostile against them. In a letter sent to various Muslim leaders and 'ulama, a top SIMI leader, 'Abdul 'Aziz Salafi, insisted that the Muslims should make it clear to the government of India as well as to Hindu militants that the Muslims 'would now refuse to sit low'.

He insisted that Muslims could no longer trust various 'secular' parties to guarantee their rights and that they should now 'establish their own political identity'. Four years later, the SIMI spelled out precisely what it had in mind.

In a statement issued in 1996 it declared that since democracy and secularism had failed to protect the rights of the Muslims, there was no alternative left for the Muslims but to struggle for the establishment of the khilafah.

It appealed to non-Muslims to recognize that nationalism and westernization were not the solution to the manifold problems facing the country, the only answer to which, it argued, was what it called the Islamic political order. It insisted that with the establishment of the khilafah, all racial, linguistic, caste and communal antagonisms would automatically be resolved and true equality and justice established. The break from the Jama'at's policy of gradualism was thus made irrevocable and complete.

As Hindu militancy increased in stridency, taking an ever-increasing toll of Muslim lives, the SIMI adopted an even more hard-line position, calling for Muslims to avenge the death of their co-religionists by following in the footsteps of the eleventh century Mahmud Ghaznavi, who led several attacks into India and is said to have destroyed many Hindu temples.

SIMI activists put up posters in several towns appealing to God to send down another Mahmud to take revenge for attacks on Muslims and their places of worship. In 1993, the arrest of a Sikh militant is said, at least so Indian sources claimed, to have revealed a 'Pakistani conspiracy' to unite Sikh and Kashmiri Muslim activists along with SIMI members to allegedly 'create disorder in India'. By this time the SIMI was alleged to have developed links with Islamist militants in Kashmir. It is said to have distributed posters and audio cassettes extolling the militants, and exhorting the Indian Muslims to follow in their path. In 2000 the arrest of a Chinese Muslim from Xinjiang and his SIMI accomplice at the border between West Bengal and Bangladesh is said to have provided the Indian police vital information on the SIMI's contacts with Islamist groups in western China struggling for independence. Indian authorities also alleged that the SIMI had established links with Osama bin Laden. In the wake of the attack on the World Trade Centre in New York in September, 2001, SIMI activists organised demonstrations at several places in India, castigating America as an 'enemy of Islam' and 'an agent of Satan', and lionizing Osama as a 'true mujahid' and a 'hero fighting the non-believers'. Posters hailing Osama and supporting the Taliban, including extolling the Taliban's destruction of the Bamiyan Buddhas, were put up in several towns, and Muslims were exhorted to 'trample over infidels'.

Shortly after the attacks on the World Trade Centre, and emboldened by the Western concern about Islamist militancy, on 27 September, 2001 the Government of India declared the SIMI a banned organization under the Unlawful Activities (Prevention) Act 1967. In the wake of the ban, the government arrested most of the top leaders of the SIMI, along with scores of its activists, closed all its offices, froze its banks accounts and seized all its assets. The two-year ban was notified by the Union Home Ministry after the governments of the states of Uttar Pradesh,

Maharashtra and Madhya Pradesh pushed for its proscription in the wake of allegations of theorganization's involvement in incidents of inter-communal strife. The ban was sought to be justified on four counts. Firstly, the SIMI's alleged links with militant Islamist groups in Jammu and Kashmir and the Pakistani secret services agency, the Inter-Services Intelligence. Secondly, its alleged links with pan-Islamist militant organizations and its agenda of working for the establishment of a 'global Islamic order'. Thirdly, its role in promoting inter-communal rivalry, hurting the religious sentiments of people of other faiths and allegations of its involvement in violent incidents.

Lastly, its involvement in allegedly working to destabilise the country, promoting secessionism and denying the basis of the Indian Constitution through its virulent opposition to nationalism, democracy and secularism. SIMI leaders rebutted all these charges, insisting that they had always abided by peaceful and democratic methods and that their work had all along been limited only to 'character building'. Its President, Shahid Badr Falahi, insisted that the SIMI was totally opposed to 'any violent or terrorist activities'. Muslim and even some secular and leftist organizations were quick to protest the government decision,branding it as partisan and blatantly anti-Muslim. It was pointed out that the government had no firm evidence of the SIMI's involvement in violent incidents. The ban was said to be yet further confirmation of the government's anti-Muslim policy and it was argued that if the government were really serious about tackling terrorism it should have also banned Hindu terrorist groups, which have a long history of involvement in anti-Muslim and anti-Christian violence. It was alleged that the government's move was motivated by political compulsions, in order to present itself as defender of the Hindus. That the government chose to ignore these criticisms was a clear indication that in the war against terrorism a consistent policy of double standards would be adopted. The message that was conveyed was that the government had different yardsticks to deal with Hindu and Muslim militants, the former treated as nationalists' and ardent patriots and the latter as 'enemies of the nation.

For Muslim organizations this came as little surprise, and although feeble protests were made, it was realized, as never before, that the aggressive confrontationist stance of groups like the SIMI could hardly serve the community. Rather, it had only made their situation as a beleaguered minority even more precarious. As to whether or not the SIMI was actually behind the recent Mumbai blasts it is too early to say. In the absence of clear evidence it would be unwise to rush to any conclusion. Yet, what is obvious is that the radicalism of Islamist groups like the SIMI, on the one hand, and Hindu fascist groups, on the other, feed on each other, both speaking the language of hatred. A consistent mass struggle against both forms of terrorism, Muslim and Hindu, and insisting that the state take vigorous action against both, is the only way to ensure that the recent events in Mumbai are not repeated.

FORMATION OF STUDENTS ISLAMIC MOVEMENT OF INDIA (SIMI)

The Students Islamic Movement of India (SIMI), proscribed under the Unlawful Activities (Prevention) Act, 1967, is an Islamist fundamentalist organization, which advocates the 'liberation of India' by converting it to an Islamic land. The SIMI, an organisation of young extremist students has declared Jihad against India, the aim of which is to establish Dar-ul-Islam (land of Islam) by either forcefully converting everyone to Islam or by violence.

FORMATION

The SIMI was formed at Aligarh in the State of Uttar Pradesh on April 25, 1977. Mohammad Ahmadullah Siddiqi, Professor of Journalism and Public Relations at the Western Illinois University Macomb, Illinois, was the founding President of the outfit. It originally emerged as a student wing of the Jamaat-e-Islami Hind (JIH). The alliance, however, lasted only till 1981, when SIMI activists protested against Palestine Liberation Organisation (PLO) leader Yasser Arafat's visit to India, and greeted him with black flags in New Delhi. Young SIMI activists identified Arafat as a western puppet, while the senior JIH leaders saw Arafat as a champion of the cause of Palestine. JIH decided to abandon SIMI and floated a new student wing, the Students Islamic Organization (SIO).

Objectives and Ideology

- Governing of human life on the basis of the Holy Quran
- Propagation of Islam
- *Jehad* for the cause of Islam

SIMI also attempts to utilize the youth in the propagation of Islam and also to mobilize support for Jihad and establish a Shariat-based Islamic rule through "Islami Inqulab". As the organization does not believe in a nation-state, it does not believe in the Indian Constitution or the secular order. SIMI also regards idol worship as a sin and considers it to be a holy duty to terminate idol worship.

SIMI is widely believed to be against Hinduism, western beliefs and ideals, as well as other 'anti-Islamic cultures'. Among its various objectives, the SIMI aims to counter what it believes is the increasing moral degeneration, sexual anarchy in the Indian society as also the 'insensitiveness' of a 'decadent' west. Ideologically, SIMI maintains that the concepts of secularism, democracy and nationalism, keystones of the Indian Constitution, are antithetical to Islam. Parallel to its rejection of secularism, democracy and nationalism is its oft-repeated objective of restoration of the 'khilafat', emphasis on 'ummah' (Muslim brotherhood), and the need for a Jehad to establish the supremacy of Islam.

The outfit is known to have adopted an extremist and militant posture on various issues of concern to the Muslim community.

According to the SIMI, Al Qaeda chief Osama bin Laden is an outstanding example of a true Mujahid, who has undertaken Jihad on behalf of the 'ummah'.

SIMI's interpretation of Islam is influenced to a great extent by the writings of Syed Abul A'ala Maududi, founder of the Jamaat-e Islami.

According to the scholar Yoginder Sikand, Nationalism, for SIMI, is seen as a false idol, and one devised by the non-Muslim 'enemies of the faith' to divide the Muslims and thereby weaken them. All non-Muslims are branded by the SIMI as 'kafirs', and no distinction is made among them. Because the 'enemies of God' are expected to show stiff resistance to Islam, violent Jihad is to be waged.

Leadership

Dr Shahid Badar Falah functioned as the national president and Safdar Nagori as the general secretary till the organization was proscribed under the Prevention of Terrorism Act, 2002. The Delhi Police arrested Falah on September 28, 2001, from its office in the Zakir Nagar area of Delhi and he has subsequently been charged with sedition and inciting communal disharmony in the State of Uttar Pradesh.

Similarly, on March 27, 2008, SIMI general secretary Safdar Nagori, absconding since September 27, 2001, was arrested along with 12 other cadres of the outfit from Indore in Madhya Pradesh. Among the arrested was Safdar's brother Kamruddin Nagori. Safdar Nagori has been named in a First Information Report (FIR) under Section 3 of the Unlawful Activities Act, registered at the New Friends Colony Police station in South Delhi. He is alleged to have established links with the operatives of Inter-Services Intelligence (ISI), Pakistan's external intelligence agency, and other Islamist fundamentalist leaders in a bid to revive SIMI cadres under the umbrella of a different outfit.

Mohammad Aamir, the chief of SIMI's Uttar Pradesh (UP) State unit and the prime accused in the Kanpur riots of March 16, surrendered before a metropolitan magistrate on April 25, 2006.

Another top SIMI leader Abul Bashar Qasmi, who had taken over the control of the outfit after Safdar Nagori's arrest, was arrested on August 16, 2008 from a village in Azamgarh in UP by a joint team of the UP and Gujarat Police. Qasmi allegedly was the mastermind behind the July 26, 2008 Ahmedabad (Gujarat) serial bomb blasts,

LINKAGES AND AREAS OF OPERATION

SIMI reportedly secures generous financial assistance from the World Assembly of Muslim Youth (WAMY), Riyadh, and also maintains close links with the International Islamic Federation of Students' Organizations (IIFSO) in Kuwait. It also receives generous funds from contacts in Pakistan.

The Chicago-based Consultative Committee of Indian Muslims is also reported to have supported SIMI morally and financially.

The SIMI has links with the Jamaat-e-Islam (JeI) units in Pakistan, Bangladesh and Nepal. It also has a close working relationship with the Islami Chhatra Shibir (ICS), the students' wing of the JeI in Bangladesh. The SIMI is also alleged to have close links with the Hizb-ul-Mujahideen (HM), and the ISI.

Beginning the autumn of 2000, SIMI cadres were known to have undergone training with the HM cadres in Jammu and Kashmir (J&K). At least three Jalgaon (in Maharashtra) residents — Sheikh Asif Supdu, Sheikh Khalid Iqbal and Sheikh Mohammad

Hanif — are believed to have died in shootouts with Indian troops near Kishtwar in J&K.

Certain SIMI leaders are reported to have close links with Pakistan-based terrorist groups such as the Lashkar-e-Toiba (LeT) and Jaish-e-Mohammed. SIMI activists, over the years, have also become a vital part of the LeT's grand plans for destabilisation in India.

SIMI also maintains ties with the Harkat-ul-Jehad-al Islami Bangladesh (HuJI-B).

SIMI is also reportedly involved in a continuous recruitment drive for the HuJI-B in Uttar Pradesh's Jaunpur, Allahabad, Kanpur, Lucknow, Ambedkar Nagar, Aligarh, Azamgarh, Sonauli, Ferozabad and Hathras areas. Further, SIMI cadres, sources indicate, are involved in the safe transportation of explosives and creation of channels for funds and securing safe houses for the HuJI-B cadres.

Groups of SIMI sympathizers reportedly exist in several places in the Gulf States. Jamayyatul Ansar, an organisation of SIMI activists comprising expatriate Indian Muslims, reportedly operates in Saudi Arabia.

Several Islamist fundamentalist organisations in India are allegedly controlled by former SIMI cadres. Prominent among them are the Kerala-based National Democratic Front and Islamic Youth Centre (IYC), and the Tamil Nadu Muslim Munnetra Kazhagam (TMMK) in Tamil Nadu.

According to official sources, in the year 1993 following the arrest of a Sikh terrorist, it was revealed that SIMI cadres, Sikh and Kashmiri terrorists, had been brought together by the ISI through the Jamaat-e-Islami in Pakistan to carry out subversive activities.

The outfit is currently regarded as having a national presence with strong bases in the States of Uttar Pradesh, Delhi, Madhya Pradesh, Gujarat, Kerala, Maharashtra (Aurangabad, Malegaon, Jalgaon and Thane), Andhra Pradesh and Assam. It reportedly has a strong base in various universities in these States. SIMI is also believed to enjoy the support of a large section of the Muslim populace in cities such as Kanpur, Rampur, Moradabad, Saharanpur, Lucknow and Azamgarh in Uttar Pradesh. Official sources are reported to have identified nine districts in Uttar Pradesh, where the SIMI is suspected of engaging in subversive activities-Lucknow, Kanpur, Aligarh, Agra, Faizabad, Bahraich, Barabanki, Lakhimpur Kheri and Azamgarh. The SIMI is also being utilised by various terrorist outfits because it has a well-knit network in Uttar Pradesh, Bihar and West Bengal.

In Kerala, SIMI operates under the cover of some 12 front organisations, at least two of which are based in the capital, Thiruvananthapuram, and a third in the port city of Kochi. Kondotty in the Malappuram District has also emerged as a hot-bed of SIMI activities. An official declaration submitted on June 1, 2006, by the Kerala Government before the tribunal examining the legality of the ban on SIMI, indicated that the outfit's cadres had 'lately' developed links with the LeT. Reports from various agencies, including the State Police Special Branch, further indicate that SIMI is operating under the cover of religious study centres, rural development and research centres. Some of these front organisations were spreading "extremist religious ideals" among sections of youth in Kerala by acting under the guise of "counselling and guidance centres working for behavioural change". SIMI is also reported to have established a women's wing in Kerala. Generous funds for such activities flow in from contacts in Kuwait and Pakistan.

In the western State of Maharashtra, areas such as Aurangabad, Malegaon, Jalgaon and Thane have remained strongholds of the SIMI. Intelligence agencies indicate that *Madrassas* (seminaries) in the Districts of Jalgaon, Nashik, Thane, Sholapur, Kolhapur, Gadchiroli, Nanded, Aurangabad, Malegaon and Pune have been brought under the scanner for SIMI activities. There are more than 3,000 *Madrassas* in the State, with about 200,000 students. As many as 500 seminaries are located in the State capital, Mumbai. Sources indicate that many of these seminaries are potential breeding grounds for SIMI's activities.

SIMI's activities have also continued in Assam and West Bengal, where the organisation has infiltrated Madrassas, Muslim clubs, libraries, and other cultural bodies for covert mobilisation of Islamist forces. In 2003, SIMI activists have operated from the platform of 'Islamic Siksha Shivirs' (Islamic Educational Camps) in Mograhat in the North 24 Parganas district in West Bengal. A two-day 'workshop' organised in the District between August 31 and September 1 had, in fact, finalised the outfit's infiltration plans.

Sources indicate that in August 2003, one Jamaluddin Chaudhory of the ICS had taken seven SIMI activists from Assam and West Bengal to residential Madrassas in Chittagong, Rangpur and Dhaka for 'higher Islamic studies'.

Additionally, some hardcore SIMI activists from Malda and South 24 Parganas had crossed over to Bangladesh for higher studies in Islamic theology at a Saudi-funded private institution in Chittagong. In the 2004 general elections, SIMI had backed the newly floated 'Indian National League (INL)', which put up candidates in six constituencies of Jangipur, Murshidabad, Diamond Harbour, Basirhat, Jadavpur and Kolkata North-West. Senior SIMI leader Hasan Saidullah Ashrafi contested the Basirhat seat from the INL platform and finished seventh among eight candidates polling just 4,780 valid votes.

In the State of Madhya Pradesh, "While SIMI activities were confined to Indore, Ujjain, Khandwa and Bhopal before the ban on it in 2001, they have spread to Burhanpur, Guna, Neemuch and Shajapur as well now," an unnamed police official was quoted as saying in Hindustan Times on August 16, 2006. Before the ban, 33 cases were registered against SIMI activists in various districts for spreading religious discord.

Since then, however, 49 cases have been filed against the group. SIMI national general secretary Safdar Nagori, an Ujjain resident in his 40s, has been absconding since the ban. "He has cases against him of spreading religious discord since 1997-98," Ajay Kumar Sharma, a Deputy Inspector General of Police, said. Since the ban, 180 SIMI activists have been arrested from across the State. And since April 2006, five SIMI members, including two women, have been taken into custody in Khandwa, four in Burhanpur and one each in Jabalpur and Ujjain.

MEMBERSHIP, INFLUENCE AND ACTIVITIES

Opposed to democracy, secularism and nationalism, SIMI has been advocating among its followers-some 400 ansars (full-time cadres) and the 20,000 ordinary members-the need to oppose "man-made" institutions and work for the Ummah.

Students up to the age of 30 years are eligible to be its members and after completing this age-limit they retire from the organization.

SIMI cadres consider Osama bin Laden as a 'true believer of Islam' and regard him as an epitome of 'Islamic Hero'. According to Safdar Nagori, a prominent SIMI leader, bin Laden is "not a terrorist" and neither is Jammu and Kashmir an "integral part of India." At its congregations, messages and recorded speeches have been relayed from the Palestinian Hamas leader Sheikh Ahmed Yasin and Qazi Hussein Ahmed, chief of the Jamaat-e-Islami in Pakistan.

Official sources have indicated that the SIMI has established links with terrorist outfits and is also supporting extremism/militancy in Punjab, Jammu and Kashmir and elsewhere. The outfit is reported to have published objectionable posters and literature, which are intended to incite communal feelings and which question the territorial integrity of India.

Shaheen Force, the outfit's wing for schoolchildren, seeks to "protect the children from present-day misguidance and vices" and keeps them "under the shade of Islamic culture". The outfit also has a wing that aims to channelise the talent of girls for the Islamist cause.

SIMI reportedly operates many special programmes for students of Arabic colleges and Islamic universities. Students receive training and other assistance in the study of languages and Islamic sciences. According to the SIMI, renaissance of the Ummah depends on Islamic scholars because the community can attain its glory only when it will be led and guided by sincere Ulema (scholars).

According to the SIMI, Israelis were responsible for the 9/11 attacks in New York. According to a press release issued by its secretary-general Safdar Nagori after 9/11, "there are strong reasons to believe that the recent attacks may be a conspiracy of the Zionist Israel, which is rapidly losing world support because of its inhuman and terrorist activities in Palestine."

SIMI AND IM: ORIGINS

Currently, most prominent Indian analysts believe that SIMI and IM are no longer (if they were ever) distinct organizations; rather, these analysts believe that IM emerged largely from militant elements of SIMI, enjoying the support of, and possibly personnel from, Pakistan-based LeT and Bangladesh-based Harkat-ul-Jihad-Islami (HUJI-B). This stands in contrast to earlier assessments that treated the SIMI and IM as distinct organizations that share a common origin, leadership, and cadres. Others have suggested that IM does not exist at all but is instead an effort by Pakistan's external intelligence agency, the Inter-Services Intelligence (ISI), to project an Indian face to the activities of Pakistan-based militant groups. This essay treats IM as an evolution of SIMI, in a narrative that begins with the origins of the SIMI and continues with an exposition about IM's formation. This narrative is subject to the caveat that the assumption that IM is an evolution of SIMI has merit.

SIMI formed in 1977 at Aligarh (Uttar Pradesh), initially as a student wing of the Jamaat-e-Islami Hind (JIH). It is believed that SIMI was established to revitalize the JIH's older student wing, the Students Islamic Organization (SIO), which was set up in 1956. SIMI's founding president was Mohammad Ahmadullah, who had been a professor of Journalism and Public Relations at Western Illinois University. JIH reportedly began distancing itself from SIMI in 1981, when several SIMI activists protested against Yasser Arafat's visit to India. SIMI's youth perceived Arafat as a puppet of the West, whereas JIH viewed him as a champion of the Palestinian cause. SIMI and JIH had other differences. JIH was discomfited with SIMI's support of the Iranian Revolution and its communal orientation. After distancing itself from SIMI, JIH reverted to relying on the older student organization, SIO.

The relationship, if any, between the SIMI and SIO is difficult to ascertain. Some reports suggest that SIMI was a competitive splinter of SIO, whereas others see the rise of SIMI as a means of revitalizing SIO. Yet others believe that SIMI was a deliberate spin off from JIH to allow JIH to pursue its goal of an Islamic state by proxy while still maintaining its moderate standing within India. Irrespective of their relationship, SIMI and SIO maintained cordial relations after the formal split.

However, SIMI continued to vex and strain relations with JIH. For example, in 1986, SIMI openly called for liberating India's Muslims. Nonetheless, JIH continued to share platforms with SIMI until at least 1992, when SIMI convened a conference in Mumbai that propounded the virtues of militant Islam. Reports conflict about the degree to which SIMI and JIH continue their organizational links to date.

At some point, perhaps as late as 1999, a militant movement within SIMI emerged. Praveen Swami reports that in that year, a SIMI convention took place in Aurangabad, Maharashtra, when Mohammad Amir Shakeel Ahmad—a SIMI cadre arrested in 2005 for smuggling military-grade explosive and assault rifles for a series of attacks in Gujarat, along with over a dozen of SIMI-linked LeT—declared that "Islam is our Nation, not India." Swami reports that Ahmad became "one of hundreds" of SIMI cadre who joined terrorist networks that attacked sites throughout India and who were linked to LeT. According to interlocutors in India and Bangladesh, SIMI is believed to be a major conduit for LeT activities working in association with HUJI-B in Bangladesh to move people and war material into and out of Pakistan and India.

The Indian Mujahideen emerged from SIMI perhaps as early as 2001, when some 25,000 SIMI activists met at what was SIMI's last public convention. During that convention, SIMI activists were called to Jihad and later mobilized demonstrations in support of Osama bin Laden. Key future IM leaders continued to migrate from moderate SIMI positions toward that of militancy. For example, Sadiq Israr Sheikh joined SIMI in 1996, when SIMI was still a legal organization. He, along with other SIMI cadres, attended the weekly meeting at the home of a Dr. Tayyeb Ali. (No further information can be found about this person in the open-source media.) Apparently several other senior Mumbai SIMI members were also in attendance, including Riyaz Ismail Shahbandri (alias Riyaz Bhatkal) and Altaf Subhan Qureshi (alias Tauqeer). Qureshi, Sheikh, and Shahbandri helped found the terrorist cell that would later become the IM. Shahbandri became a key commander of the IM/SIMI networks responsible for staging numerous urban bombings since 2006.

Although members of SIMI embraced militancy and began merging into what is now IM, IM as an organization did not appear formally until much later. In November 2007, IM claimed responsibility for several simultaneous blasts targeting lawyers in court premises in three cities in Uttar Pradesh (Varanasi, Ayodhya, and Lucknow). IM explained that these attacks were "Islamic raids," precipitated by the purported refusal of the lawyers to take on the cases of accused terrorists. In the wake of these attacks, Indian agencies increased pressure on the organization. At least six senior IM members reportedly fled to Pakistan, including Shahbandri.

SIMI was banned in September 2001, under the Unlawful Activities (Prevention) Act of 1967, due to alleged working relations with al Qaeda, the Taliban, and other Islamist terrorist groups. SIMI has unsuccessfully challenged the ban in the Supreme Court to seek its revocation.

ORGANIZATIONAL STRUCTURE, LEADERSHIP, AND MEMBERSHIP

Organizational Structure and Roles

Before being banned, SIMI claimed some four hundred full-time workers known as *ansars* (helpers), 20,000 sympathizers known as *ikhwans* (brothers), and the Shahin force for enlisting children between the ages of seven and eleven. In addition, SIMI set up the Tehrik-e-Tulaba-i-Arabia to reach madrassah students and *ulema* (learned religious scholars).

It is believed that IM has a complicated organizational structure. As should be apparent, the below noted description of IM bares considerable similarity to the notes on SIMI. Given the nature of Indian reporting, which tends to treat SIMI and IM as one organization, it is difficult to discern whether the descriptions were derived independently for IM or whether they were derived from earlier information about SIMI.

Core group : There is a core group of twelve leaders of which the only known member is Altaf Subhan Qureshi (alias Tauqeer). This estimate of twelve is apparently derived from leaked Indian intelligence sources and therefore cannot be confirmed.

Call of Islam : The largest group is code-named Call of Islam. Members of this group are reputed to be over 35 years of age and may number as many as 60,000. They are dispersed across the country and tend to be professionals—teachers who appear to be "law abiding citizens but issue instructions to those below them based on orders they get from top leadership."

Ikhwan : Below the Call of Islam are the ikhwan, with about 6,000 core members. They are described as "sleepers" that are called into action for a particular purpose, and then they return to their sleeper status.

Ansars : Below the ikhwan are the ansars. Ansars are deeply involved in the terrorist attacks.

Shaheen : Below the ansars are the Shaheen (white falcon) members whose job is to enlist and indoctrinate new children between the ages of seven and eleven years of age.

Muslim Brotherhood : Finally, there is a group code-named the Muslim Brotherhood, whose main function appears to be fundraising through *hawala* (an informal Islamic financial transaction system) and from Muslims serving in the Gulf. Reportedly, they have enlisted some one million (10 lakh) regular donors, many of whom are in the Gulf.

Recent arrests of IM cadres provide further insights into the command structure of the IM/SIMI.

Shahabuddin Ghouri Brigade : Headed by Amir Raza and based in Kerala, this group is responsible for planning and executing attacks in southern India.

Muhammad Ghaznai Brigade : This group (leader unknown) is responsible for targeting high-value civilian targets in northern India.

Shaheed-al-Zarqaqi Brigade : This group targets high-value personalities and organizes suicide attacks.

Media wing u Headquartered in Pune (Maharashtra), this group dispatches email and print communications (e.g., manifestos) before or after IM attacks.

LEADERSHIP OF SIMI AND IM

IM emerged from militarized elements of SIMI. The following discussion offers some known details about SIMI's leadership and those SIMI elements that forged IM.

Shahid Badar Falah served as the president of SIMI, with Safdar Nagori as the general secretary, until the organization was proscribed in 2001. Falah was arrested in 2001 and Nagori was arrested subsequently in 2008. Despite being banned, SIMI remained the principle platform for Islamist violence in India.

Nagori, who was 38 years of age at the time of his arrest, split away from moderate elements of SIMI in 2005. He is believed to have been a primary ideologue and organizer for attacks, although Indian analysts do not believe he personally carried out attacks. Nagori is believed to have nurtured SIMI's organizational networks in Central and Western India.

Mufti Abu Bashir, who is approximately 29 years of age as of 2009, is an Islamic preacher from Azamgarh in Uttar Pradesh; he also taught in a madrassah in Hyderabad. A primary ideologue of IM, he was arrested in 2008. Bashir oversaw the planning of terrorism attacks along with Altaf Subhan Qureshi (alias Tauqeer) and Qayamuddin Kapadia.

Though several SIMI/IM activists have been arrested in recent years, Altaf Subhan Qureshi remains at large. Qureshi, age 37 as of 2009, is believed to have been the mastermind of the blasts in Bangalore (July 2008), Ahmadabad (July 2008), and New Delhi (September 2008). He is a software engineer by training and worked for a leading computer firm before joining SIMI. He is the author of the virulent emails dispatched prior to every IM attack.

Qayamuddin Kapadia, around 28 years of age as of 2009, is a petty merchant in Vadodar (Gujarat) and leader of the Gujarat

IM unit. He escaped arrest when Nagori was apprehended and is believed to be the second-in-command to Qureshi. Analysts believe that he was the main coordinator of the Ahmadabad blasts.

Membership

SIMI and IM activists are all Indian. Analysts such as Praveen Swami note that the personal backgrounds of some SIMI and IM activists involve direct or indirect experience with communal violence, and these experiences may have served as a motivation for joining these groups. Cadres in SIMI and IM hail from all over India, attesting the geographical reach of these groups across India. Yoginder Sikand notes that SIMI's activists come from lower- and middle-class families and appeal to those who have felt underprivileged and increasingly victimized by the rise of Hindu nationalism and a state that privileges Hindu interests. SIMI also attracted those Muslims who believe in the intrinsic superiority of Islam both over a decadent and morally depraved West and over polytheistic Hindus.

To accommodate those who espoused such concerns about society's immorality and decadence, SIMI organized an "anti-immorality" week where it supposedly burned obscene literature. One year later, the group held an "anti-capitalist week" in Kerala to compete with the state's left-wing constituents. Unlike the left, however, SIMI argued that it is Islam—not socialism—that can mitigate the ills of capitalism. SIMI also worked with victims of communal violence and provided educational opportunities for poor Muslims residing in riot-affected areas.

Curiously, many high-profile SIMI/IM cadres are computer-literate and, in some cases, have had impressive private sector employment; they joined the movement upon experiencing religious discrimination within multinational corporations. Other cadres have had other professional careers, such as Mohammad Abrar Qasim, who was a dentist. Qasim joined SIMI in 1993 after attending his first meeting at a mosque (Jamia Masjid) in Mominpura, a slum where LeT formed Indian networks. Qasim used his earnings from dentistry to serve as SIMI's chief in Bihar. In another instance, SIMI/IM leaders set up a Bangalore Jihad cell that recruited at least six IT workers through a front organization called Sarani.

Many members of IM/SIMI enjoyed mafia links as well, especially with networks of the Bombay underworld "don," Dawood Ibrahim. These connections between the Indian mafia and SIMI/IM were mutually beneficial. The mafia link allowed the Islamist militants to acquire and move materials as well as personnel in and out of various countries for training and to position personnel and material in order to perpetrate terrorist attacks. In turn, the relationship afforded the mafia an opportunity to claim that it was helping a vulnerable community.

Indian analysts and officials also believe that the organizations receive money from the ISI. This suspicion is bolstered by Nagori's admission upon being arrested that SIMI received funds from the ISI.

Ideology and Motivation

Ideologically, SIMI rejects Hinduism, secularism, democracy, and nationalism, which are keystones of India's constitutional establishment. Similarly, SIMI embraces the restoration of the Khilafat (Caliphate) and emphasizes the importance of the *ummah* (Muslim community) and the need to wage a Jihad to exert Islam's supremacy. SIMI contends that Osama bin Laden is an exemplary *mujahid* who has embraced Jihad at the behest of the ummah.

Reflecting IM's emergence from SIMI, the organization's ideology and motivation are nearly isomorphous with that of SIMI. Given that IM typically issues email messages to the media prior to attacks, its ideology and motivation are relatively easy to discern. These messages aim to exposit IM's positions on controversial subjects such as the 1992 destruction of the Babri Mosque (Ayodhya), the anti-Muslim pogroms in 2002, and other events in which Muslims have been disproportionately affected. According to various public pronouncements, IM advocates spreading Islam throughout India, waging Jihad against non-Muslims, and establishing a government based on the Koran.

IM, in its manifestos, seeks to cultivate support among members of India's large Muslim population that harbor, to varying degrees, grievances regarding access to public-and private-sector jobs, development, educational opportunities, the rising tide of Hindu nationalism, and anti-Muslim violence, among other issues.

In 2008, IM claimed responsibility for at least four high-profile attacks, which are described below. IM justified the attacks by characterizing the terrorism campaign as the "rise of Jihad" and the "revenge of Gujarat." Other IM recruitment materials include CDs containing footage of U.S. forces killing Muslims in Iraq and Afghanistan.

SIMI/IM appears to be an important vector of LeT infiltration and cultivation of Indian leaders and cadres. Indian recruits to LeT, like those identified as SIMI or IM, appear to have been motivated by anti-Muslim violence in India. Even women were moved to join LeT after having experienced the violence of the 2002 pogroms in Gujarat. LeT has publically called for Indian Muslims to embrace Jihad since then. In 2004, Swami observed that LeT had been able to recruit several dozen Indian Muslims in the wake of the 2002 pogrom. It is not clear whether LeT nurtured the splits within SIMI and the formation of the IM or whether LeT was simply well-positioned to benefit from these developments.

TIES TO OTHER TERRORIST ORGANIZATIONS AND OTHER INTERNATIONAL LINKAGES

Since the destruction of the Babri Masjid and consequent anti-Muslim violence, as well as the 2002 pogrom in Gujarat, the LeT has been effective at recruiting Indians for group actions. For example, the July 11, 2006, attack on multiple targets in Mumbai appears to have been an LeT operation outsourced through SIMI. One of the main Indian masterminds of that attack was Raheel Abdul Rehman Sheikh (along with Zabiuddin Ansar and Zulfikar Fayyaz Qazi). Sheikh grew up in an economically impoverished area, and actually became involved with the Markaz-i-Ahl-e-Hadith, a Salafist organization. Swami argues that while there is no evidence directly linking Sheikh to SIMI, he likely forged his contacts with LeT through SIMI's convention in 1999. If true, this would attest to the networked nature of the groups operating in

India and their ties to Pakistan-based groups. Sheikh also worked with mafioso Dawood Ibrahim, who used his own network to ship weapons and used several mafia operatives to move people via Dhaka to Karachi on fake passports. Thus, it would appear that the criminal underworld is a shared collaborative resource for India's militant groups.

SIMI is believed to have enjoyed considerable international support, including that of the World Assembly of Muslim Youth (WAMY) in Riyadh. Terrorism analysts believe that WAMY has ties to terrorist groups throughout the world. The organization has chapters in 55 countries and was founded by Osama bin Laden's nephew. It holds conferences and distributes literature that promote Jihad as well as raises funds for terrorist groups such as Hamas. WAMY has been tied to the 1993 World Trade Centre bombing. (The organization provides a very different account of itself on its website, focusing on peaceful assembly and networking among Muslims.)

SIMI has also benefited from its ties to the International Islamic Federation of Students' Organizations in Kuwait, another organization with alleged ties to terrorist groups. SIMI continued to grow especially after 1982 with the support of these and other organizations, which helped the group establish numerous magazines in many vernacular languages that promoted the notion of Islamic revolution. These magazines include the *Islamic Movement* (in Urdu, Hindi, and English), *Iqra* (in Gujarati), *Rupantar* (in Bengali), *Sedi Malar* (in Tamil), and *Vivekam* (in Malayalam).

In addition, SIMI/IM maintains links with Jamaat-e-Islami (JI) organizations in Pakistan as well as in Bangladesh. SIMI has, for example, maintained linkages with the student wing of JI-Bangladesh, Chatra Shabir.

Despite these allegations, SIMI/IM denies such linkages with the ISI or any Pakistan or Bangladesh-based militant groups.

Potential Cleavages?

There is a lingering—if unanswerable—question surrounding the contemporary relationship between SIMI and IM and about the coherence of SIMI itself in the wake of IM's emergence. Some analysts interviewed by the author during fieldwork in India in July 2009 argued that SIMI is now IM. Others were more dubious about this sweeping statement. Praveen Swami, for example, believes that part of SIMI would like to renounce any ties to violence or support thereof. Indeed, there is evidence that SIMI members would like to disassociate themselves from violent extremism, while those committed to violence have formed the rump of IM.

Several SIMI activists have even turned themselves in with the hope of eventually regaining some degree of legitimacy for the organization and to reintegrate themselves back into society. For example, the above noted Abrar Qasim walked into a court in Nagpur and announced that he wished to surrender. The clerks were befuddled when he explained to them that he was wanted by the Maharashtra Police in connection with the Mumbai serial bombings of July 2006. Qasim sought to clear his name. In the weeks following his surrender, he told authorities that most of SIMI's rank and file wanted to emerge from the underworld. He said that "moderates in SIMI want to come over ground….for we have nothing to hide." Qasim joined SIMI in 1993, following the controversial destruction of the Babri Masjid.

Using the cover of a summit for the National Urdu Promotion Council, SIMI elected several new office bearers who were charged with lobbying political and religious leadership to remove the ban on SIMI. Swami reports that most members of this new team were anti-Jihad political Islamists, and several believed that SIMI's ties with jihadi groups undermined the group as well as the Indian Muslim community writ large. Among those espousing this view was the new SIMI president, Misbah-ul-Islam, from West Bengal.

Later in January 2007, SIMI leadership again met with a senior New Delhi-based JI leader, who sought to encourage the militant elements within SIMI to surrender and demanded to know why SIMI helped perpetrate the 2006 Mumbai attack. In the absence of a possible compromise, SIMI's political Islamists convened again in Kozhikode (Kerala) in mid-November 2007. Misbah-ul-Islam argued at that time that, if SIMI were to ever function as a political organization, its leadership would have to face prosecution. Qasim was the first to volunteer. Swami reports that a senior SIMI functionary believed that the leaders wanted to see if coming out would open doors for SIMI to recuperate itself. During interviews with the author, Swami explained that many of SIMI's members would like to restore their organization's credibility and legitimacy.

While this may have been the majority view and the view of the new senior leadership, there were important dissenters. For example, Shibly Peedical Abdul (a computer engineer from Kerala) was among those operatives that retained a commitment to militancy. During the January 2007 meeting, Abdul responded that jihadist activities will continue and accused JI and other leadership of "selling out." Abdul set up an important cell, which with his organizational assistance executed the July 2006 serial attacks in Mumbai. It is believed that this attack was conducted as an LeT operation working through these SIMI/IM activists. After the bombing, Abdul fled while other SIMI operatives were arrested in conjunction with the attack. Abdul apparently recruited a dozen or more men through the religious front organization Sarani. After the Mumbai attacks, officials began examining Abdul's networks, which spanned the country and included SIMI activists associated with the Jammu-Kashmir Islamist leader, Syed Ali Shah Geelani. Abdul had also set up Fatah Business Solution, which is believed to have laundered money for terrorist activities.

It would appear that while moderate SIMI activists were and are trying to find a way to become a legitimate organization again, the militancy-inclined members among SIMI were also rethinking their strategy to redouble efforts toward Jihad. It is likely that the more militant-inclined among SIMI's ranks formed the IM.

MAJOR IM/SIMI OPERATIONS

SIMI/IM is likely responsible for numerous attacks from at least 2000; however, the Indian media frequently attributes these attacks to LeT. Below is a sampling of recent attacks for which SIMI/IM has claimed responsibility.

Jaipur (Rajasthan), May 2008: Nine blasts in markets; killed over 60 people and injured many more.

Bangalore (Karnataka), July 2008: Eight simultaneous low-intensity blasts; killed 2 people and injured 7.

Ahmadabad (Gujrat), July 2008: Sixteen synchronized bomb blasts occurred in largely crowed urban centers; 38 were killed and more than 100 were injured. (Curtis claims that 56 were killed in this attack.)

New Delhi, September 2008: Five bomb blasts occurred in heavily trafficked market areas, killing 30 people and injuring more than 100.

As noted, these are only the most recent and high-profile incidents; SIMI/IM may have been involved in many more attacks.

INDIAN INTERNAL SECURITY CHALLENGES

Given Pakistan's long-standing history of supporting terrorism in India, and the inability of India or the United States to compel Pakistan to cease such activities, India is likely to continue facing threats from external and internal actors. Yet, India has been slow—if not outright unwilling—to take the necessary steps to improve internal security. In the wake of the 1999 Kargil War, the Kargil Review Committee was established to review both how the Pakistani Northern Light Infantry was able to seize territory kilometers within India's borders and what deficient security arrangements precipitated India's inability to detect the territorial incursion until months after it had taken place. In addition, the committee made a number of recommendations to ensure that India is neither vulnerable to such a territorial assault nor unprepared to contend with the challenge should it arise again. That report offered several initiatives to fortify India's defense and internal security situation. Some ten years later, however, most of those recommendations have yet to be implemented.

Following the November 2008 attack in Mumbai, the Indian government announced that it would undertake numerous reforms to address the country's internal security challenges. On December 11, 2008, India's home minister, P. Chidambaram, proclaimed that the government would *inter alia* create a Coastal Command to secure 4,650 miles of shoreline, establish twenty counterterrorism schools and standing regional commando units, create a national agency to investigate suspected terrorism activity, and strengthen anti-terrorism laws.

India's parliament surprisingly acted quickly to make some of these reforms a reality. On December 17, 2008, India's lower house (the Lok Sabha) approved new anti-terrorism legislation, which was approved by the upper house (the Rajya Sabha) the next day. The new Unlawful Activities (Prevention) Act provides new powers to the security services, including the ability to hold suspects for six months without charges. It also makes provisions to establish a national investigative agency that will be responsible for investigating terrorism and gathering and processing intelligence. Some of these provisions (such as lengthy detentions without charge) have drawn domestic criticism. In July 2009, however, interlocutors had already grown wary of the Indian political system and most believed that—like Kargil—the Mumbai attack would not jolt the Indian system into action.

India's external intelligence agency, the Research and Analysis Wing (RAW), does not interface well with domestic intelligence agencies, which are responsible for dealing with the police (a state subject). There is no FBI equivalent in India. Unfortunately, corruption is an enormous problem that ultimately will undermine efforts to fortify India's internal security—especially efforts to professionalize the police. As one columnist astutely noted only days before the Mumbai attack:

The police are treated as subjects of whatever local politicians reign in a particular state. The political parties use the police to serve their own ends, so police behavior reflects the agenda of the political party that governs that state. Political changes are quickly reflected within the police force. Given the fact that a considerable number of Indian politicians are criminals, it is no surprise that the police they control mirror them in this respect.

Thus, while India tends to claim that the Mumbai attack was India's September 11, the attack—however horrific—has not comprehensively moved the Indian system to undertake massive reform of its domestic security arrangements. Having said that, Chidambaram is extremely concerned about these issues and has made reforming India's internal security arrangements a priority. It remains to be seen how effective he will be in moving a large, lethargic bureaucracy on these politically challenging issues.

Conclusion

In the early years after September 11, analysts remarked that India's Muslims have not become part of the global Jihad, a view that Indian officials readily endorsed. This claim was tenuous at best. If, as India claims, the groups operating in Kashmir were international, then the local population's support, however limited, would undermine that statement. Indeed, Pakistan-based groups have, for years, enjoyed logistical support among Indians, even if they had not developed Indian militant leaders or cadres.

In recent years, Indian officials have had to concede that the country does indeed have an internal security problem stemming from "home grown" militants. The Indian government seems to believe—or adopts the public position—that if Pakistan were to cease support for India's terrorist groups, these domestic and foreign terrorists would disappear, be captured, or killed in action. Few embrace the possibility that it is India's domestic socio-political arrangements and inequitable treatment of Muslims that present opportunities for militants and outside support. Yet, as Praveen Swami has noted, people....Many Muslims have done well in independent India...But despite the constitutional promise of equality, Muslims remain underrepresented in government jobs, suffer significant discrimination in employment, income levels and land-holding, and are worse-off even than India's scheduled castes in education.

Swami has argued that it is these domestic conditions that motivated the rise of Indian jihadists, and, indeed, though SIMI and IM endorse the al Qaeda message, they appear to motivate cadres and leaders by focusing on the plight of India's Muslims rather than those of the larger Muslim world. SIMI/IM—unlike al Qaeda—does not advance an agenda for the global umma. Unfortunately, India's inadequate security arrangement and lethargic political institutions seem ill-prepared to contend with the emerging threat.

2

Students Islamic Movement of India: A Profile

Following the October 2005 deadly bombings in New Delhi, the Union Home Department claimed that Islami Inquilabi Mahaz, or the Islamic Revolutionary Front (a hitherto unknown outfit), which accepted responsibility for the Delhi blasts, is associated with the outlawed Students Islamic Movement of India (SIMI), a radical Islamist organization. Intelligence sources revealed that the masterminds behind the October blasts had several meetings with SIMI cadres in the southern cities of Gulbarga and Hubli. SIMI is also suspected of involvement in the blast at Ahmedabad railway station in Gujarat on February 19 and the twin blasts in Varanasi on March 7 that killed 18 people and injured over a hundred others (Daily News and Analysis, February 22; Hindustan Times, March 30). Although SIMI was outlawed immediately after 9/11, the Indian government claims its subversive activities have continued relentlessly. In 2005, SIMI allegedly struck twice in a single month; for instance, on July 5, suspected SIMI operatives staged an attack on the disputed temple complex in Ayodhya, and, on July 28, SIMI operatives allegedly played a role in the bombing on board the Shramjeevi train that killed 12 passengers and injured at least 52 others (The Hindu, August 1, 2005).

BACKGROUND

SIMI was founded on April 25, 1977 at the Aligarh Muslim University, Uttar Pradesh, as a radical student outfit with a mission to revive Islam in India and transform the entire country into an Islamic state. SIMI's founding president was Mohammad Ahmadullah Siddiqi, currently a professor of journalism and public relations at the Univeristy of Western Illinois. The group's three core ideological concepts were: Ummah, Caliphate and Jihad. SIMI's ideological inspirations were Muslim thinkers who had launched major Islamic movements in the subcontinent, in particular Shah Waliullah, Sayyid Ahmad, Haji Shariat Allah and the legendary Maulana Maududi, the founder of Jamaat-e-Islami (JI).

Specifically, SIMI was deeply inspired by Maududi's goal to make Islam the supreme organizing principle for the social and political life of the Muslim community. In its annual report, SIMI reiterated these tenets, urging Muslim youths to struggle for the revival of Islam in the light of the Quran and Sunnah (South Asia Analysis Group, October 30, 2003). In fact, the Maududi influence was so deep-rooted that in the early years of SIMI's existence the organization was dominated by the Indian wing of JI, called Jamaat-e-Islami Hind (JIH). In due course, SIMI emerged as a coalition of student and youth Islamic bodies, namely the Muslim Students Association, Students Islamic Union, Students Islamic Organization and Muslim Youth Association.

SIMI's pro-Taliban stance in the wake of the 9/11 terrorist attacks, anti-U.S. demonstrations in the Indian states of Madhya Pradesh, Uttar Pradesh, Maharashtra, Gujarat and Rajasthan and the glorification of Osama bin Laden as the "ultimate jihadi" prompted the Indian government to impose a ban. Since the ban, some reports suggest that SIMI has been operating under the banner of Tahreek Ihya-e-Ummat or Movement for the Revival of the Ummah (The Milli Gazette, January 2002).

SIMI is believed to have 400 full time cadres called "Ansars" and some 20,000 ordinary members known as "Ikhwans." The leadership is in complete disarray following the ban in September 2001. The last known leaders of the outfit were Shahid Badar Falah and Safdar Nagori as the national president and secretary-general, respectively. While Falah was arrested and charged with sedition and communal tension in north India in September 2001, Nagori has so far evaded arrest. It has been reported that Nagori is trying to revive SIMI and has established links with Pakistani intelligence operatives, the Palestinian group Hamas and other like-minded organizations beyond India's borders (The Pioneer, July 21, 2003).

The ideological affinity with Hamas was revealed by SIMI's financial secretary Salim Sajid following his arrest in June 2002. According to Sajid, Hamas' former spiritual leader Sheikh Ahmad Yasin had endorsed the "freedom struggle" in India's Jammu and Kashmir state and the reconstruction of the demolished Babri Masjid in Uttar Pradesh (Times of India, June 29, 2002). Sajid's interrogation also exposed SIMI's covert connections with Saudi Arabia's Jamayyatul Ansar (JA) and Bangladesh's Islamic Chhatra Shivir, the student wing of Jamaat-e-Islami Bangladesh (Times of India, June 29, 2002). JA is primarily comprised of expatriate Indian Muslims working in Saudi Arabia and is suspected of channeling funds to SIMI. Other sources of funding have included the World Assembly of Muslim Youth in Riyadh, the International Islamic Federation of Students Organizations based in Kuwait and the U.S.-based Consultative Committee of Indian Muslims (The Hindu, September 28, 2001).

While SIMI's strong ties with Jamaat-e-Islami units in Pakistan, Bangladesh and Nepal are well documented, not much is known about its ties with Pakistan's notorious Inter-Services Intelligence Directorate (ISI). According to some reports, SIMI cadres were being trained by the ISI to launch terrorist attacks in India (rediff.com, April 27, 2004). One arrested Sikh militant revealed in 1993 that SIMI cadres, along with Kashmiri and Sikh militants, had been brought together by the ISI through the Jamaat-e-Islami in Pakistan to carry out training and subversive activities in India (The Hindu, September 28, 2001). Moreover, it has been reported that the ISI has maintained contact with key SIMI operatives during their trips to Saudi Arabia and other Middle Eastern countries, either for Haj or fund-raising activities (Daily Excelsior, October 9, 2001). In early 2003, a senior police official in Lucknow (tasked with investigating SIMI in Uttar Pradesh state), warned that the group was trying to re-organize with the help of the ISI. His claim was based on the confessions of two detained SIMI operatives,

Obaid Ullah and Mohammed Arif (Press Trust of India, January 27, 2003).

Intelligence sources have stated that after proscription, large numbers of SIMI cadres fled to the northeastern parts of India and neighbouring Bangladesh for sanctuary, training and bonding with other Islamic groups. In previous years, SIMI had formed local branches in West Bengal, especially in the border districts of Malda, Murshidabad, North and South Dinajpur and even Kolkata. They organized regional meetings in West Bengal and in Chittagong (Bangladesh) under a different banner in 2003 where they were reportedly planning to infiltrate Islamic education centers, libraries, and other cultural bodies (Daily Excelsior, December 12, 2003). SIMI is also believed to be active outside the Indian subcontinent, mainly in Saudi Arabia and other Persian Gulf states. In 2003, as many as 350 Indian Muslims working in Jordan, Libya, Saudi Arabia, Kuwait, Oman, Qatar and other Middle-Eastern states were allegedly recruited by SIMI to fight U.S. forces in Iraq at the behest of the International Islamic Front (Intelligence Online, August 28, 2003).

Additionally, Pakistani terrorist outfits like Hizbul Mujahideen (HM), Lashkar-e-Taiba (LeT) and Jaish-e-Muhammad (JeM) have had strong logistical and operational ties to SIMI. In late 2002, Maharashtra police seized as many as 30 compact discs containing speeches of Maulana Masood Azhar, chief of Jaish-e-Muhammad, along with clippings of communal riots in Gujarat from SIMI offices in Aurangabad. Furthermore, there is clear evidence of operational ties between HM militants and SIMI. The arrest of Sayeed Shah Hasseb Raza and Amil Pervez with explosives in the Kolkata railway station in 2002 substantiated earlier claims of terror ties. Both Raza and Pervez were senior members of SIMI and earlier worked for HM. Investigation officers believed that the duo were in Kolkata to carry out subversive activities and recruit youth for jihadi activities (Times of India, March 2, 2002).

Conclusion

The major concern for the Indian government and the United States revolves around al-Qaeda's possible penetration of SIMI.

While there is no evidence linking SIMI to al-Qaeda, SIMI leaders are known to have made declarations of support for Osama bin Laden and his organization. In October 2001, Safdar Nagori stated in Lucknow that declaring bin Laden as an international terrorist was part of "an evil design of the U.S." He later admitted to distributing audio cassettes of bin Laden's speeches in and around Kanpur city (The Milli Gazette, October 2001). This was not a single instance of SIMI's brazen anti-Americanism. Earlier, in July 1998, SIMI cadres held demonstrations in the major cities of India against the presence of U.S. troops in Saudi Arabia, which they called "a sinister plot on the part of the enemies of Islam to desecrate and capture its holiest site" (South Asia Analysis Group, October 30, 2003). Furthermore, during a special operation, security forces recovered CDs, tapes, books, journals, posters of bin Laden and documents urging all Muslims "to take revenge for the Babri Masjid demolition, to support the secession of Kashmir as well as the Jihad of bin Laden in West Bengal" (The Statesman, October 5, 2001).

ORGANIZATIONAL HISTORY OF SIMI

Among its various objectives, the Students Islamic Movement of India (SIMI) aims to counter the jahiliya (unbeliever) section of society that Indians have embraced. The group wants to restore the Caliphate to promote the unity of ummah (Muslim community) through Jihad.

SIMI's vision of Islam derives from the writings of the journalist and Islamist ideologue, Sayyed Abdul al Maududi, the founder of the Jamaat-e-Islami. According to Maududi and SIMI, the mission of the Prophet Muhammad is viewed as the establishment of true monotheism, referred to as tawhid. In this context, it is the nature of Muslims to dominate over infidels to establish the supremacy of the Islamic faith. Usama bin Laden is considered the consummate mujahid by the SIMI rebels.

The SIMI has its roots in the Jamaat-e-Islami (JEI), one of the principal Islamist movements in South Asia. In the early 1950s the JEI established a school at Rampur, in present-day Uttar Pradesh, to provide Islamic education to university graduates. The goal was to get people with advanced education involved in the Islamist cause. To this end, the Students Islamic Organization (SIO) was established in 1956, with headquarters at Aligarh (Uttar Pradesh). By 1971, the SIO had established branches in 40 towns in Uttar Pradesh and had established contact with Muslim student groups in Bengal, Bihar, Kerala, and Andhra Pradesh. In 1975, a meeting of various Islamist student groups, all of whom shared a common vision, was held in Aligarh, and an All-India committee was established to coordinate the work of Muslim students. Two years later, on April 25, 1977, the SIMI was formed at Aligarh under the auspices of Mohammad Ahmadullah Siddiqi. The alliance with JEI ended when SIMI protested the arrival of Yasser Arafat to India. SIMI members believed the leader of the Palestinian Liberation Organization (PLO) was a puppet of western powers. The JEI disagreed with this view and cut its relationship with the more conservative SIMI activists.

SIMI originally emerged as a legal organization; however it was proscribed under the Prevention of Terrorism Act, 2002, for involvement in terrorist attacks. Group members have been charged with associating with Pakistani ISI officials in an effort to revive group efforts under a larger umbrella organization. Much of SIMI's leadership has been incarcerated in the past few years, although through strong relationships with other militant Islamic groups in the region as well as growing recruitment strategies, the group continues to thrive.

Structure

The group is largely hierarchical, although some group members have been forced to operate in a clandestine fashion, forming more of a cellular structure. The main structure consists of six main groups: the Core Group, made of up 12 leaders; the Call of Islam, a collection of subgroups tasked with transmitting instructions from the Core Group; the Ikhwan, sleeper cells who respond as needed to the leaders above them; Ansars, the group of people responsible for most terrorist attacks; Shaheen, tasked with recruiting new members; and the Muslim Brotherhood, responsible for fundraising for SIMI.

Furthermore, according to Indian police forces, there are four other divisions which they discovered among the organization: the Shahabuddin Ghouri Brigade is responsible for violent activities in southern India, the Muhammad Ghaznai Brigade is tasked with planning high-value civilian incidents in northern India, the Shaheed-al-Zarqaqi Brigade chooses high-value targets and organizes suicide attacks, and the Media Wing is responsible for releasing communiqués and messages to the public concerning group activities and attacks.

Arsenal

SIMI members employ a number of different weapons, including AK-56 rifles, Chinese made pistols, and other types of light weaponry. More alarming is evidence that the group has experimented with chemical weapons, including lethal potassium cyanide. Other substances the group is known to have experimented with include sulphuric acid and nitric acid. SIMI is known to have access to advanced plastic explosives, as well as ammonium nitrate, to make explosive compounds.

Recruitment

Many of SIMI's members join the organization following some level of religious discrimination by their professional or social communities. Members hail from all regions of India, attracting both illiterate and literate populations. Many have been drawn to the group because they were alienated by a rising Hindu nationalism in their respective neighborhoods. There are branches under the SIMI hierarchy, called Shaheen and the Tehrik-e-Tulaba-i-Arabia, who recruit children between the ages of seven and eleven and reach out to the religious students in the area.

Funding

SIMI reportedly receives generous funding from a number of different overseas organizations. Past organizations, including the World Assembly of Muslim Youth (WAMY), and the International Islamic Federation of Students Organizations (IIFSO) in Kuwait. Arshad Ayub, a SIMI member, was formerly in charge of the IIFSO, which was founded in Saudi Arabia in 1969. Further ties to the Gulf were discovered in October 2001 when a SIMI headquarters in Kozhikode was raided. Police found account logs showing financial contributions from Gulf-based individuals. The money was received through Hawala transactions.

Tactics

The group has been involved in various public as well as clandestine activities. Many members have carried out extensive bombing campaigns, including the Ahmedabad bombings in the state of Gujarat in late July 2008. Other groups affiliated with SIMI have succeeded in killing hundreds, if not thousands, of civilians during complex bombing or assault plots across the country.

ISLAMIC FUNDAMENTALIST ORGANIZATION OF SIMI

The Students Islamic Movement of India (SIMI) is an Islamic fundamentalist organization, which advocates the 'liberation of India' by converting it to an Islamic land.

The SIMI was formed at Aligarh on April 25, 1977. Mohammad Ahmadullah Siddiqi, Professor of Journalism and Public Relations at the Western Illinois University Macomb, Illinois since 1987, was the founding President of the outfit. Currently, Shahid Badar is the national president of the SIMI and Safdar Nagori serves as the secretary-general.

It originally emerged as an offshoot of the Jamaat-e-Islami Hind. The SIMI is an organisation of young fanatical students. Students up to the age of 30 years are eligible to be its member and after completing this age-limit they retire from the organization. The SIMI has declared *Jehad* against India, the aim of which is to establish Dar-ul-Islam (land of Islam) by either forcefully converting everyone to Islam or by killing.

According to news sources, SIMI is reportedly securing generous financial assistance from the World Assembly of Muslim Youth, Riyadh and also maintains close links with the International Islamic Federation of Students' Organizations, Kuwait. The Chicago-based Consultative Committee of Indian Muslims has also been found to support SIMI morally and financially. It also has links with the Jamaat-e-Islam (JeI) units in Pakistan, Bangladesh and Nepal. The SIMI is also alleged to have close links with the Pakistani-supported terrorist outfit Hizb-ul-Mujahideen.

Opposed to democracy, secularism and nationalism, SIMI has been advocating among its followers-some 400 ansars (full-time cadres) and the 19,000 ordinary members-the need to oppose "man-made" institutions and work for the *ummah* (Muslim brotherhood). The cadres of SIMI consider the Afghanistan-based Osama bin Laden as a 'true believer of Islam' and look up to him as an epitome of 'Islamic Hero'. According to Safdar Nagouri, General Secretary of SIMI, the outfit believes that Osama bin Laden is "not a terrorist'" and neither is Jammu and Kashmir an "integral part of India." At its congregations, messages and recorded speeches have been relayed from the Palestinian Hamas leader Sheikh Ahmed Yasin and Qazi Hussein Ahmed, the *Amir* of the Pakistani Jamaat. SIMI is widely believed to be against Hinduism, western beliefs and ideals, as well as other anti-Islamic cultures. Among its various objectives the SIMI aims to counter what it believes is the increasing moral degeneration, sexual anarchy in the Indian society as also the 'insensitiveness' of a 'decadent' west.

SIMI publishes several magazines in various languages which include *Vivekam* (Malayalam),*Sedhi madal* (Tamil), *Rupantar* (Bengali), *Iqraa* (Gujarati), *Tahreek* (Hindi) and *Al Harkah*(Urdu). The outfit is currently regarded as having a national presence with strong bases in Uttar Pradesh, Delhi, Madhya Pradesh, Gujarat, Kerala, Maharashtra, Andhra Pradesh and Assam. The SIMI is being utilised by various terrorist outfits because it has a well-knit network in UP, Bihar and West Bengal. News reports indicate that terrorist outfits had also found a fertile ground in the SIMI for the recruitment of new sympathisers.

SIMI is believed to enjoy the support of a large section of the Muslim populace in cities such as Kanpur, Rampur, Moradabad, Saharanpur, Lucknow and Azamgarh in Uttar Pradesh. Two SIMI activists and their three associates were arrested in Lucknow in September 2000 for delivering inflammatory speeches and inciting communal violence in the city. Official sources are reported to have identified nine districts in Uttar Pradesh where the SIMI is suspected of engaging in subversive activities-Lucknow, Kanpur, Aligarh, Agra, Faizabad, Bahraich, Barabanki, Lakhimpur Kheri and Azamgarh. It is also alleged that 12 SIMI cadres, some of them students at the Aligarh Muslim University had abducted and tortured a Deputy Superintendent of Police attached with the local branch of the Intelligence Bureau.

The Deputy Chief Minister of Maharashtra, Chhagan Bhujbal disclosed in the State Legislative Assembly on March 12, 2001, that the Karachi-based mafia chief, Chhota Shakeel in league with the Students Islamic Movement of India was inciting communal riots in some parts of the State. Sajid Sundke, the city unit chief of SIMI and four of his associates were arrested in Pune on March 11, 2001, for their suspected involvement in communal riots in Ganj Peth and Ghorpade Peth areas of the city. Ilyas Gausn, main accused in the communal violence surrendered before a judicial magistrate on April 10, 2001. The police had registered a case against Gaus on charges of fanning communal passions by making inflammatory speeches during the Friday prayers on March 1, 2001 at a mosque in the Ghorpade Peth area of the city and distribution of pamphlets. The Maharashtra government has confirmed SIMI's role in creating law and order problems in 21 different cases in the State in which 206 cadres of the outfit have been arrested. On May 9, 2001, the police arrested 13 SIMI activists, including zonal President Irshad Khan in Kurla and Vikhroli for allegedly possessing weapons (choppers) and several incriminating documents. The police alleged that among the seized documents were texts of speeches, which were reportedly intended to create communal tension in Mumbai. The State Deputy Chief Minister Chhagan Bhujbal, who also holds the home portfolio, told the Legislative Assembly that the State government had asked the Centre to proscribe the SIMI for its anti-national activities. SIMI activists were involved in the untoward incidents that occurred at various places in Maharashtra over the screening of controversial Hindi film 'Gadar'. Eleven cases had been registered and 68 persons arrested in the incidents that had taken place in cinema halls in Sangamner, Washim, Parali and Bhiwandi leading to riots, communal tension and the death of one person.

In the March 16, 2001 clash between SIMI activists and the police in Kanpur six persons including an Additional District Magistrate were killed. Violence erupted when the police prevented SIMI activists from assembling at the Parade Choraha immediately after the Friday prayers to register their resentment against the alleged burning of Quran in New Delhi. Mohammad Aquil, a former student of Aligarh Muslim University (AMU) and an active member of the SIMI was arrested by the UP Police in a bomb blast case, which occurred on August 15, 2000 in the Sabarmati Express near Faizabad. The bomb blast had caused the death of 10 passengers and had injured 40 others.

The SIMI in also alleged to be responsible for the twin blasts in Delhi on May 9, 2001 in which one person was injured. The first bomb went off near the Army Headquarters and another bomb exploded in a parking lot on Dalhousie Road.

The Gujarat government in a letter to the Union Home Ministry called for a ban on SIMI on the basis of the anti-national activities of the outfit in the state. The State police in May 2001 had arrested many SIMI leaders in Bhuj on the charges of arousing a communal flare up. The police had also invoked stipulations of the National Security Act against SIMI in Kutch after the cadres were found selling posters of Maulana Masood Azhar, Chief of the Pakistan-based Jaish-e-Mohammed who had been released in the terrorists-for-hostages swap in Kandahar.

Similarly, the Madhya Pradesh government in May 2001 urged the Government of India to proscribe the Students Islamic Movement of India. The State government while giving details in a report stated that SIMI cadres had become a threat to peace and security in the state. In Madhya Pradesh, 41 cases have been registered against the outfit's activists. In the state, Indore and Ujjain are currently considered to be strong bases of the SIMI.

HISTORICAL BACKGROUND OF STUDENTS ISLAMIC MOVEMENT OF INDIA

Till mid nineteen thirties student community in India was not communally divided. The thundering slogan of 'Vande Mataram' (Salute to Motherland) during freedom movement thrilled the students and youth of the country irrespective of their religious faith. The All India Students Conference, which subsequently formed All India Students Federation (AISF) during freedom struggle unitedly fought against the colonial rule till 1936 when a group of Muslim students seceded from it on the plea that it was a Hindu dominated organisation. They subsequently organised a group on communal lines in January 1937 and formed the All India Muslim Students Federation (AIMSF) with Mohammad Nauman as President and Mohammad Waseeque as Organising Secretary.

Initially, the Muslim students of AMU and Lucknow University strongly opposed the division of students on communal line but AIMSF worked as an adjunct to tail of Muslim League with the patronage of Mohammed Ali Jinnah and Mohammed Iqbal and finally became the main voice of Muslim students during freedom struggle. Starting its campaign with strong reservation against the non-Islamic crest in Calcutta and Nagpur universities and also against the then vibrant slogan of 'Vande Mataram' on the plea that it was anti-Islamic, AIMSF attracted the Muslim masses in favour of Pakistan Movement.

Mohammed Iqbal (1877-1938) " sent a message of encouragement cheering the Muslim students on their great achievement" (Muslim Students and Pakistan Movement-Sarfaraz Hussain Mirza, XXII, 1988). Though he could not accept the invitation of the AIMSF to preside over its first annual session (December 28, 1937) on grounds of health, he " exhorted the Muslim students to carry on their good work for the national cause (Muslim nation) without being hampered by any kind of opposition" (Ibid. PageXXIV). The theory of separate statehood for Muslim as enunciated by Iqbal in 1930 worked as a motivational factor for AIMSF.

The resolution adopted in the first annual session of AIMSF with presidential address of Jinnah hardly had anything to do with the modern and secular education to the Muslims. Its 'working scheme' had an important clause, which read "that 'Fath-e-Mecca' be observed as Muslim Students Day and demand should be made for the introduction of compulsory religious instructions for

Muslim children in all schools" (The Punjab Muslim Students Federation by Sarfaraz Hussain Mirza, Introduction, 1991).

AIMSF though made a significant contribution to the creation of Pakistan, it left a legacy of endemic Hindu-Muslim tension to be carried forward by their successive generation in democratic and secular India. Since prescription of Iqbal and Jinnah was not relevant in new state of India, Muslim students maintained a relatively low profile after partition.

With the defeat of the Indira Gandhi after emergency and emergence of the Janata Party Government at centre in 1977 a group of Muslim students under the patronage of the Jamaat-e-Islami Hind (JEIH) assembled at Aligarh on April 25, 1977 and formed Students Islamic Movement of India (SIMI). "The meeting was attended by representatives of Students Islamic Organisation from Aligarh,Calicut, Mallapuram, Madras, Hyderabad, Lucknow, Allahabad, Sholapur,, Patna, Azamgarh, Jaipur and S. Madhupur" (Radiance dated May 1, 1977). An "amalgamation of a number of students and youth bodies like Muslim Students Association, Students Islamic Union, Students Islamic Organisation, Muslim Youth Association" (Radiance, an Organ of JEIH), SIMI gradually became a platform for fanatical Muslim students, who were opposed to democracy, secularism and nationalism.

Though, SIMI was not the main voice of Muslim students of the country, in the absence of any visible resistance from them a general impression was created that it was the sole representative body of the latter. In a changed political environment SIMI planned for reviving resurgent Islam in India in a more coordinated manner with an overall objective to Islamise this biggest democracy for challenging the hegemony of Christian tradition at international level.

In its political pronouncement SIMI gave a call for restoration of the Caliphate for the unity of Ummah(Muslim community as a whole) by rejecting the concept of nationalism, democracy and secularism. Its political ideology was dominated by the mainstream Islamic fundamentalism propounded by Maulana Maududi, the founder of the JEI. Till October 1987 all the successive presidents of SIMI were the senior members of the JEI.

In Islamic history the people, who had helped the Prophet in Madina, when he was driven away from Mecca-were called Ansaars. Accordingly SIMI drew inspiration from this historical event and recruited Ansaars (helpers) as its cadres from the Muslim students below thirty years of age. While the Prophet strengthened his position in Madina with the support of Ansaars and fought beck Mecca, SIMI intended to fight against the present political system in the country with the support of its cadres (Ansaars) for establishment of Islamic State.

SIMI drew ideological inspirations from the Muslim thinkers, who launched Islamic movements in India after the decline of Muslim rule in this country in eighteenth century. Prominent among them were:

* Shah Walliullah: He had invited Ahmad Shah Abdali of Afghanistan to fight against Marathas in 1760.
* Sayyid Ahmad: As a staunch follower of Shah Waliullah, he had launched Islamic Jehad "to liberate all India from foreign domination and establish a genuine Islamic state. He was however, killed in a battle with Sikh in 1831 at Balkot" (Islamic Movement, a monthly organ of SIMI, Volume 3, January 1992).
* Haji Shariat Allah: He had launched Fara'idi movement in nineteenth century to create pure Islamic order in the society.

Maulana Sayyid Abul Ala Maududi: He was the founder of JEI.

Emergence of SIMI in democratic and secular India was a reminder to the formation of AIMSF in 1937. While the emergence of AIMSF was to strengthen movement for Pakistan, the SIMI was born to carry forward the legacy of Indian Islamic Movement launched by Muslim thinkers from Shah Waliullah to Maulana Maududi and to complete their unfinished agenda of establishing Islamic rule in the country. AIMSF countered the movement for social integration of Hindus and Muslims launched by the Congress under the leadership of Mahatma Gandhi whereas the SIMI followed Jinnah, in rejecting the concept of nationalism. While Jinnah had a secret support from the then British authorities for his communal demand, SIMI got similar support from Pakistan and other fundamentalist groups from Muslim world for its movement against secularism and democracy. Relying upon the jehadi power of Islam Jinnah succeeded in creation of Pakistan, SIMI equally depended on jehadi passion of Islam for its resurgence in India.

SIMI maintained, "it is the responsibility of this (Muslim) 'last community', the 'best community', the 'middle community', to rise up and face the challenges that surround it, to revive Deen, to lead and guide not only the Islamic world, but all of humanity along the 'Straight Path' and rescue it from the clutches of Satanic power. It is the demand of the time that Muslim youth should struggle for the superiority and establishment of Deen and revival of Islam in the light of Holy Quraan and Sunnah"(SAGA OF STRUGGLE-Annual Report 1998-2000, page 3, published by SIMI, New Delhi).

According to SIMI "the end of Khilafah(Caliphate) led to our (Muslim) disintegration into different countries on the basis of nationalism, language and other sectarian prejudices. Naturally therefore, our main responsibility is to strive in those areas, which are directly related to the reinstating of Khalifah" (Ibid. Page 8). Since its inception SIMI has kept Caliphate at the centre of discussion from local to central level and had been in communication of thought on this issue with the like-minded Islamic organisations of the world. It claimed to be in touch with 25 organisations from all over the world through Internet and its delegation participated in workshops conducted by Dawah Academy in Sri Lanka in 1999 and attended the Ijtema of Jamat-e-Islami in Pakistan in 1998. SIMI is also known to be in touch with number of Islamic organisations of the world like:

* Federation of Students Islamic Societies (FOSIS) -United Kingdom and Ireland.
* Ittehad al-Tallab al-Muslimeen -Myanmar
* Islami Chhatra Shibir -Bangladesh.
* Islami Jamiat-e-Talaba -Pakistan.
* Muslim Youth Movement of Malaysia (ABIM)-Malaysia.
* World Assembly of Muslim Youth (Riyadh)

* International Islamic Federation of Students organisations (Kuwait)
* Consultative Committee of Indian Muslims (Chicago)
* Jamaat-e-Islam units of Pakistan, Bangladesh and
* Nepal (Islamic Movement, a monthly organ of SIMI, VOL. 3, January 1992 and Internet news).

On the issue of secularism SIMI "feels it is essential to emphasise that no political party or organisation can bring about a solid and constructive change through secularism in the light of their erratic ideologies. The only way to bring about real change through ...... establishing an Islamic system of life" (Ibid. Page34). Interpretation of secularism and democracy as un-Islamic, rejection of nationalism and propagation of Islam as "only way to bring about real change" suggest that SIMI believed in confrontative Islam.

With units in different parts of India SIMI often raised voice against national and international issues, which were not in tune with its Islamic movement. In September 1985 it played a vibrant role in joining protest demonstrations all over the country against the Supreme Court verdict in Shahbano case. It campaigned against singing of Vande Mataram in U.P. schools, and protested against blasphemy regarding the Prophet. Since its inception SIMI made a protracted attempt to project itself as the main voice of Indian Muslims. Unfortunately, no Muslim student organisation came forward to counter it.

After demolition of Babari Mosque in 1992, SIMI exploited the enraged sentiments of Muslim mass. By the closing decade of twentieth century it increased its influence in a sizeable section of Muslim populace in different cities of Utaar Pradesh, Bihar, Maharashtra, Andhra Pradesh, Kerala, Tamil Nadu, Madya Pradesh, Gujarat and Assam. It always maintained pro-Pakistan stand on Indo-Pak conflict and spoke in the language of Pakistan on the issue of Jammu and Kashmir. By mid nineties its defiant and militant posture even annoyed its patron the JEIH, which started maintaining distance from it possibly due to tactical reason.

SIMI projected the Muslims killed in communal riots as martyrs and complemented those who were detained by Police with the honour of Islamic warriors sacrificing for the cause of faith. With these activities SIMI succeeded in generating some interest in middle class Muslim society that was earlier immune to violent interpretation of jehad in Islam. Its hate campaign against Qafirs (non-believers) only increased the widening gulf of mistrust between Hindus and Muslims.

SIMI considered USA as enemy of Islam and joined radical Islamists for their aggressive criticism of the presence of American troops in Soudi Arabia. "The Saudis invited in the U.S. military shortly after Saddam Hussein invaded Iraq's oil-rich neighbor Kuwait, on August 2, 1990. To help protect the kingdom and prepare to expel Iraq from Kuwait, the United States sent about 500,000 troops to Saudi Arabia". "U.S. presence was opposed by some in the kingdom — the site of Islam's holiest sites — and was among reasons cited by Saudi-born Osama bin Laden for his al-Qaida attacks on America on Sept. 11, 2001. .... The base became the centre of the U.S. presence in the country in 1997 after the Khobar Towers bombing that killed 19 airmen and injured 400 others" (http://www.chron.com/cs/CDA/ssistory.mpl/nation/2070489Aug. 28, 2003, 8:10AM-Most U.S. forces withdrawn from Saudi Arabia,Associated Press)

By 1997, when the base of American troops in Saudi Arabia, became a centre of U.S. presence, radical Islamists all over the world took it as a danger to their faith. In July 1998 SIMI held demonstration in Bombay, Calcutta and Delhi against the presence of American troops in the Holy Land of Hijaz. For SIMI, it was "not only a gross violation of some of the last instructions or will of the Prophet, but also represents a sinister plot on the part of the enemies of Islam to desecrate and capture its holiest site" (Annual Report 1998-2000 of SIMI,page 9).

SIMI publishes monthly and weekly organs in different languages like:

- Islamic Movement (Monthly) in English, Hindi and Urdu.
- Sethi Mandal (Monthly) in Tamil.
- Iqraa (Monthly) in Gujrati.
- Rupaantar (Monthly) in Bengali.

- Vivekam (Bimonthly) in Malayalam.
- Tehreek (Weekly) in Hindi.

By the closing decade of twentieth century particularly after the BJP came to power at the centre the SIMI succeeded in expanding its influence to a visible extent among Muslim students. Moreover, the Muslim middle class, a product of western education and not yet reconciled with its lost medieval supremacy-provided open space to SIMI,s cadres. With financial help from oil-rich Muslim countries to carry forward the Arab legacy of Islamic imperialism and material support from Pakistan to create disorder in India strengthened the morale of SIMI leaders. In view of inflammatory statements, alleged involvement in inciting communal violence in certain places in Maharashtra, Uttar Pradesh and other states and arrest of its leaders, some of the state Governments recommended for a ban on SIMI. Arrest of a SIMI activist in bomb blast case in Sabarmati Express near Faizabad (August 15, 2000), its alleged involvement in bomb blast incident in Delhi (May, 2001) and provocative statements of its leaders supported its jehadi design. Keeping in view its activities detrimental to national interest, Government of India ultimately put a ban on SIMI in September 2001 by declaring it an unlawful association.

Justice S.K.Aggarwal of Unlawful Activities (Prevention) Tribunal confirmed the ban notification of the Government and said:

"It is clear that the members, office bearers and activists of SIMI association have been indulging in unlawful activities.... I hold that there is sufficient cause for confirming the notification issued under sub-section(1) of Section 3 of the Act, declaring SIMI to be an unlawful association and the same is confirmed" (The Pioneer dated May 10, 2002).

Although, SIMI's challenge to democratic and secular system was temporarily defeated, propagation of radical Islam by thousands of its Ansaars will remain a source of concern for India particularly in a predominantly non-Muslim environment. Restoration of Caliphate might be the dream of radical Islamists but they ignore the historical records that suggest how Caliphate shifted to monarchy. Marshal G. S. Hodgson in his book-'the Venture of Islam' opined: "At the height of Islamic history during the Abbasid (Dynasty of Caliph) period, the Caliphate, as the traditional Islamic system of Government was an absolute monarchy. The historical records show, as a symbol of his power, there stood beside him the executioner ready to kill the most exalted personage at a word" (The Challenge of Fundamentalism by Bassam Tibi, 1998, page 160-61).

Conclusion

Purpose of this discussion is not to criticise the Muslim students but to suggest them to denounce the clerics favouring medieval interpretation of Islam. They should in fact change the mode of their thinking as exhorted by Malaysian Prime Minister Mahathir during the recent Islamic summit held in Malaysia. Pointing out to the angry mood of Muslims against anti Muslim forces, he said, " Angry people cannot think properly. And so we find some of our people reacting irrationally. In contemporary India it is also the responsibility of the present generation of Muslim students to give a wake up call to their co-religionists for developing a twenty-first century mindset, which does not approve religious hegemony of any community.

Religion is basically a spiritual path to reach the Divine. Its role in politics if any is to bring peace in society with its spiritualisation. Permeating communal interpretation of Islam in modern world in the minds of Muslim students is not only harmful to the country but it is also a major hindrance to the meaningful progress of Muslim society as a whole. Contrary to it deeply ingrained religious intolerance and violent burden of historical luggage carried by SIMI-have adversely affected the Islamic ethos of forbearance and liberalism as projected by some saner section in the community. World Tower incident in USA and attempt to attack Indian Parliament has only negated such Islamic ethos. The fundamental postulate of SIMI was Islamisation of India by recruiting Ansaars for jehadi onslaught on non-believers. Generating negative energy in the name of religion by the self-appointed guardians of Muslim students only accelerated the widening divide between Hindus and Muslims. Ironically, Muslim intellectuals, politicians or Muslim students looked other way and did not come forward to counter the divisive move of this radical outfit in assertive way.

Mahatma Gandhi tried to educate the people to " shed fear, hatred and violence for the unity, equality and brotherhood of man. He passionately believed in the unity of all religions and the universality of the essential teachings of all faiths" (Hindu dated September 28, 2003). The President A.P.J.Kalam " called upon the youth to make India economically strong with an integrated spiritual life, if they wish to live in a peaceful, prosperous and safe country" (Hindu dated September 27, 2003). But those, who created Pakistan, termed Mahatma Gandhi as a Hindu leader although he sacrificed his life for the cause of Muslims. For SIMI the saner words of Mahatma Gandhi and A.P.J. Kalam have no relevance, as they still believe in revival of Caliphate in a democratic and secular society in which majority are 'non-believers'.

3

Incidents and Statements Involving SIMI: 2000-2012

2012

December 31: An investigation by the NIA has revealed that Pakistan is relying on narcotics smugglers to push FICNs into India. In the charge sheet filed against three alleged narcotics smugglers, Dilbagh Singh, Bikramjit Singh and Gurpratap Singh, the NIA has stated that Pakistani intelligence agency ISI is using smugglers in Punjab.

Investigators have found evidence that links IM 'India chief' Yasin Bhatkal with the Delhi High Court unsuccessful bomb blast attack of May 25, 2011. The case is being investigated by the NIA.

December 20: Four IM militants, already in Delhi Police custody arrested by Maharashtra ATS in connection with Pune serial blasts (August 1, 2012) and remanded in Police custody till January 1.

December 19: With regard to the cases of serial blasts in the courts of Lucknow, Faizabad and Varanasi (all in Uttar Pradesh) of November 23, 2007, the ATS is saying the blasts were jointly carried out by HuJI and IM.

December 16: The Interrogation Report of IM militant Fasih Mehmood, revealed a detailed account of IM's foundation, his first interaction with IM masterminds Yasin Bhatkal, Riyaz and Iqbal Bhatkal.

December 15: The judicial custody of five India IM militants accused in Pune (Maharashtra) blast case of August 1, 2012 and that of Fasih Mehmood was extended by a Delhi court till December 17, 2012.

December 11: The Kurla Police Station in Mumbai (Maharashtra) that is probing a threat letter allegedly sent by IM to a shop owner, Paras Gupta, owner of Deepak Farsan, found the threat letter's origin in Bangalore.

The Union Minister of State for Home Affairs, R.P.N. Singh said LeT, IM, BKI and KTF are interested in carrying out terrorist attacks in India but there are no inputs about the Taliban.

December 10: A special MCOCA court rejected the bail application of SIMI cadre, Ehtesham Siddiqui facing trial among others in the July 11, 2006 train bomb blasts in Mumbai (Maharashtra).

December 4: NIA has announced a reward of INR 4, 00,000 on information leading to the arrest of absconding IM terrorist Abdul Subhan Qureshi alias Touqeer.

December 1: The Delhi Police has charge-sheeted a suspected IM operative, Kamal Hassan alias Bilal for his alleged role in the Jama Masjid (Delhi) blast-cum-shootout case of September 19, 2010. He is also an accused in Bangalore's (Karnataka) Chinnaswamy Stadium blast case of April 17, 2010.

November 27: Union Minister of State for Home Affairs R. P. N Singh said various terrorist groups, including LeT, IM and JeM are engaged in terrorist activities in the country, often supported by their parent outfits based abroad, particularly in Pakistan. Singh said other terrorist outfits which are active in India include HuM, Al-Umma, Al Badr, HuJI, HM, BKI, KZF and KTF.

November 22: Mumbai (Maharashtra) CB has arrested a software engineer, identified as Tajool Kazi, from Hyderabad (Andhra Pradesh) for his alleged role in BEST bus at Ghatkopar attack (Mumbai, Maharashtra) on December 6, 2002, which killed four people. Kazi is an active cadre of SIMI.

November 8: LeT operative Syed Zabiuddin Ansari aka Abu Jundal sent money to India from Saudi Arabia at least twice after the Mumbai attack.

The Maharashtra ATS filed a supplementary charge sheet against Jundal in the May 9, 2009 Aurangabad (Maharashtra) arms haul case before MCOCA Court.

Jundal also told Gujarat Police that LeT used Gujarat riots (2002) as an emotional trigger to introduce Gujarat youths to terrorism. A strong terror network has been built in the state.

November 6: IM operative Fasih Mahmood has reportedly admitted to the Police that he co-founded IM along with fugitive terrorists Riyaz, Iqbal and Yasin Bhatkal, with the help of some ansars and ikhwans of the SIMI after it was banned by the Central Government in 2001.

UMHA Sushil Kumar Shinde showed concern over the efficacy of red corner notices on terrorist vis-a-vis Pakistan providing shelter to the perpetrators of March 12, 1993 Mumbai (Maharashtra) serial bomb blasts and November 26, 2008 (26/11) Mumbai terror attacks, like Dawood Ibrahim and Hafiz Saeed.

November 5: Investigations into the plan to attack Delhi during Deepawali by four IM terrorists, arrested on October 11, 2012, by Delhi Police, have revealed that its 'moderator', identified as Raju Bhai, may be in Delhi-National Capital Region.

Police learnt that "several cadres of LeT and IM are hiding in Mumbai (Maharasthra), Karnataka and Andhra Pradesh. LeT and IM are coordinating with associates of Fayaz Kagzi in Saudi Arabia and Pakistan.

November 4: The Indian authorities have approached the Saudi Government with a fresh request for four more IM cadres, suspected to be hiding there.

In a list submitted to the UAE, the Government has urged to deport Ubed Kola, an accused in Mumbai"s 13/7 triple bomb blast case. Kola is suspected to have played a vital role in transferring hawala money from Dubai to India.

Special Cell of Delhi Police has also learnt that Saudi Arabia-based IM 'commander' Fayyaz Kagzi had been staying there using the name of "Abdul Rehman".

November 3: The Maharashtra ATS filed a supplementary charge sheet in the special court against suspected LeT operative

Zabihuddin Ansari alias Abu Jundal in the 2006 Aurangabad arms haul case.

November 2: The questioning of suspected IM operative Fasih Mahmood has revealed details of the logistical support he provided for the terror strike at the Chinnaswamy Stadium (April 17, 2010) at Bangalore (Karnataka).

November 1: The custody of IM operative Fasih Mehmood, deported from Saudi Arabia and arrested by the Delhi Police Special Cell on October 22, 2012 was handed over to the Bangalore (Karnataka) City Police.

October 31: A Delhi trial court sent a suspected IM terrorist,Sayed Firoz *alias* Hamza, allegedly involved in the, August 1, 2012, Pune serial blasts to 14 days of judicial custody.

A classified report recently circulated in top government circles revealed that India's most wanted terrorist and IM head, Yasin Bhatkal, is hiding in Bangladesh, having established a good network in Dhaka and Chittagong with the help of Pakistan's ISI.

October 29: Tight security measures have been put in place at the Mahabodhi temple in Gaya District of Bihar, to ward off any possible terrorist attack by the IM.

October 26: Maqbool has revealed that the Pune serial blast carried out by IM is linked to the recent arrest of 16 terrorists in Karnataka who plotted to kill some politicians, Hindu leaders and journalists.

Mumbai ATS chief Rakesh Maria said that Maqbool has no connection with the Pune serial blasts of August 1, 2012.

October 25: Fasih Mahmood, the IM 'treasurer' recently deported from Saudi Arabia, revealed the identities of two more ideologues associated with IM.

The ATS of Mumbai Police moved a court seeking the custody of four suspected IM terrorists, Asad Khan, Imran Khan, Feroze Hamza and Irfan Mustafa Langda, allegedly involved in the Pune serial blasts of August 1, 2012.

October 24: According Zabihuddin Ansari alias Abu Jundal, Abu Ismail had worked as a compounder at a Civil Hospital in Karachi, in Pakistan, before joining the terror outfit camp.

Fasih Mahmood disclosed that Pakistan's ISI has stationed officials in Saudi Arabia with whom he had been working in close co-ordination. The primary task of ISI operatives in Saudi Arabia is to ensure greater cooperation between IM and LeT and promote anti-India terror activities from Saudi soil.

October 23: Delhi Police arrested another suspected IM terrorist, identified as Sayed Maqbool alias Zuber, from Hyderabad (Andhra Pradesh) for his alleged involvement in the August 1, 2012 Pune serial blasts. The total number of arrests in the Pune blasts has gone up to five.

October 22: Syed Zabiuddin Ansari alias Abu Jundal is being probed by Gujarat ATS that whether did he set up sleeper cells for terrorists in Gujarat. ATS officials produced Jundal before a local court which granted him remand till November 3.

Top IM leader Fasih Mohammad, a key fund-raiser for the outfit, was arrested by the Delhi Police from Delhi's IGI Airport soon after his deportation from Saudi Arabia.

October 21: Delhi Police prepared a list of 460 important places that may be attacked by IM terrorists during Diwali. LeT have threatened to blow up important places around Diwali.

Abu Jundal was brought to Ahmadabad by a team of State ATS.

Jundal revealed how Pakistan's ISI officer Major Sameer Ali had a long conversation with Zaki-ur-Rehman Lakhvi, chief operational commander of LeT, a few hours before the attack.

October 19: Abu Jundal has said that he had seen US national David Headley while undergoing training in Muridke city of Lahore District in Punjab Province of Pakistan.

A youth from Aurangabad District of Maharashtra, who deposed before the Court said that he used to live in Beed District earlier and had seen Baig working with terror suspect Abu Jundal in 2006.

According to Special officials from Delhi police-on August 1, 2012 three IM terrorists travelled by a PMPML bus from Kasarwadi (Maharashtra) to Jangli Maharaj Road (Maharashtra) to orchestrate the serial blasts.

October 18: Fayyaz Kagzi, LeT operative, helped Abu Jundal in fleeing the country when he was under the radar of the ATS after the Aurangabad arms haul case of May, 2006.

IM militants, who executed Pune (Maharashtra) serial blasts of August 1, 2012, used phones and free software to evade security agencies as they communicated with Riyaz Bhatkal, the IM 'chief' of India.

October 17: IM terrorist Irfan, allegedly involved in the Pune (Maharashtra) serial blasts (August 1, 2012), had also welcomed Pakistan nationals Shaqir and Ahmed, who had come to India as specialist bomb-makers. They were the same men who had carried out the July 13, 2011, (13/7) serial blasts at Zaveri Bazaar in Mumbai (Maharashtra) under the assumed identities of Waqas and Tabrez.

Police have also learnt from the arrested men that several LeT and IM operatives are hiding in Mumbai and other parts of Maharashtra, Karnataka and Andhra Pradesh. LeT and IM are in constant touch with Pakistan and Saudi Arabia-based associates of Fayyaz Kagzi.

The Police custody of three suspected IM operatives Asad Khan, Imran Khan and Syed Feroze alleged for their alleged involvement in the Pune serial blast has been extended till October 27, 2012.

October 16: Special cell of the Delhi Police searched the two-room tenement in Kasarwadi (Pune District) where IM militants stayed before the Pune (Maharashtra) blats of August 1, 2012 and found traces of ammonium nitrate, wires and batteries at the tenement.

Revelations made by Abu Jundal disclosed that LeT has permeated Bangladesh administration.

Jundal has revealed that at least 12 IM and LeT modules have been trained to target major Indian cities.

According to the supplementary charge sheet filed against Abu Jundal, he imparted training to the gunmen in spreading wrong information about the real purpose of the attack.

Intelligence agencies have established that the bombs used in both Zaveri Bazaar blasts in Mumbai (July 13, 2011) 13/7 and Pune

(Maharashtra) serial blasts (August 1, 2012) were made by two Pakistani LeT militants.

Asad Khan, Imran Khan and Feroz, who were recently arrested by Delhi Police for Pune serial blasts and for plotting a similar attack in the national capital.

October 14: Terror outfit IM has set up base in West Asia, with Saudi Arabia emerging as preferred destination to launch its operations in India. Pakistan's ISI is arranging safe havens for the terror operatives in West Asian countries.

The Saudi link and the activities on social media are phenomena that have surfaced following the recent arrest of IM terrorists in Delhi linked with Pune (Maharashtra) blast of August 1, 2012.

The Special Cell team investigating the August 1, 2012 Pune (Maharashtra) serial blast case claims to have gathered evidence to indicate that the attacks were also meant to avenge the murder of alleged IM militant Qateel Siddique in Yerawada Jail.

Delhi Police have identified a house where the conspiracy for Pune blast hatched. Sayyed Feroze led a team of the Delhi Police Special Cell to a house which he and five others had rented as a meeting ground a month prior to the bid.

Despite the arrest of three suspected IM terrorists who were planning major strikes in Delhi during the Diwali season, sources in Delhi Police say that the threat is not over.

October 12: Investigators have learned that the three IM terrorists, arrested for the August 1, 2012 Pune (Maharashtra) serial blasts, had conducted a recce at five crowded places in Mumbai on July 24. The targets included Borivli railway station, Juhu beach, Vashi, Bandra and Andheri. They also planned to attack the Maharashtra ATS headquarters at Nagpada.

The Mumbai plan was dropped, though, on the instructions of Riyaz Bhatkal from Pakistan.

Three had met Yusuf Himayat Baig through Kashif Biyabani, brother of Akhef Biyabani who was arrested for the 2006 Aurangabad arms haul case.

The two terrorists in this IM module-Shaqir and Ahmed who are currently absconding-were involved in previous blasts as well.

According to Police, Raju Bhai, an important link in the Pune blasts case, got the Pul Prahladpur flat in Delhi on rent for the three IM militants using a fake name.

A team of Pune ATS officers have reached Delhi and are coordinating with the Delhi Police's Special Cell. Karnataka Police officers will reach here on October 13.

IM was planning to carry out a fidayeen attack at the Bodhgaya (Bihar) temple to avenge the recent killing of Muslims allegedly by Buddhists in Myanmar.

LeT leader Fayyaz Kagzi, said to be the mentor of three IM terrorist arrested in New Delhi, did not engage Asad, Imran and Sayed but they volunteered to carry out jehad.

Aurangabad ATS continued to question people in touch with IM operatives Imran and Asad Khan in Aurangabad and Nanded (Both in Maharashtra) to gather more information about the duo and their dealings.

IM is worth INR 500 million and its major donors are the rich Sheikhs of Saudi and Gulf countries. Pakistan's ISI has entrusted LeT to arrange funds for IM during holy month of Ramadan when rich donate for zakaat.

October 11: Syed Afaque Iqbal has now been booked by the SIT for reviving banned SIMI in Hyderabad (Andhra Pradesh). Two days after taking the custody of Iqbal, Hyderabad Police has claimed to have gathered sufficient leads to charge him of revving banned SIMI in the city.

Delhi Police busted a gang of IM terrorists-Asad Khan, Imran Khan and Sayed Feroz alias Hamza, all belonging to Maharashtra, which carried out the serial blasts in Pune on August 1, 2012 and had planned to attack Delhi and Bodh Gaya (Bihar) during the coming festival season.

The terrorists were carrying 5kg of explosives and 10 detonators as part of the plot to explode at least 10 bombs in Delhi and the pilgrim city of Bodh Gaya.

One of the arrested persons, Asad, is allegedly linked also to the Aurangabad arms haul case in which Jundal is also an accused.

Delhi Police stumbled upon the IM module by tracing their phone calls and email conversations with their contacts, suspected to be the Bhatkal brothers and Kagzi in Pakistan and Saudi Arabia.

Aurangabad ATS, led by Navinchandra Reddy searched residence of Asad Khan in Naigaon (Pune District), and seized documents. Asad's younger brother, Hussain Khan, has been picked up for questioning.

It was through Kagzi that Asad was introduced to Riyaz and Iqbal. He then remained in touch them through email and phone.

The arrested had made three attempts to plant a bomb on the premises of the Yerawada central jail and a local court in Pune.

October 10: IM terrorist, identified as Langde Irfan, allegedly involved in the Pune (Maharashtra) serial blasts (August 1, 2012) was arrested in Jaipur by the Delhi Police. With this, the total number of arrests in the case has gone up to four.

October 9: IM 'chief' Yasin Bhatkal started his recruitment from a room near Darbhanga airport. Bhatkal would spot recruits and Kafeel used to indoctrinate them into IM, said ATS officials.

October 8: Abu Jundal was remanded in the NIA custody till October 20, 2012 by a Delhi court.

Yasin Bhatkal, 'chief' of IM India operations, planted the bomb at Dadar in the July 13, 2011 (13/7) Mumbai (Maharashtra) serial blasts himself, according to the confessional statement of Nadeem Sheikh, a key accused in the triple blasts.

The Maharashtra ATS which is probing the case has also learnt that on July 7, 2011, six persons including Bhatkal, Ahmed, Waqas, Tabrez, Munnabhai and Sheikh had met at Habib building in Byculla to plan the serial blasts.

October 1: Feroz, an IM terrorist, which carried out the serial blasts in Pune on August 1, 2012 and had planned to attack Delhi and Bodh Gaya (Bihar) during the coming festival season, was arrested by Delhi Police from Nizamuddin railway station in Delhi.

September 26: Asad and Imran, IM terrorists, which carried out the serial blasts in Pune on August 1, 2012 and had planned to attack Delhi and Bodh Gaya (Bihar) during the coming festival season, were arrested by Delhi Police from their Pul Prahladpur accommodation.

October 3: Thane Police booked former SIMI militant Saquib Nachan and four others under the MCOCA. Saquib Nachan, is also accused in Mulund bomb blast of 2003, was arrested by police for allegedly firing at an advocate in Bhiwandi on August 3, 2012.

October 2: Alleged IM and SIMI operative Afaq Iqbal alias Danish Riyaz was brought to Hyderabad from Gujarat by the SIT of Hyderabad Police. He was sent to fourteen-day judicial custody.

September 30: Maharashtra ATS and Central agencies probing the August 1, 2012 Pune (Maharashtra) blasts are now closing in on fronts funding IM and its activities. One such key front based in south India projects itself as dedicated to social service but is modelled along the lines of the banned JuD in Pakistan; the LeT parent body.

September 26: NIA has registered a fresh case against the members of the banned outfit IM for recruiting, financing and running terror camps. The agency said that the IM has received large amount of money over a period of one year from Pakistan, Saudi Arabia and other Gulf countries.

According to the UMHA, there are more than 52 militants of the IM who have been identified by the Police and are presently on the run.

Investigations have revealed that IM, has links with the international Islamic organization HuT banned in Germany and Bangladesh.

Delhi Police had filed two charge sheets against IM members and the alleged handler in 26/11) attacks case, Syed Zabiuddin Ansari alias Abu Jundal.

September 24: The Mumbai (Maharashtra) High Court, granted bail on INR 50,000 to Mohammad Atik Iqbal, an alleged IM operative.

IM militants had been instructed to take to crimes like dacoity and snatching to fund their terror activities in India without depending on hawala money. besides Madhya Pradesh, the terror imprint has been found on robberies committed even at Pune (Maharashtra), Patna (Bihar), Jaipur (Rajasthan) and Ahmedabad (Gujarat).

September 23: Saudi Arabia has asked for more evidence from India about involvement of IM operative Fasih Mohammed in terror activities especially in the conspiracy behind the bomb blasts in Bangalore and Delhi.

September 21: The prosecution in the German bakery bomb blast (February 13, 2010) case got an enhance on September 21, 2012 as the role of IM 'chief' Yasin Bhatkal, the man wanted for a string of terror attacks across the country, came to light for the first time while recording evidence of a key witness.

September 16: ATS investigating the August 1, 2012 Pune (Maharashtra) serial blasts have detained a jeweller for processing INR 2.2 million *hawala* transaction from Dubai and delivering it to two persons, suspected to be part of the sleeper cells of IM.

A garment trader, identified as Arvindkumar Jain, was arrested in Mumbai in an eight year old case of FICN, booked by the Thane crime branch.

Abu Jundal key conspirator of 26/11 told interrogators that he was assisting the LeT in maintaining their website for six to seven months prior to the 26/11 strike.

September 15: It was reported that IM perpetrators were paid INR 1 million, sent through *hawala*from UAE, for 13/7 blasts.

September 13: A court, awarded five-year rigorous imprisonment to three militants, identified as Khalid, Sami and Shahja of SIMI in a 2008 case for possessing arms and distributing objectionable pamphlets in Shyamnagar area of Dhar District in Madhya Pradesh.

September 12: With the fourth anniversary of September 13, 2008 Delhi serial blast, Delhi Police has started tracking the members of IM especially Yasin Bhatkal *alias* Shahrukh, as they fear an IM strike.

September 11: UMHA has asked the NIA to lodge a fresh FIR against IM. UMHA named all the absconding members as accused.

Sources said the FIR would have names of about a dozen absconding IM members, including those holed up in Pakistan.

September 9: The IM is out to resurrect the outfit by dumping former cadres of the Students Islamic Movement of India and starting recruitments afresh, the Delhi Police have warned.

September 7: The Delhi Police, in a conference presentation said the IM was targeting disenchanted youth comprising 'petty criminals' and 'highly-paid software professionals' for assembling bombs, Internet hacking and is extensively using social networking sites to avoid detection.

September 4: MHA has asked West Bengal government to keep tabs on the activities of SIMI in the state.

The UMHA is concerned about the steady rise in terrorist activists in the Marathwada region of Maharshtra particularly Aurangabad, Jalna, Parbhani, Beed and Nanded Districts. It was found that activists of the banned Student SIMI, IM and certain organisations from neighbouring Andhra Pradesh, were focusing on the Marathwada region.

August 30: Initial reports had said the four suspected IM activists involved in the April 17, 2010, Chinnaswamy stadium (Bangalore) blast case were picked up by Police.

Mumbai Police arrested another desecrator of Amar Jawan memorial at the Azad Maidan in Mumbai (Maharashtra) during the August 11, 2012, violence. The arrestee was identified as Shahbaz Abdul Kadir Sheikh. He along with other desecrators Abdul Kadir Mohammad Yunus Ansari and Salim Chaukiya, who allegedly snatched a rifle from a Police official, were said to be the key rioters in the case.

August 27: The Supreme Court refused to direct the Union Government on extradition or deportation of IM militant Fasih Mohammed from Saudi Arabia Authority. After going through all the correspondence between the Centre and the Saudi Arabia Government, a bench of justices P Sathasivam and Ranjan Gogoi said it is for the Centre to pursue the case further as it cannot pass any direction for bringing him back.

August 22: In its recently submitted inquiry report, the Maharashtra CID said that the murder of suspected IM militant Qateel Mohammed Siddiqui inside Pune's Yerwada Central Jail on June 8, 2012.

August 21: The Government has officially called the August 1 Pune (Maharashtra) serial blasts a terror act. The Centre had maintained so far that all angles were being probed and that the blasts, which injured one person, could be an act of terrorists.

The Bangalore and Delhi Police are preparing documents in Arabic for the extradition of 28-year-old IM operative Fasih Mohammed from Saudi Arabia as sought by the Saudi authorities. Fasih is wanted in connection with blast that occurred outside the Chinnaswamy Stadium in Bangalore (Karnataka) on April 17, 2010, and a shootout at Jama Masjid in Old Delhi onSeptember 19, 2010.

Bangalore city Police are planning to send a proposal to the state Government, seek its approval for setting up a special court to speed up the trial of the Chinnaswamy stadium blast case. They will also ask the Government to appoint a special public prosecutor for the case.

August 20: Cyber security agencies have detected the hand of the PFI in Kerala and Bangladesh-based HuJI, while tracking SMSs that led to the exodus of Northeast people, said a cyber expert.

According to Police officials, Mohammed Sajjid, founding member of banned IM is a key suspect in the August 1 Pune (Maharashtra) serial bomb blast.

August 16: Initial investigation shows role of SIMI in the violence at Azad Maidan in Mumbai. Security agencies have pinpointed SIMI operative Saquib Nachan to be the mastermind of the attack.

CCCI probe into the SMSs and the uploaded morphed pictures circulated among the minority community which led to provocation at Azad Maidan Mumbai on August 11 has so far not found any IP to suggest that it had originated from Pakistan.

August 12: A communication between terrorist of two terrorist organisations, LeT and IM, intercepted by the central IB has revealed that terror operatives failed to plant a bomb-laden car in Ahmadabad.

A high alert was sounded at Jaipur (Rajasthan) airport by the CISF and the city Police in the wake of an IB alert on a possible hijack plan at four probable spots in the country, including Jaipur.

Mujib Shaikh, IM mitant and an accused in the serial blasts that took place in Ahmedabad (Gujarat) on July 26, 2008, told the Ahmadabad Crime Branch officials that Abus Subhan *alias*Tauqeer-a terror operative and one of the masterminds of Ahmadabad serial blasts-could be behind the August 1 Pune serial blasts.

Mujib Shaikh told the Ahmadabad Crime Branch officials that Abus Subhan *alias* Tauqeer could be behind the August 1 Pune serial blasts and is now heading the IM.

August 9: A strand of hair found on a defused bomb at Chinnaswamy Stadium on April 17, 2010, helped Police establish the identity of a terrorist named Mohammed Qateel Siddiqui (30), who planted it. Siddiqqui was killed in a brawl in Pune central jail.

August 8: The forensic experts' report on August 1 Pune bomb blast reveals the use of a cohesive mixture of ammonium nitrate and furnace oil as well as use of several.

August 6: The Ahmadabad crime branch has taken into its custody IM suspect in the Ahmadabad serial blasts case, Mujib Sheikh. Sheikh has been brought to the city for further questioning regarding the Ahmedabad serial blasts of 2008 and the planting of bombs in Surat.

SC granted two weeks time to the Centre to file its written submission on the whereabouts of suspected IM member Fasih Mohammed, who is currently in the custody of Saudi Arabia Police, in connection with several terror acts in India.

Rajasthan State ATS intensified its search for the four absconding suspects associated with the IM terror outfit of the Jaipur serial blasts of May.

A SC bench of justices P Sathasivam and Ranjan Gogoi granted two weeks time to the Centre to file its written submission on the whereabouts of suspected IM member Fasih Mohammed, who is currently in the custody of Saudi Arabia Police, in connection with several terror acts in India.

August 5: The intensity of the four explosions on Jungli Maharaj Road, Pune on August 1 would have been higher had all the charges gone off, and if the ammonium nitrate used was not outdated or if RDX had been used, said officials from the BDDS.

The involvement of IM has worried Gujarat Police, because the state has always figured high on the terrorists' hit list.

The Ahmadabad crime branch has taken into its custody IM suspect in the Ahmadabad serial blasts case, Mujib Sheikh, after he was brought to the city on a transfer warrant from Madhya Pradesh. Sheikh has been brought to the city for further questioning regarding the Ahmedabad serial blasts of 2008 and the planting of bombs in Surat.

August 4: Karnataka ATS raided the houses of suspected IM militants Shaikh Altaf and Shaikh Ramzan in Bijapur in connection to the Pune blasts.

Investigators based on a host of factors and indications are convinced that the low-intensity serial blasts in Pune on August 1 were executed by the IM.

Abu Jundal, told the Police that the Pune German Bakery blast conspiracy was planned in 2008 but it could not be executed as the LeT bosses wanted a Mumbai operation first.

Abu Jundal told the crime branch of Mumbai Police that the brothers Riyaz Bhatkal and Iqbal Bhatkal are hiding in Pakistan, but he doesn't know much about them. The Bhatkal brothers are involved in several serial blasts across the country and had fled to Pakistan in 2009.

Karnataka ATS raided the houses of suspected IM militants Shaikh Altaf and Shaikh Ramzan in Bijapur (Karnataka) in connection to the Pune blasts.

Investigators based on a host of factors and indications are convinced that the low-intensity serial blasts in Pune on August 1 were executed by the IM. While it may have been executed by some new recruits of the terror outfit, IM leadership that is mostly intact and believed to be hiding in Pakistan may have planned the attack, sources say.Further, the investigators have ruled out the possibility of Maoists or Hindu fringe groups being responsible for the four blasts and two unexploded IED, sources said.

August 3: Justice V. K. Shali Tribunal has submitted its report confirming the ban on SIMI that it has links with Pakistan-based terror outfits, including the LeT and its frontal outfit, the Indian Mujahideen IM.

Maharashtra Police officials said that they prepared sketches of two persons who may have planted explosives in Pune on August 1. The investigators suspect involvement of at least three persons in executing the serial bomb blasts in Pune.

The court of additional sessions judge N P Dhote deferred the hearing in the February 13, 2010, German bakery bomb blast case that killed 17 people and injured 64 till August 24, 2012. The hearing was deferred as the special public prosecutor Raja Thakare had sent a plea.

ATS officers from Karnataka and Gujarat reached Pune to probe link of August 1, blast to their states in any manner. The Karnataka Police interrogated Dayanand Patil, the only injured in the blast and a suspect, and his wife, as they are a natives of Kohinoor village in Basavakalyan *taluk*(administrative unit) of Karnataka's Bidar District.

The investigating agencies suspect that a new terror module engineered August 1 blasts in Pune. According to officials, the suspicion stems from the nature of the material used in the bombs and the modus operandi of the group. The investigators believe five to six persons may have carried out the blasts.

August 2: NIA members said that entire operation of August 1 Pune (Maharashtra) serial blasts looks as though it had been planned locally. Right from the timer devices, a locally-made clock and locally purchased bicycles, all indications are that the entire operation was planned in Pune.

"Although the IM [Indian Mujahedeen] had resurfaced from Bihar, it would not be correct to say that their modules are dead in Pune, which was once their headquarters," Intelligence Bureau officials said.

Home Minister R R Patil said that Pune police had received a letter warning revenge over the death of alleged IM operative Qateel Ahmad Siddiqui in Yerawada jail.

Top police officers in Pune refuted reports of having received a specific report from the SID or letters warning them about the bomb blasts on the busy Jangli Maharaj road a day earlier.

An unnamed official as saying that a design flaw in the bombs caused them to explode partially and prevented the shrapnel from spreading. Without naming any group, an unnamed Home Ministry official in New Delhi said there were "credible leads" pointing to a "big plan" by a terror outfit. "

Investigation in the serial low-intensity blasts in the city has hit a hurdle as some CCTV cameras at the explosion sites have been found to be non-functional. Sources in the investigative agencies said that the CCTV cameras installed at Dena Bank, McDonald's and Bal Gandharva traffic square, near where the explosions occurred, have not yielded any clue so far and some of them were non-functional.

August 1: Four low-intensity blasts rocked the busy Junglee Maharaj Road in Pune injuring one person. Two other bombs were defused by the Anti-Terror Squad. All explosives were kept in cake boxes and placed within a kilometer range.

Home Secretary RK Singh said that the injured person is being treated as suspect and questioned by the police. Mr. Singh also suspects a terror angle as it was a planned attack. After the blasts all cities across India are on high alert. A bomb disposal squad swept Jantar Mantar in New Delhi where Anna Hazare and his activists are on a hunger strike, supported by a large crowd.

Police sources said that the preliminary report of the FSL indicates that ammonium nitrate was used in the Pune blasts. According to the city's Police Commissioner Gulab Rao Pol, the man who was suspected to have carried one of the four bombs that exploded in Pune on August 1 night, and was injured has been identified as Dayanand Patil, a local tailor. He is a local resident and works as a tailor in Junglee Maharaj Road.

The Pune Police commissioner Gulabrao Pol have denied the

August 1 attack to be a terror attack; however, ATS suspect it to be work of IM.

According to a report, bicycle has once again become the vehicle of terror after the August 1 Pune blast suggests the use of bicycle to carry out attack.

July 27: Jundal reiterated the presence of IM founder brothers Riyaz and Iqbal Bhatkal in Karachi, Pakistan.

July 26: PFI is the new face of banned extremist outfit SIMI and is engaged in anti-national activities, Kerala Police's Intelligence Wing Chief, Siddique Rawther, told the Kerala High Court.

Jundal has told the Mumbai crime branch that he was associated with the activities of the banned SIMI in Beed since early 2000. But it was in 2005 that he got close to LeT operative Aslam Kashmiri, who he met in Beed, and started participating in terror activities.

Delhi Police Commissioner Neeraj Kumar said that there could not be a set time-frame for the deportation of alleged IM operative, Fasih Mohammed, from Saudi Arabian, as it involved legal procedures. The CBI on behalf of the Karnataka and the Delhi Police had got a red-corner notice issued against Fasih through the Interpol.

July 25: Jundal further revealed that, the SIMI, a banned outfit, has been acting as the 'backbone' for militant organisations providing them with critical logistical support to carry out terror strikes in the country. He said, SIMI has links with JeM, HM and the ISI.

July 23: The STF of Kolkata Police believes suspected IM militant; Haroon Rashid was probably planning a strike during Mamata Banerjee's Martyrs' Day rally on the same day. Haroon wanted in connection with the 13/7 Mumbai blasts and other terror acts in Andhra Pradesh and Gujarat.

Jundal said LeT was planning to revamp its Indian agency, IM, but admitted he had never met the Bhatkal brothers. The IM was setting up modules in India with the help of its Saudi Arabian modules.

July 21: Abu Jundal provided first-hand evidence of recent vintage that "Project Karachi", an ISI backed terror scheme to provide shelter to Indian terror fugitives, continues to present a danger to India.

Some prominent members of the IM believed to be in Pakistan and the names of those who have cropped up in Jundal's interrogation include Riyaz and Iqbal Bhatkal, Aslam Kashmiri, Fayaz Kagzi and Aakif.

July 19: Jundal revealed that Yasin Bhatkal, one of the most wanted terrorists in the country and 'chief' of the IM, is now hiding in Bangladesh with the support of ISI.

India has decided to formally move for Fasih Mehmood's deportation from Saudi Arabia so that the role of IM in several blasts in the country can be investigated.

July 17: Kolkata Police's STF arrested a suspected terrorist, identified as Harun Rashid, of banned SIMI, believed to be active behind the Islamic terrorism in India and having close links with terror outfit IM.

Interpol has informed the MHA that IM Fasih Mohammed terrorist, who is wanted in several terror cases and is in the custody of Saudi Arabian authorities, cannot be extradited to India.

Haroon Rashid, suspected IM militant arrested from Kolkata on July 17.

July 15: Investigation in bomb blast cases has thrown light on the fact that not only low level militants but also top rung of IM have cheated their sponsors of big amount of cash.

LeT militant, Abu Jundal, has revealed that the 26/11 attacks were most probably planned spanning across five countries-Pakistan, Sri Lanka, US, Italy and France.

July 13: The questioning of IM militants-Kafeel and Kamaal Ansari by Delhi Special Cell has revealed that the IM's Indian head, Yaseen Bhatkal, had entrusted them with the job of conducting recees and arranging for arms and ammunitions to the strike force that actually carried out the attacks.

The questioning of IM militants-Kafeel and Kamaal Ansari by Delhi Special Cell has revealed that the IM's Indian head, Yaseen Bhatkal, had entrusted them with the job of conducting recees and arranging for arms and ammunitions to the strike force that actually carried out the attacks.

A year after the 13/7 blasts, the probe led by Maharashtra's ATS has gone transnational as the key wanted accused are believed to be operating from Saudi Arabia, Dubai, Nepal and Pakistan.

July 12: The arrested LeT handler Syed Zabiuddin Ansari *alias* Abu Jundal has told the Intelligence and Delhi Police officials that "10 SIM cards, used by 10 terrorists, including lone survivor Ajmal Kasab, in Mumbai were procured and sent to Pakistan by Abu Zar, Lashkar-e-Taiba's commander in Jammu and Kashmir", said a source.

Fasih Mohammed, an accused in the April 17, 2010, Chinnaswamy Stadium (Bangalore) blast and the September 19, 2010, shooting incident near Jama Masjid (Delhi) and detained in Saudi Arabia, is likely to be deported to India next week.

July 11: IM India chief and one of the main conspirators and executors of the triple blasts in Mumbai on 13/7)Mohammed Ahmed Sadibappa *alias* Yasin Bhatkal used to impart *jihadi*speeches to the youth in a school library at Darbhanga in Bihar.

July 10: After the arrest of top LeT militant Abu Jundal, Indian security agencies have over the past few days intercepted several wireless messages close to the LoC in the Kashmir Valley in which LeT commanders operating out of Muzaffarabad in PoK are telling counterparts across the border to launch major terror strikes in the region.

26/11 attack handler Abu Jundal has been in custody of the Delhi Police's Special Cell since June 21, but insiders say that his 'real' interrogation is yet to begin. According to IB and the Delhi Police are seeking to establish the exact links between LeT and the IM.

July 9: A Delhi court remanded to 10 days Delhi Police custody two suspected militants of IM identified as Kafil Akhtar and Kamal Hasan for their alleged involvement in reviving the banned outfit.

Syed Zaibuddin Ansari aka Abu Jundal, the key handler of 26/ 11 attack was given eight different aliases by LeT leadership since his induction in the outfit till his stay in Saudi Arabia, which also suggests that the organisation used more than one *Quniyat* (nickname) for its militants.

Delhi Police will be writing to Interpol asking for details of Ansari's Pakistani SIM card. A source said "we will seek SIM card of Jundal from FIA of Pakistan through Interpol.

The Union Government revealed the whereabouts of Fasih Mohammad, a suspected terror accused, and said he is in custody of the Saudi Arabia Police.

July 8: Abu Jundal has told interrogators that it was LeT 'operation head' Muzammil Butt, then operating in Kashmir, who along with dozen terrorists in Army fatigues went to Chhattisinghpora village in Jammu and Kashmir's Anantnag District on March 25, 2000 and killed 35 Sikhs.

Abu Jundal claimed that, Abu Hamza, who has been linked to several terror strikes in the country, including the December 28, 2005 attack on the Indian Institute of Science (IISc) in Bangalore (Karnataka), is dead.

Delhi Police has approached Interpol to get the statement of the Taiwanese tourist, Ku Ze Wei, who was injured in IM orchestrated attack on Jama Masjid on September 19, 2010.

July 6: Jundal revealed Major Sameer Ali came to PoK to hand over two cartons of AK-47 bullets to the terrorists who were to carry out the 26/11 attacks.

Delhi Police is planning to send a Letter Rogatory (LR) to Saudi Arabia seeking more details about Jundal's stay, his job and about computers used by him.

The Indian agencies for the first time sent an elaborate report to the FBI on LeT operative David Coleman Headley's involvement in 26/11, based on interrogation of Abu Jundal.

July 5: Union Home Minister P. Chidambaram said that India has conveyed to Islamabad that information from the interrogation of LeT terrorist Abu Jundal clearly pointed to involvement of non-state actors and state actors in Pakistan who were behind 26/11 terror attack in Mumbai.

NIA is reported to be currently conducting fresh raids in

Maharashtra, Gujarat and Karnataka based on crucial leads provided by Jundal.

Abu Jundal told interrogators, the Pakistani handlers of the 26/11 Mumbai terror attack believed for some time that three cabinet ministers and a cabinet secretary had been held in Hotel Taj (Mumbai) and thought that they could demand anything from the Indian government for their releaseas.

Abu Jundal has told interrogators that LeT 'military commander' Zakiur Rehman Lakhvi is being guarded in Adiala jail in Rawalpindi, Pakistan by LeT militants.

Abu Jundal told Delhi Police that LeT has jointly set up bases with IM all over India for future operations.

July 4: IM has been banned in the UK, Britain's Security Minister James Brokenshire told lawmakers. IM has become one of 47 other organisations on the UK banned list.

Union Home minister P. Chidambaram said it had become increasingly clear that 'state actors' were involved in executing the 26/11 terror attacks and that without state support the terror control room could not have been established in Pakistan.

Abu Jundal has told investigators that 12, and not 10, LeT terrorists had been trained for the 26/11 attacks.

NIA told a Delhi court that it wants custodial interrogation of Abu Jundal.

Union Home Minister P. Chidambaram admitted officially for the first time that IM operative Fasih Mahmood had been detained in Saudi Arabia.

State Home Minister Thiruvanchoor Radhakrishnan told the Kerala State Assembly that the SIMI is not functioning in Kerala but former activists of the banned outfit were carrying out their activities under cover. Seven terror related cases, including the camp held by SIMI activists at Wagamon (Idukki District), were handed over to the National Investigating Agency, he said.

Jundal has told interrogators the Karachi 'control room' was destroyed by sleuths of Pakistan's Federal Investigation Agency weeks after the barbaric Mumbai attack.

July 3: Recent investigations have revealed that IM's Bihar module, was not the "latest" but the "oldest" module formed by the terror outfit.

Jundal's passport (number-QL1790941) was made on January 28, 2009, valid till January 2014, with his address shown as village Daowkay, Post Office Mohammad Rehman Pura in District Sheikhupura (in Punjab Province). He was shown as the son of one Mohammad Khushi.

Abu Jundal reportedly used chat services to communicate with his module members.

India decided to give a dossier on LeT operative Abu Jundal to Pakistan.

The jailed mastermind of 26/11 attack, Zaki-ur-Rehman Lakhvi, is still active, commanding the main LeT communication centre from within Adiala jail in Rawalpindi.

July 2: A senior LeT militant, identified only as "major general saheb", and two ISI personnel were among the 10 people present in the control room set up in Karachi to orchestrate the 26/11 terror attack on Mumbai.

LeT terrorist and 26/11 Mumbai attacks handler Abu Jundal's passport has revealed his present and permanent addresses in Pakistan as Muridke near Lahore.

Jundal was planning to attack the Nashik Police Academy in Maharashtra, following the successful strike on the Lahore Police Academy in Pakistan allegedly by the Taliban on March 30, 2009.

Jundal told the Special Cell of Delhi Police that the LeT has brought in an ace Chinese para-glider to northern Pakistan where he has been training militants in paragliding for the past two years. The training is being conducted somewhere in the Baltistan area of north Pakistan bordering the Xinjiang Autonomous Region of China.

Jundal has shown no regret for 26/11 attacks, in which 166 people were killed and 238 injured.

Jundal refuses to give information about the involvement of Pakistan's state agencies, say investigators.

Statements of LeT operative David Coleman Headley and Abu Jundal, match in one key respect as they have both named the same three Pakistani officials as being involved in the planning and execution of the 26/11 attacks. Sources in the Maharashtra ATS) said Jundal has named Major Iqbal, Major Sameer Ali and Colonel Shah of the Pakistani Army.

July 1: Abu Jundal told his interrogators, that LeT militants are trained in 'internet activities' and the outfit has a dedicated band of "trained and educated" boys.

Jundal has also given information about LeT's training camps running all over Pakistan.

Fasih Mahmood is one of the founding members of IM and that he studied in the same engineering college as Riyaz and Iqbal Bhatkal-the Bhatkal brothers.

Fasih was one of the five men who transformed SIMI into the IM almost overnight a decade ago, Delhi Police sources claim.

June 30: Sources further said that they found around 60 "interesting" numbers in Jundal's mobile phone and Jundal has allegedly claimed that of these about 15 are of ISI officers and LeT members in Pakistan. The other numbers are of contacts in the UAE and Saudi Arabia.

Jundal has told officials that German Bakery blast accused Fayaz Kagzi, who was Ansari's accomplice and who inducted him into the LeT, is living in Abu Dhabi. The officials said Jundal had obtained the SIM card for his mobile from Pakistan.

Abu Jundal has told interrogators that at least two officers of Pakistan's ISI were present in the control room set up in Karachi.

Jundal has revealed he had recruited 50 persons during his nearly two-year stay in Saudi Arabia and was also instrumental in hawala funding through his contacts in Riyadh and Dubai to LeT's sleeper cells in Kerala and Maharashtra.

June 29: Asserting the role of Abu Jundal, Union Home Minister P. Chidambaram commented, "In fact many missing pieces of the 26/11 conspiracy are now known to us through interrogation of Abu Jundal. He was a key operative, he was assigned the key responsibility to putting the 10 terrorists in intensive training and the customs followed by Mumbaikars."

Intelligence sources said that Abu Jundal, in his interrogation disclosed that following the Mumbai massacre the LeT shifted its headquarters from Muridke to Dolai region in PoK to avoid suspicion.

Abu Jundal has revealed that one Major Abdurrehman and key 26/11 accused Sajid Mir*alias*Sajid Wajid had visitedIndiaas cricket fans and conducted reconnaissance of important sites inDelhiand Mumbai for about a fortnight.

CBI source said that "The Saudi Arabian authorities have finally confirmed to the CBI that Fasih Mehmood is in their custody. The CBI has begun the process to get him back toIndia soon". In addition, Indian security establishment is looking at almost half a dozen persons in Saudi Arabia who may have had significant role in terrorism targeted against India.

A source said among the key Indian terror suspects they believe to be hiding inSaudi Arabiais C A M Basheer, the former SIMI leader.

Union Home Minister, P. Chidambaram stated that according to Abu Jundal's revelations, a new 'chief' is heading LeT. After arrest of Zakiur Rehman Lakhvi on December 2, 2008, by Pakistan for 26/11 attacks, another handler named Muzameel took charge of the terror outfit.

Abu Jundal, the alleged handler of 26/11 terrorists, has further revealed that Mumbai attackers had undergone training in al Qaeda camps in Afghanistan.

Jundal claimed there was a 'great degree of coordination now between LeT, al Qaeda and even the Taliban'.

Jundal claims that though he did visit LeT's training facility at the Pakistan-Iran border but he was not present during the time that the Mumbai module was undergoing training there.

The LeT militant Faiyaz Kagzi, an accused in 26/11 blast case, had given bomb-making training to Pune German Bakery blast (February 13, 20120) accused Mirza Himayat Baig in Sri Lanka capital Colombo in 2008.

June 28: After 26/11 Mumbai terror attacks, when pressure mounted on Pakistan to arrest LeT 'operations chief' Zakiur Rehman Lakhvi from a camp near Muzaffarabad in PoK, LeT's Indian command Abu Jundal was bailed out by ISI. After being bailed out, Jundal was asked to stay off the radar and he left forSaudi Arabiain early 2010.

Jundal revealed that all LeT members had done some communication practice for VoIP internet calls and understand the network areas of the targets. The LeT bosses also checked theSIMcards and handsets before the 10 terrorists left for Mumbai and a last-minute drill was also conducted.

UHM is unlikely to oblige a Pakistani request to share information about Syed Zabiuddin aka Abu Jundal's arrest.

Jundal has revealed before the Special Cell of Delhi Police that LeT is running several training camps in Muzaffarabad in PoK.

NIA moved for his custody and registered an FIR against him and another terrorist Fayaz Kagzi for planning to organise terrorist attacks inIndia.

According to the reports, Jundal was sent toKathmanduin 2005 for training for two months in arms and explosives. After coming back, he got involved with theFebruary 19, 2006Ahmedabad blast.

Jundal revealed that two days before the 26/11 attack, LeT militants carried out a mock drill inPakistan.

According to Bengal Police, he used Bongaon District inWest Bengal, to sneak fromIndiaintoBangladeshbefore moving on toPakistanin 2006. While he was inBengal, he recruited youths from Murshidabad, Malda and North 24-Parganas Districts.

Abu Jundal had nine Facebook accounts and email ids that he allegedly used to hunt for new recruits in Saudi Arabia and in India for LeT.

Abu Jundal confessed that he had met LeT's operational commander Zakiur Rehman Lakhvi in thePakistanjail. Jundal said that after 26/11, he fled toPakistanand was running a business of sale and purchase of cars inRawalpindi.

June 27: The Indian Government said it is in touch with authorities inSaudi Arabiato bring back alleged IM operative Fasih Mahmood.

Union Home Minister P Chidambaram said that the arrested 26/11 attack handler, Syed Zabiuddin alias Abu Jundal, had confirmed the role of Pakistani state actors in the plotting and execution of Mumbai attacks.

The role of Pakistani state actors is also being suspected from the location of LeT's control room in Karachi as pointed out by Jundal.

The interrogation of Abu Jundal, the 26/11 handler, has turned out to be an expose of LeT links with the IM, Jundal has confessed his links with IM.

Jundal is the highest ranking Indian in LeT and was recruited in 2005. Jundal has told his interrogators that he was recruited by LeT's 'commander' of Jammu and Kashmir range Aslam Kashmiri.

Jundal confessed that the plan to carry out 26/11 type terror strike was plotted in 2006, however, when the security agencies track down arms, ammunitions and explosives from Aurangabad in Maharashtra it was postponed and then he was asked to come down to Pakistan by his LeT bosses.

Delhi Police revealed that LeT trained Jundal to fly planes. Lashkar had planned to use him and two others (Fayyaz Kagzi from Beed and Mohammad Rahil Sheikh from Thane) in 9/11-style kamikaze attacks on Indian highrise buildings and big dams.

Abu Jundal was planning to attack the RSS Headquarters inNagpuras well as theUSAand Israeli embassies inNew Delhi.

Jundal has been put on a suicide watch. Accordingly, Delhi Police's SWAT commandoes have been deployed to prevent Jundal from harming himself in the custody.

June 26: Anti-India terror outfits operating fromPakistanhave been trying to lure youth from Kerala under a slogan 'Organise without organisation'. There is a wide network that recruits youth from Kerala for LeT. C A M Basheer, the elusive SIMI leader from Aluva (Ernakulam District), now operating fromSaudi Arabia, is the key figure.

Indian Government sources confirmed reports of more terror operatives' detention inSaudi Arabia, Suspected IM operative Fasih Mohammad was one of those detained in Saudi, sources said.

Foreign Minister S.M. Krishna confirmed that Jundal, a key player in 26/11terror operation, was arrested with the help of Saudi authorities.

Adil*alias*Ajmal, a Pakistani national told Police that in 2009, Jundal reportedly trained 90 men at LeT Bhawalpur training camp in the Punjab Province of Pakistan, many of them later joined the IM.

Further investigation revealed that Abu Jundal was the conduit betweenPakistan's ISI and LeT and SIMI and IM in India.

US had prevented Jundal's deportation toPakistanas he was earlier arrested inSaudi Arabia(2011) in a forgery case, andPakistanwas trying hard to get him deported.

June 25: Union Home Minister P. Chidambaram said, "The person who goes by the pseudonym of Abu Jundal has been apprehended and has been remanded to the custody of law enforcement agencies".

LeT has re-activated its naval wing last year (2011) with terrorists trying their hand at maritime techniques including sailing off theKarachishore, the interrogation of Abu Jundal has revealed.

June 23: LeT terrorist Abu Jindal (Jundal), who is in Delhi Police's custody, has confessed his active role in 26/11 attacks, saying that JuD 'chief' Hafiz Saeed was present in the Karachi (Pakistan) control room when the 26/11 masterminds were controlling the events.

According to IB sources, during the interrogation, Abu Jindal has admitted to handling the attack on Nariman House during 26/11. Jindal reportedly told the Police that he was the one who trained the 10 terrorists.

Sources said, "Abu Jundal knows the Bhatkal brothers-Riyaz and Iqbal, bosses of Indian Mujahideen based inKarachi— very well. He claims that the Bhatkal brothers used to come to joint meetings of Lashkar and IM. For the Jama Masjid attack, the

Bhatkal brothers asked Jundal to provide a man, an expert in firing".

June 17: India has for the first time lodged a strong protest with Pakistan and given concrete evidence proving that IM, which has been responsible for a series of bomb blasts across the country, is a front of terror outfit LeT.

New Delhi has also categorically told Islamabad that LeT was using the Pakistani soil to give training and other logistical support to the IM. The issue was discussed at length during the recently concluded home secretary-level talk in Islamabad.

Pakistan's intelligence agency, ISI, has for long been trying to project that IM was India's internal problem of 'home grown terror' as most of its members were Indians. The basic idea of ISI, intelligence sources said, behind floating IM was to show that terrorism was India's own domestic issue and that Pakistan has nothing to do with it. But Indian intelligence and security agencies have now busted that myth giving a complete list during the secretary-level talks to Pakistan of LeT's terror camps in Pakistan where IM cadre, comprising mostly Indian recruits, were being trained.

The details of this elaborate dossier reveals that LeT was using at least five camps in PoK to train IM terrorists in use of making IEDs and training of arms and ammunitions. These important camps, which have been on the radar of Indian agencies, are: Bait-ul-Mujahideen at Shawai Nalla; Al Massada, Ibn Taymiyya, Abdullah Bin Masood, Masker Al Aqsa. All these training camps are in Muzaffarabad in PoK. The dossier also states that most of these men are 'launched across the border' mostly through the Maskai-e-Ummalkura which is basically a tent camp used for transit close to the Indian border.

The details provided by the Indian side go on to reveal that the top LeT commanders like Abu Muzammil and Abu Sama, are actively involved in training the IM terrorist. These two LeT operatives often cross over into India also to supervise Lashkar operations in the Kashmir Valley, particularly in North Kashmir. In addition, India also reiterated that the two founders of IM, Riaz and Iqbal Bhatkal, continue to live in Karachi under the ISI's protection.

"Information was also provided to Pakistan as to how Indian youth from various parts of the country are taken to Pakistan through Nepal and Bangladesh for training. This is the first time that India has taken up the IM issue with Pakistan so strongly," a senior home ministry official said. The current chief of IM in India, Yasin Bhatkal, who is still on the run, is also suspected to have been trained by the LeT at these training centres in Muzaffarabad.

June 15: Investigations into the 13/7 Mumbai triple blasts revealed that one of the wanted accused and IM operative Muzaffar Kola, had been using two SIM cards which were obtained under fake identity.

Police said that Kola, who originally belongs to Bhatkal (Karnataka), owns a private firm, Muzaffar Kola Enterprises, in Dubai. ATS chief Rakesh Maria said, "This firm is also involved in hawala business. One of the arrested accused, Haroon Rasheed Naik, had given INR 10 lakh to this firm to send it to India. The money was send from Dubai to a New Delhi based *hawala* operator, Kanwalnayan Pathrija, who in turn gave this money to Indian Mujahideen leader, Yaseen Bhatkal alias Shahrukh alias Shivanand. This money was used to execute the triple blasts".

ATS investigators said that two other arrested accused, Naqi Ahmed and Nadeem Akhtar, had provided SIM cards obtained on forged and fake documents to several Indian Mujahideen leaders. "We have got evidence to prove that the two SIM cards which Kola had been using were obtained on forged documents," said an officer.

The officers of the Maharashtra anti-terrorism squad (ATS) interrogating Indian Mujahideen (IM) operative Mohammed Kafeel Ahmed, in connection with July 13, 2011 (13/7) triple blasts in the city, have said that he is the key conduit in what is believed to be a well-spread out *hawala* (illegal money transfer) network that channels underworld money to the terror group. Kafeel, the caretaker of a local mosque and well-versed with scriptures, travelled across the country to spot and train fresh recruits into the IM cadre, ATS officials said.

The interrogation has also revealed that Kafeel knows how the INR 3.75 crore ransom collected in the 2001 kidnapping of shoe baron Partho Roy Burman in West Bengal was routed through*hawala* channels. The Intelligence Bureau (IB) and Research and Analysis Wing (RAW) believe that the money was used to fund the 9/11 World Trade Centre attack in US, as well as the attack on the American Centre at Kolkata in 2002, and that the kidnapping was carried out by persons who went on to form the home-grown IM.

His interrogation has revealed over a dozen names that play a crucial role in the IM set up. Kafeel, along with Muzaffar Kola could throw light on terror financing through *hawala* networks, said police sources. Kola, whom the ATS alleges to be the key person who channelled INR 10 lakh to 13/7 mastermind Yasin Bhatkal through his hawala network, was also involved in the transfer of ransom money in the Burman case.

June 11: The Centre again denied that engineer (and alleged Indian Mujahedeen operative) Fasih Mohammad from Bihar, who had gone missing from Saudi Arabia after being allegedly picked up by Indian intelligence sleuths on May 13, was in the custody of any Indian law enforcement agency. The Delhi Police also filed an affidavit in the Supreme Court to this effect.

Appearing for the Union of India, Additional Solicitor General (ASG) Gourab Banerji also said the Government of Saudi Arabia, with whom the Indian ambassador had held two meetings on the issue, were "neither confirming nor denying" if Fasih is in the custody of that country's police.

To a question from the Bench if Fasih was alive or not, the ASG said, "We have no knowledge as they (Saudi authorities) are not saying anything." He said there would be "some information" within 10 days.

June 8: IM operative Mohammad Qateel Siddiqui, accused of executing terror attacks in Bangalore and Delhi and involved in the attempt to blow up Pune's Dagadusheth Ganapati temple, was strangled to death by two other prisoners in a high-security cell of Pune's Yerawada central jail on June 8, 2012. Siddiqui was in custody of the Maharashtra ATS since May 3, 2012. He was handed over by Delhi Police, who arrested him on November 22, 2011. The terrorist was believed to be a close associate of Yasin Bhatkal, the main suspect in a string of terror attacks.

Prison Superintendent S.V. Khatavkar, who was later suspended by the Maharashtra government for the security lapse, said that Siddiqui was found dead in his 10 ftx10 ft cubicle in the 'anda' cell of Yerawada. "We later learned that gangster Sharad Mohol and his aide Alok Bhalerao, who were also lodged in the anda cell, had strangled Siddiqui to death with a drawstring from a pair of shorts around 9.45am," he said.

Further, the Maharashtra government has now asked prison authorities to separate terror accused from other high-profile criminals, according to *Hindustan Times*. The directive was issued soon after Siddiqui's murder came to light, said Police sources. The directive is significant considering Arthur Road, Yerawada and Nagpur central jails hold high value criminals including Ajmal Kasab, the Pakistani national convicted for his role in the 26/11 terrorist attacks.

Apart from him, the state is particularly concerned about the key IM operatives arrested in the 13/7 Mumbai serial blasts which includes Haroon Rashid Abdul Hamid Naik, Naquee Ahmed, Nadeem Sheikh and Kanwar Nain Wazirchand Pathrija. All the four accused are currently in Arthur Road jail in Mumbai which also houses key Chhota Rajan henchmen facing trial in various cases.

June 6: The Delhi High Court gave four weeks time to the centre to respond to a Public Interest Litigation (PIL) seeking verification of users of networking sites on the lines of mobile subscribers, to augment national security.

The PIL seeks strict scrutiny and verification of each user of social networking sites in India to ward off cybercrimes and terrorism. Referring to a report of Mumbai ATS, the PIL claims the accused of the 13/7 blast in Mumbai (Maharashtra) were in touch with each other and the IM operatives through internet since 2008.

The centre told the Supreme Court that a red corner notice has been issued IM operative Fasih Mehmood for his alleged role in various terrorist activities, but refuted his wife's claim that he was abducted in a joint operation by Indian and Saudi Police in Dubai.

Additional Solicitor General Gaurab Banerjee also submitted to the bench of justices K.S. Radhakrishnan and J.S. Khehar, a copy of the "red corner notice (RCN)" which was issued through Interpol and carried a warning, that Fasih "may be armed, dangerous and violent."

The notice stated that 30-year old Fasih, a resident of Bihar's Darbhanga district, was a member of the IM and responsible for the Pune German Bakery blast on February 13, 2010; Bangalore Chinnaswami Stadium blasts on April 17, 2010 and Delhi's Jama Masjid shootout and blast on September 19, 2010.

During the course of investigation, 7 persons were arrested and interrogated. They voluntarily confessed that they along with Fasih Mehmood and other absconders belong to the banned outfit called IM. The absconding accused Fasih Mehmood is an active member of IM since 2003. At present the absconding accused is hiding himself in Kingdom of Saudi Arabia.

It was submitted that several cases under various IPC sections like 120B (criminal conspiracy), 121 (waging or attempting to wage war against India), besides various provisions of the Explosives Substances Act and Prevention of Damage to Public Property Act have been lodged against Fasih.

Further, the centre told the Supreme Court that its agencies had no role in alleged arrest of Fasih Mehmood on May 13, 2012.

Responding to the court's notice, Gaurab Banerjee told a bench of Justices K S Radhakrishnan and J S Khehar that its investigating agencies neither accompanied Saudi Arabian Police in effecting the alleged arrest nor had he been brought to India.

Banerjee said "The external affairs secretary and the home secretary have conveyed that neither Indian agencies nor its officials were part of any alleged action to arrest Fasih in Saudi Arabia. It is not correct to say that Indian police arrested him. He is not in India". The Maharashtra ATS claimed that it was aware of the whereabouts of a 13/7 accused, Muzaffar Kola, listed as wanted in the case charge sheet. He has not been arrested so far owing to his medical condition. Muzzafar Kola, owner of the Dubai based company Muzzafar Kola Enterprises, was in Bhatkal, Maharashtra, even as the ATS charge sheet listed him as a wanted accused.

ATS chief Rakesh Maria said, "We have given it in the charge sheet. We know he is in Bhatkal. He has undergone surgeries. Because of his medical condition we have not arrested him. What's the point of arresting him when he would be in the hospital instead of jail? We have said in the charge sheet that his passport has been confiscated so that he does not move out of the country."

June 5: Investigators probing the 13/7 triple blasts have learnt that Delhi-based *hawala* operator Kanwalnayan Pathrija not only transferred funds for the bombings, but also used three SIM cards obtained on fake documents. The SIM cards were from a set of cards provided to operatives of IM.

According to the chargesheet filed by the ATS, suspected Pakistani bombers Waqqas Shaikh and Tabrez *alias* Danish, arrested accused Naquee Ahmed and Nadeem Akhtar and wanted accused Tehseen Shaikh and Muzaffar Kola had used SIM cards which were obtained using forged documents. "Pathrija (42) used three such SIM cards," said an ATS officer. "We have obtained the call detail records of these SIMs."

The ATS chargesheet in the 13/7 case also mentions that the DNA of a woman was found in Byculla's Habib Mansion, the building where the suspected bombers stayed. "We had sent several seized items to the state forensic science laboratory for analysis. The forensic reports state that one of the three toothbrushes seized by the police from the room contains a woman's DNA," said an ATS officer. "It is likely that a family stayed in the room before the bombers rented it. Our probe has not reaveled the involvement of a woman, but we are probing all angles," the officer added.

Investigations into the 13/7 Mumbai serial blasts has led government agencies to Haryana's Mewat District, known as the birthplace of the Tabhligi Jamaat religious movement. It is learnt that some of the most wanted terrorists in the country have used the District, as a safe haven or a transit point.

During the interrogation, arrested IM operatives have disclosed that top IM terrorists Riyaz Bhatkal and Haroon Rashid Abdul Hamid Naik had stayed at Mewat to escape arrest. Ahmad Zarar Siddibappa, *alias* Yasin Bhatkal, too, has narrowed down on the District, Police sources said.

Yasin had stayed in Mewat after his cover in Darbhanga (Bihar) and Delhi was busted by the Delhi Police special cell along with the IB, added police sources. Mewat has been the place where most top IM terrorists have sought refuge after they conducted the blasts at Varanasi in 2006, and Jaipur and Delhi in 2008.

Police sources further said Riyaz's presence was last reported in 2008, after which he crossed over to Pakistan. Apart from the district's proximity to the Capital, the area is on National Highway No 71-B and provides connectivity to West Bengal, Bihar and Uttar Pradesh.

Investigations revealed that the IM operatives had used social networking websites, and that's how they managed to stay under the investigators' radar. The investigators also found that some IM operatives were trying to conduct recruitments through their Facebook accounts.

The IM has been quick in the use of technology when it came to planning and executing their operations. They started out with the use of email, then moved on to chats and later Skype, a video conferencing application.

June 4: The Maharashtra ATS has claimed that the funds received by IM operative Yasin Bhatkal from Dubai through the *hawala* channel were used to send recruits to Pakistan to receive terror training. Apart from being used in the 13/7 blasts, the funds were also used to pay the deposit for the Habib Mansion flat in Mumbai.

The ATS, in its chargesheet, said, "During the course of investigation it has transpired that Yasin Bhatkal has utilised the money received by him through hawala for paying the deposit of the rental room in Mumbai and other places. The funds were also distributed to other members for the purpose of causing terrorist acts and sending Muslim youths to Pakistan for terror training".

Until now, the investigators had claimed that only Bhatkal, *alias* Shivanand, was in touch with arrested Delhi-based *hawala* operator Kawalnayan Pathreja. However, investigations have now revealed that Wakas Shaikh, one of the planters in the case, was also in touch with Pathreja. "We had seized two broken mobile phones and two pocket diaries from Pathreja's residence, but one of the diaries contained a page of the month of July wherein the name of Wakas Shaikh was written by Pathreja. This means Wakas was in touch with him and some dealing had taken place in the month of July between them," said the officer.

Further, Investigations revealed that suspected Pakistani bomber Waqqas (Wakas Shaikh) had helped his co-accused steal two Activa scooters from Grant Road and V P Road areas a day before the explosions.

Last week, the ATS arrested Naqi Ahmed and Nadeem Akhtar for stealing two bikes and two Activa scooters. In its chargesheet, the ATS said that Waqqas had accompanied Ahmed and Akhtar when they went to steal the vehicles.

According to sources, Waqqas had joined a gym in Byculla and went there regularly to work out. "He stayed in a rented room in Habib Mansion in Byculla for almost nine months with the other suspected Pakistani bomber, Tabrez. Waqqas also participated in assembling of the bomb in the rented room. On the day of the blasts, Waqqas and Tabrez went to Opera House on one of the stolen scooters around 1.30pm and the former planted the bomb there near a hawker. The bomb was not fitted into this scooter," said a source.

June 2: The Lucknow bench of the Allahabad High Court has ordered an inquiry into lapses in security of three judges who delivered the verdict on the title suite of the Babri Masjid, Ayodhya, in September 2010. The court has also directed the Central government and governments of Uttar Pradesh (UP) and Uttrakhand to take immediate steps to provide adequate security to the judges. The three judges who delivered the Ayodhya verdict are Justice Sudhir Agarwal, Justice SU Khan and Justice DV Sharma.

The court issued order after UP ATS informed court that activists associated with the SIMI may attack the three Judges. In the statement submitted before the court by Rajiv Sabarwal, DIG, ATS, submitted that during the course of investigation, even in the months of March and April, 2012, it was found that the judges who decided Ram Janam Bhoomi case are still under continuous threat and the SIMI activists are in process to constitute a fresh module to assault the Judges. The statement given by Sabarwal also revealed that imminent threat to the life of the judges.

May 31: The Interpol issued a red-corner notice, an international arrest warrant, against Fasih Mehmood (28), an engineer from Bihar who is wanted for his alleged involvement in the Chinnaswamy Stadium blasts in Karnataka and the explosion outside Jamia Masjid in Delhi, in 2010.

Union Home Minister P. Chidambaram denied reports that Mehmood had been detained by Indian intelligence agencies and said such media reports were "completely wrong".

May 28: Terror suspects and IM operatives Naquee Ahmed and Nadeem Shaikh were arrested for stealing two motorcycles from VP Road and Dongri areas of Mumbai days before the 13/7 bomb blasts.

A magisterial court in Pune (Maharashtra), granted permission to the state ATS to conduct an identification parade of IM operative Qateel Siddiqui (27) of Bihar. Siddiqui has been accused for attempting to plant a bomb near the Shrimant Dagdusheth Halwai Ganpati temple in Pune on February 13, 2010.

Madhya Pradesh ATS has issued notices to five major telecom companies asking "why they should not be charged under sections of Unlawful Activities Prevention Act (UAPA) for providing SIM cards to the suspected terrorists without proper verification process.

Credible information available with Indian intelligence agencies suggests that Pakistan's intelligence agency, the ISI, has directed the IM to launch a fresh spate of high value terror attacks in the country.

Intelligence inputs also suggest that the ISI is using Bhatkal brothers, Riyaz and Iqbal, who in turn have directed Yaseen Bhatkal, the India chief of IM, to carry out this operation.

Mohammed Kafeel Ansari, suspected to be the close associate of elusive IM 'chief' Yasin Bhatkal and also the accused in 13/7 serial blasts case, was remanded in Maharashtra ATS custody till June 8 by a Maharashtra Control of Organised Crime Act (MCOCA) court in Mumbai.

Judicial magistrate first class A.G. Santani, granted permission to Maharashtra ATS to conceal names of witnesses in the case in which IM operative Qateel Siddiqui (27) of Bihar was arrested for allegedly making a bid to plant a bomb near the Shrimant Dagdusheth Halwai Ganapati temple in Pune on February 13, 2010.

May 28: Among the 641 witnesses listed by the ATS in the July 13, 2011 (13/7) Mumbai (Maharashtra) triple blasts case chargesheet, at least eight men who were working in the Sakhli Street Byculla workshop of accused Naquee Ahmed's brother Rafi Ahmed at that time claim to have spotted the two accused, Naquee and Nadeem Akhtar, meet and interact with one Imran and two others in February 2011. The Police believe that Imran is an alias used by the main conspirator of the blasts, Indian Mujahideen (IM) leader, Yasin Bhatkal.

Another witness included in the chargesheet is a key maker who allegedly made duplicate keys for two bikes. The ATS has said that of the four bikes stolen by Naquee and Nadeem, two were used to plant bombs at Opera House and Zaveri Bazaar. The police have recovered the duplicate keys. In his statement, the key maker said that two young men came to his shop in the first week of July 2011 and one of them asked him to make duplicate keys on urgent basis for a Honda Activa and a Unicorn Motorbike.

May 27: The link between underworld and IM has surfaced with Maharashtra ATS naming Dubai-based Muzaffar Kola, an associate of jailed 1993 serial blasts accused Mustaffa Dossa, as a wanted accused in 13/7 blasts case.

ATS sources said, "Kola has been associated with Dossa and

his absconding brother Mohammed Dossa. On Kola's instructions, *hawala* [illegal money transfer] operator Kanwar Pathrija (arrested in the 13/7 blasts case) allegedly handed over Rs. ten lakh [INR 1 million] to one Shivanand, who later turned out to be Yasin Bhatkal". "With this link, we now cannot rule out underworld help in this terror attack," the source added.

May 25: The chargesheet filed by the ATS before a special Maharashtra Control of Organized Crime Act Court on May 25, states that the serial bombings that hit Mumbai (Maharashtra) on July 13, 2012 (13/7) were planned and coordinated by IM leaders from Pakistan.

The nearly 4,800-pages-long document names at least 10 accused and says that the objectives behind the bombings at Opera House, Zaveri Bazar and Dadar were to "create instability in the state" and to "weaken the country's economy".

The chargesheet says that "the entire criminal conspiracy was hatched by Riyaz Bhatkal and Yasin Bhatkal of IM. The banned terrorist group, it adds, was created by Pakistani spy agency ISI "to spread terror in this country". Riyaz and his brother Iqbal Bhatkal "operate from Pakistan with the help of their associates based in India by imparting instructions to them" via electronic means through Yasin. Riyaz and Yasin are two of the wanted accused named in the chargesheet. Among the remaining wanted accused are two suspected Pakistani nationals identified as Waqqas Ibrahim Shaikh and Danish alias Tabrez, Shaikh Mohammadd Tahsin Akhtar, currently believed to be on the run in Andhra Pradesh; and an Indian-born hawala operator based in Dubai named Muzzafar Kola.

Apart from the above mentioned named, the 10 names in the chargesheet also include Naquee Ahmed, Nadeem Shaikh, Kanwar Pathrija and Haroon Naik who are facing trial under the stringent Maharashtra MCOCA, the IPC and other laws.

India and Pakistan pledged to fight terrorism together, calling it "a continuing threat to peace and security". The Indian side had also demanded the handing over of fugitives allegedly sheltering in Pakistan, including terrorist Dawood Ibrahim and several IM leaders.

May 23: A 324-page chargesheet has been filed in a Delhi court, listing IM's plans in India. The chargsheet have been filed against 11 IM operatives-Mohammad Irshad Khan, Asadullah Rehman, Mohammad Adil, Bashir Hasan, Abdul Rehman, Mohammad Kafil, Mohammad Qateel Siddiqui, Gauhar Aziz Khomani, Gayur Ahmed Jamali, Mohammad Aftab Alam and Tariq Anjum Hasan.

The chargesheet mentions that IM leaders Riyaz Bhatkal, Iqbal Bhatkal and Amir Reza Khan (based in Karachi, Pakistan) came to Delhi after the 2008 Batla House encounter and held a meeting in Shaheen Bagh with its operatives, including the India chief of the group, Ahmad Zarar Siddi Bappa *alias* Yasin Bhatkal *alias* Shahrukh. The meeting took up the revival strategy for the organization.

The first objective states, "the aim of their *tanzeem* (group/ organization) is to carry out bomb blasts and shootouts in India to take revenge against the atrocities being meted out to the Muslim communities by the kafirs and spread the message of Jihad". The second objective "of tanzeem is to implement the Islamic law in India" and, lastly, it wants "to weaken the Indian economy by way of circulation of fake currency and discouraging foreign investment through violence".

Police claim the Shaheen Bagh meeting was held at Tarique's house. Following the meeting, IM operatives opened the Meer Vihar (Delhi) arms factory on the premises of Irshad Khan on the direction of absconding Yasin Bhatkal, the IM chief in India.

May 21: IM operative, Mohammad Qateel Mohammad Jafir Siddiqui, has reportedly revealed information about the hideouts in Bihar where IM 'operational head' Yasin Bhatkal and he used to go after committing crimes.

Police have claimed to have stumbled on to a hawala network which the IM had used to park money in India and carry its 2010 terror attacks.

May 17: The District court in Bhopal has framed charges against four alleged cadre of SIMI for indulging in anti-national activities.

Police is suspecting that Faseeh Mahmood was the treasurer of IM and was responsible for wiring money into bank accounts in India. He also used to spot potential operatives and remunerate them according to their capability.

May 16: IM operative Mohammed Tariq Anjum reportedly told interrogators that the IM had carried out the twin bombings in the city to avenge the May 18, 2007, Mecca Masjid bomb explosion. Sources said that Anjum has given some vital leads about 'most wanted' IM founder Riyaz Bhatkal.

Investigators believe that Faseeh Mehmood, an engineer from Bihar who was arrested by the Saudi Arabian Police, is the IM's original link to Bihar.

May 14: Shakeel, a suspected IM militant, allegedly involved in motivating youth to join the outfit, was arrested by the Delhi Police near Lucknow.

May 13: IM operative Faseeh Mehmood, an engineer from Bihar who was arrested by the Saudi Arabian Police in Dammam.

Investigations into the arrest of Pune time-bomb planter, IM operative, Qateel Siddqiui, revealed that he had shared a cab with three other persons while travelling to Mumbai from Pune with the bomb.

May 11: Maharashtra ATS has claimed that alleged IM operative Mohammed Qateel Mohammed Jafar Siddiqui has confessed that he conducted a recce of the Dagdusheth Halwai Ganpati Temple in Pune and showed the places he visited, and the spot where he unsuccessfully tried to place a bomb.

Judicial Magistrate (first class) S.S. Bose granted Police custody to Siddiqui till May 21.

ATS told a magistrate court that they have identified the flower vendor at Dagdusheth Ganpati temple who refused Siddiqui to keep the bag carrying bomb on the day of German Bakery bomb blast.

May 10: Mohammad Khafeel Akhtar *alias* Khafeel, the suspected IM operative has been remanded in Police custody till May 22.

May 9: Maharashtra ATS officers found out that Yasin Bhatkal, who heads IM, invested INR 1.4 million in the under-construction Poonam Paradise in Nalla Sopara (east) of Thane District in Maharashtra in 2010.

May 8: NIA moved a trial court in Delhi seeking to interrogate six of the eight alleged IM suspects, arrested recently by Delhi Police in connection with the May 25, 2011, Delhi High Court blast.

May 6: ATS arrested a SIMI cadre, identified as Anwar Hussain (40), from Indore (Madhya Pradesh).

Interrogation of the arrested 13/7 bomb blasts suspects has revealed that the two Pakistanis militants who are involved in the attacks along with IM militant, Yasin Bhatkal, had been using stolen cellphones to mislead the Police.

A joint team of the Andhra Pradesh and Karnataka Police arrested Kafeel Akhtar from Keoti in Darbhanga, in connection with the April 17, 2010, blasts outside Bangalore's Chinnaswamy Stadium.

May 3: A Pune court granted eight days' Police custody to IM militant Mohammad Quateel *alias*Mohammad Jafir Siddiqui.

NIA informed the tribunal handling matters related to the ban on SIMI that the outfit is still actively present in Kerala.

May 2: The Maharashtra ATS has found traces of RDX along with other explosives in a flat in Habib building at Byculla in Mumbai, where IM militants suspected to have been involved in the July 13, 2011 Mumbai blasts (also known as 13/7) stayed.

Tiger Hanif, an associate of Dawood Ibrahim, wanted by Gujarat Police for a bomb attack on a train in 1993, and absconding in Britain, was ordered by the Westminster magistrates' court in London (UK) to be extradited to India.

Commenting on the issue of delay in implementing the death sentence of 26/11 Mumbai (Maharashtra) attacks convict Ajmal Kasab, Union Home Minister P. Chidambaram, said in Parliament that Kasab needs a fair trial.

May 1 : Delhi court gave the ATS of Pune (Maharashtra) the custody remand of IM militant Mohammad Qateel Siddiqui (27) to interrogate him for his alleged role in the German Bakery bomb blast (February 13, 2010) in Pune.

The court also allowed the plea of Hyderabad (Andhra Pradesh) ATS for a month's custodial remand of another IM militant, Mohammed Tariq Anjum (31). He is said to be a member of banned SIMI.

Taqi Ahmed, a key suspect in the 13/7 serial blasts case, is believed to have told investigators that his first contact with IM militants happened at a cricket ground in Darbhanga in Bihar during a local match in the summer of 2009.

April 30: The MHA named Maharashtra based Khair-e-Ummat Trust as one of the fronts/pseudonymous organisations of Students Islamic Movement of India (SIMI). The MHA's "background note on the Student Islamic Movement of India (SIMI)," mentions four more organisations as being SIMI 'fronts' at the national level Tahreek-e-Ehyaa-e-Ummat (TEU), Tehreek-Talaba-e-Arabia (TTA), Tahrik Tahaffuz-e-Shaaire Islam (TTSI) and Wahdat-e-Islami. The MHA has not banned these groups.

April 29: Kerala Government wants the ban on Students Islamic Movement of India (SIMI) to continue in the context of its continued presence in the State despite the ban. The report prepared by the Internal Security Wing to be submitted to the tribunal handling matters related with SIMI, headed by Justice V.K. Shali, says that though the Police had not come across incidents of secret meetings or training camps as had happened before 2008, several raids had yielded pamphlets and other materials.

State Power Minister Aryadan Muhammad, said that operatives of extremist organisations had been infiltrating into certain mainstream political parties. "These are very dangerous organisations," he said. He further commented, "I can name these organisations. They are the NDF (presently Popular Front of India), SDPI… then SIMI… Most of these organisations come under the Jama'at-e-Islami," he added.

According to intelligence agencies, the preliminary plans of most of the Lashkar-e-Toiba (LeT) terror attacks carried out in Indian cities in 2008 were prepared at the SIMI camp held at

Panayikkulam near Kochi (Kerala) on August 15, 2006. SIMI had also held a training camp at Vagamon hill resorts in Idukki District in December 2007 in preparation for terror strikes.

April 28: A joint Anti-Terrorism Squad (ATS) team comprising of Maharashtra and Madhya Pradesh Police arrested a Students Islamic Movement of India (SIMI) cadre, identified as Anwar Hazi (40), in Indore Anwar was a close associate of Abrar, who is in custody in Aurangabad (Maharashtra), the Police said.

April 2: Three suspected activists of SIMI, identified as Abu Faisal *alias* Doctor, local module chief, Ejajuddin and Ikrar Sheikh *alias* Guddu, were presented for identification by Bhopal Police at an Indore Court in Madhya Pradesh in connection with their arrest in 2006 at hotel Vaadi in Chhoti Gwaltoli Police Station area.

Pune Police has served notices on cadres of the SIMI in Maharashtra, following a notification issued by the UAPA at New Delhi declaring SIMI as an unlawful association.

March 30: Maharashtra Home Minister R. R. Patil told the State Assembly that IM terrorists had conducted a trial run at the Shrimant Dagadusheth Halwai Ganpati Temple in Pune three days prior to the German Bakery blast (February 13, 2010).

March 27: An IM operative from the Bihar module, Assadullah Rehman *alias* Dilkash was arrested from his Karawal Nagar hideout in northeast Delhi. Dilkash had recently come to the city to re-establish the IM base and plot terror attacks.

Maharashtra ATS arrested two suspected SIMI cadres from Chikhli area of Buldhana District. The ATS team arrested Akil Ahmad Mohm Yusuf Khilji and Mohd Zafar Hussain, both residents of Khandwa, MP.

The terror module was attempting to set up bases in Aurangabad, Jalna and Buldhana Districts of Maharashtra and recruit people in the State. They were also planning to assassinate some prominent Hindu leaders in Maharashtra.

The arrest of 2008 Ahmadabad serial blasts accused Mohammad Abrar Babu Khan by ATS on March 26 is being viewed as a significant development by Central intelligence agencies with officials claiming that the dreaded terrorist was controlling the entire network of IM and banned SIMI in western and central India.

March 26: A suspected SIMI cadre was killed while two of his accomplices-one of whom is said to be involved in the July 26, 2008, serial blasts in Ahmadabad-were arrested after a gun battle with the ATS in Aurangabad, Maharashtra. The slain suspect has been identified as Khalil Akhil Khilji while those arrested are Abrar Babukhan *alias* Munna and Mohammad Shaker Hussain.

March 23: Maharashtra ATS claimed to have information on two persons suspected to have played a role in the triple blasts in Mumbai on July 13 last year. The two suspects were identified around the second week of March.

March 22: Maharashtra ATS told the court that one of the four arrested-Nadeem Shaikh-for 13/7 blasts had confessed and that his statement has been recorded before a magistrate. The four arrested-Naquee Ahmed, Nadeem Shaikh, Kanwar Pathrija and Haroon Naik were produced before the Mazgaon metropolitan court and sent to judicial custody till April 4.

A joint team comprising personnel from the ATS, Bangalore, and Delhi Special Police searched Bhatkal town (Karnataka) to identify the house which is presumably laden with huge quantities of explosive material including RDX, with help from four terror suspects. The explosives from the Bhatkal dump are believed to have been used in the blasts at Chinnaswamy Stadium in 2010 and the Delhi High Court blast in September last year, besides several other strikes across the country carried by IM.

March 14: SIMI leader Habib Falahi was produced before NIA Special Court in Kochi and was included as accused 32 in the Wagamon SIMI training camp case. After ascertaining the role of Habib Falahi, NIA is now on the lookout for another Uttar Pradesh-based SIMI leader Fariz who attended this camp.

March 9: Two militants of IM, Haroon Naik and *hawala* operator Kanwar Nain Wazeer Chand Patrija who were behind bars for Opera House (Mumbai) blast (13/7) case were remanded in ATS custody by a local court in connection with the Dadar explosion that took place on the same day.

March 7: Andhra Pradesh State Intelligence Officials claimed that several members of the banned SIMI have joined PFI and that it was this controversial organization that was behind some recent communal disturbances in the state of Andhra Pradesh including 2011 Adoni riots.

March 6: Delhi Police revealed it has identified four more militants of Indian Mujahideen (IM) who are currently hiding in Bihar.

March 2: Mazgaon Court in Mumbai extended the Police custody of Haroon Naik and Kanwal Nain Patrija, alleged operatives of IM, arrested for their role in the 13/7 bomb blasts, till 9th March.

Kerala Government submitted before the Kerala High Court that Susan Nathan-a British-born Jewish writer-has close connections with some extremists in the State, including the SIMI and NDF and should be deported.

February 26: NIA claimed to have got some leads to suggest that the low intensity blast outside Delhi High Court on May 25, 2011 was a handiwork of the banned terror outfit IM.

February 24: Arrested IM militant Mohammad Kafeel Ahmed has disclosed that he was one of the main conspirators behind the blasts orchestrated by IM's boss in India, Yasin Bhatkal *alias*Shahrukh. Kafeel also gave information about more active IM members in Bihar.

Maharashtra ATS, which is probing the July 13 Mumbai triple blasts case obtained the custody of Haroon Naik and Kanwar Pathrija till March 2 in connection with the blast at Zaveri Bazaar.

February 23: Interrogation of IM militant Mohammed Kafeel Ahmed has confirmed that the vast network of banned outfit SIMI is now being used by IM.

February 22: Arrested IM man Mohd. Kafeel Ahmed was brought to Delhi and produced in the court of Chief Metropolitan Magistrate at Tees Hazari court. Kafeel was a close aide of Yasin Bhatkal *alias* Shahrukh and a chief recruiter for IM.

A Delhi court, remanded four of the nine IM members, arrested for their suspected roles in various terror cases across the country, to the Karnataka Police custody to ascertain their roles in the April 2010 Chinnaswami Stadium blast case.

Former national chief of SIMI, Muneer Deshmukh, who was arrested in Bhopal in November 2010 and is on bail since July 14 last year, is suspected to have stashed US Dollars 50,000 in US accounts.

February 21: A top IM militant (organization ideologue) Mohammad Kafeel Ahmed was arrested from Darbhanga in Bihar by the Delhi Police. He was a messenger and also the main recruiter for the IM.

February 10: Investigating agencies are probing the role of IM co-founder Yasin Bhatkal alias Shahrukh's role in the 2010 blast at the Dasashwamedh Ghat in Varanasi.

February 7: ATS has found out that Haroon Naik, arrested on February 1 for 13/7 Mumbai blasts, had met LeT operations chief Zaki-ur-Rehman Lakhvi and was present at an "inspirational" lecture by slain al Qaeda leader Osama Bin Laden in Pakistan just a month before the 9/11 attack.

IM ideologue Talha Abdali *alias* Bashir Hasan *alias* Israr and popularly known as Masterji among its cadres, was a close associate of Safdar Nagori,during interrogation has revealed that he had been associated with militant outfits for a long time and knew about the blasts carried out by IM since 2007.

February 5: Delhi Police's special team investigating the IM terror cell arrested a key ideologue and founding member of the group, identified as Talha Abdali *alias* Israr, from Barabanki.

February 3: An alleged founding member of IM, Mohammad Tariq Anjuman Ehsan, was arrested by the Delhi Police at Nalanda. According to Police sources, Tariq (31) is an IM ideologue and is suspected of being involved in a number of blasts, including Jama Masjid in Delhi.

February 2: One more accused in the 2008 Bangalore serial blasts has been taken into custody. Saleem (30) is a close associate of Tadiyandavide Nasir and stayed in Kannur, Kerala. Nasir is the prime accused in the nine blasts that killed a woman and injured many in July 2008. He is also the South Indian commander of the IM.

The Union Government has decided to continue the ban imposed on SIMI. The ban has been extended in light of SIMI's alleged links with certain Pakistan-based terrorist outfits including LeT and its front, Indian Mujahideen.

February 1: Haroon Rashid Naik (33), a Mumbra (a Mumbai suburb) resident, was arrested by the ATS in the 13/7 triple blasts case. He is the fourth man to be arrested in the case for facilitating the hawala racket from where Mumbai blasts were funded.

January 31: Maharashtra ATS and Delhi Police's Special Cell have arrested a Delhi-based hawala operator, Kanwar Nain Pathrija, in Delhi for arranging funds for the 13/7 Mumbai blasts.

January 29: Habib *alias* Habibfalahi Shaikh (25), an accused in the 2008 Ahmedabad bomb blast and Surat bomb planting cases, was arrested by the Ahmadabad city Police.

The NIA informed that Muhammed Shameer, a native of Kannur in Kerala, who was arrested in Delhi, in connection with the 2008 Bangalore Blast case, on January 25 was a vital link for the inflow of money for terrorist purposes.

The NIA has undertaken two major FICNs cases in the State, after some Pakistan links were established in both the cases.

January 26: New Delhi airport immigration officials have arrested a terror suspect linked to the July 25, 2008 Bangalore (Karnataka) blasts as he was trying to fly out of the country.

A Police source said Sameer is the 24th accused arrested in the Bangalore serial blasts.

Prior to executing the 13/7 blasts in Mumbai, IM operatives Yasin Bhatkal and Riyaz Bhatkal bargained extensively on the amount to be spent to execute the terror attack. Though Yasin demanded INR 1.7 million to bomb three places in Mumbai, he was paid only INR 1.2 million by IM leaders, investigations have revealed.

Maharashtra ATS revealed that the hawala money to fund the attacks was routed through UAE.

January 24: Maharashtra ATS chief Rakesh Maria said that the IM first recruited youths from Cheetah Camp in Trombay (Maharashtra), then Kondwa in Pune (Maharashtra), then Azamgarh in Uttar Pradesh and now Darbhanga in Bihar.

The investigations into the bogus SIM cards racket led the Police to the accused in the July 13, 2011 Mumbai triple blast case (also known as 13/7).

The ATS recovered 400 documents provided by Tikole through which prepaid SIM cards were bought by the IM module members.

Eight persons have been arrested by the ATS in the 13/7 case so far.

Union Home Secretary R.K. Singh said that Bihar man held by the Maharashtra Police on the charge of playing a key role in organising the 13/7 attack was a Delhi Police and Intelligence Bureau informant.

As reported earlier, the Maharashtra ATS has said it has held three men involved in planning and executing the 13/7 attack-one of them a witness, who had cooperated with the Delhi Police and the IB in the search for two Pakistani nationals who allegedly planted the explosive devices.

January 23: Maharashtra ATS claimed to have made a major breakthrough in the triple Mumbai blasts July 13, 2011 that claimed 27 lives, with the arrest of two of the accused hailing from Bihar.

Yasin Bhatkal, the mastermind of the 13/7 Mumbai blasts, might have succeeded in evading the Police, but he remains in India, officials of the Maharashtra.

January 19: Investigators probing the IM Bihar module, part of which was busted by the special team of Delhi Police in 2011, has found that the chief of IM operations in India, Yasin, had been making frequent trips to several areas of Bihar towards the beginning of this decade for recruitment to the terror cause.

Sources have also confirmed that at least two members of the present module were present near L-11, Batla House, the encounter site on September 13, 2008, though till then they had no knowledge of the exact role played by the Azamgarh module. "We believe that these men were not part of any bombings prior to 2010, but we have evidence which suggest that they assembled as early as December 2008 and decided to take forward the IM agenda," said a source.

Investigators had believed that the Bihar module had only become active after the Azamgarh (Uttar Pradesh) module, operating under Atif Ameen, was busted in the Batla House encounter in September 2008.

Counter-terrorism agencies have narrowed down on the terror-financing module that is operating out of New Delhi, and is believed to have aided IM operatives in executing the July 13 triple blasts in Mumbai and the Delhi blast.

Police officials revealed that during their stay at Habib Mansion, right behind the Byculla Police Station, IM operative Yasin Bhatkal and Pakistanis Tabrez and Bakas had reconnoitered several vital installations in the city.

January 16: three men who planned and executed serial blasts in Mumbai and Delhi High Court blast in 2011, were holed up in an apartment in Byculla, not more than 15 minutes' walk from the Anti-Terrorist Squad's Nagpada headquarters, till just a few weeks ago.

January 15: IM militants Salman *alias* Chotu and Shahzad Ahmed *alias* Pappu have allegedly confessed to the Bangalore Police that they had got explosives for the 2008 Delhi serial blasts from Udupi, a coastal town in Karnataka.

In their confessional statement, they allegedly told the Bangalore anti-terrorism cell that their associates Mohammed Saif (now in jail) and Khalid (absconding) went to Udupi on August 31, 2008, and brought the explosives to Delhi on September 3, 2008. The Delhi blasts took place on September1 3, 2008.

January 6: There is fresh input that the IM in alliance with the ISI, is likely to carry out attacks like 13/7 in Mumbai. BARC, DRDO organizations, defence establishments like Mazgoan dock, naval dockyard, ONGC at Uran plant, economic institutions, aviation sector, oil and power sectors etc are vulnerable, the inputs states.

As opposed to 18 people, a majority of whom belonged to banned outfits were arrested in 2010, 25 full-blown terrorists were arrested in 2011. A special team of Delhi Police scanned the length and breadth of the country to bring the IM to its knees in a blitzkrieg operation.

January 2: Four IM operatives recently arrested by Delhi Police have reportedly confessed that three of them were involved in planting bombs at the Chinnaswamy stadium in Bangalore during an IPL match in 2010. An unnamed senior Police official of the anti-terrorist cell said Mohammed Qateel Siddiqui (27), Ghayur Ahmed Jamali (21) and Aftab Alam Farooq (27) planted bombs on April 18, 2010.

Investigators have said that the IM module led by Yasin Bhatkal may have also been involved in the serial blasts in Mumbai on July 13, 2011. Mohammed Ahmed Sidibapa *alias* Yasin Bhatkal*alias* Shahrukh, who led the IM module, may have been in Mumbai during the blasts, investigators believe.

As reported earlier, in a nationwide investigation, Police Forces, supported by intelligence agencies, had arrested seven IM members. Yasin managed to escape.

The Ahmadabad city crime branch officials believe that Habib Phalai *alias* Taiyab, arrested in Uttar Pradesh on December 28 in the Ahmadabad serial blasts case, may be connected to the other accused from Azamgarh involved in various serial blasts across India.

2011

December 28: The UP ATS in coordination with Ahmadabad Crime branch team arrested an alleged SIMI operative wanted in 2008 Ahmadabad blast case.

December 25: Ahmad Siddi Bappa *alias* Yasin Bhatkal alias Shahrukh, is recruiting youths for IM, motivating them on religious grounds and also cash incentives, according to a report.

December 21 :December Government gave its sanction to the NIA to charge sheet nine persons, including two serving ISI officers, Major Iqbal and Major Samir Ali, Pakistani-American LeT operative

David Coleman Headley, LeT founder Hafiz Saeed, al Qaida operative Ilyas Kashmiri, for plotting terror strikes in India, including the 26/11 Mumbai attack.

Delhi Police told a Delhi court that six of the seven IM operatives arrested in November have confessed about their involvement in the September 2010 blast near Jama Masjid. The police made this submission to Chief Metropolitan Magistrate Vinod Yadav while seeking extension of their custody for further interrogation to gather evidence of their involvement in the blast.

December 20: the Centre said a terror module busted in Delhi recently had links with Pakistan-based terrorist group LeT. This IM module was suspected to be involved in February 13, 2010 Pune German bakery blast (in Maharashtra), blast in Chinnaswamy Stadium in Bangalore (in Karnataka) on April 17, 2010 and shoot out at the Jama Masjid (New Delhi) on September 19, 2010.

Union Minister of State for Home Jitendra Singh said, "factory manufacturing arms and ammunition being run by the IM in New Delhi was unearthed recently". However, he did not specify the details about where the factory was located in the national capital.

The Centre said a terror module busted in Delhi recently had links with the LeT.

December 18: Police have intensified the hunt for IM sleeper cells in Tumkur District of Karnataka after revelations of the arrested IM operatives in Delhi (Mohammed Qateel Siddiqi, Gayur Ahmed Jamali and Farooq) that those involved in the April 17, 2010 Chinnaswamy Stadium blasts in Bangaluru had taken shelter in Tumkur. Police sources in addition said that IM had executed the terror attack with the help of locals and students.

December 15: A Delhi Court extended the Police custody of seven suspected IM militants who have been arrested for their alleged role in blasts across the country by six days. The seven arrested accused are Mohammed Qatil Siddqui, Gohar Aziz Khumani, Mohammed Adil, Abdur Rehman, Mohammed Irshad, Gayur Ahmed Jamali and Aftab Alam.

December 14: It has also been revealed that chief of IM, Siddi Bappa alias Shahrukh, had instructed all module members to use different SIM cards for calling each other and he himself carried several phones with different connections.

December 9: Unearthing more anti-national links by the SIMI operatives, the NIA has zeroed in on the plans by an accused in the Vagamon SIMI camp case with other anti-national activities. Danish Riyaz, an operative of the IM and SIMI operative who is also the 34th accused in the Vagamon SIMI camp case, has been involved in a conspiracy to attack the judges of the Allahabad High Court who pronounced the verdict in the Ayodhya case.

Interrogation of six suspected IM operatives, arrested recently for their alleged role in various terror attacks across India, reveals that Pune's [Maharashtra] famous Dagdusheth Halwai was also on their radar. It is also revealed that the agenda of the refurbished Indian Mujahideen is targetting religious places, voicing the concerns of Pakistan and large-scale destruction.

December 8: investigating agencies have learnt from the arrested IM militants that the terrorists had been converting the Udupi town, so far known for its religious places, into a hub of explosives manufacture.

A Delhi court remanded suspected IM operative, Aftab Alam alias Farooq, a Pakistai, arrested from Bihar on December 6 for his alleged role in various blasts across the country, to seven days' police custody. The police sought his custody, saying he needs to be thoroughly interrogated to track his terror network and arrest his other accomplices.

December 5: IB personnel and Bihar Police arrested a suspected IM terrorist of the module led by Yasin Bhatkal alias Ahmed Siddi Bappa alias Imran from Purnia in Bihar. Radicalised in Salafi mosques of north Bihar, Farooq along with Bhatkal, Mohammed Qateel Siddiqui and Gayur Ahmad Jamal were the four persons directly involved in 2010 Chinnaswamy stadium bombing in Bangalore. While Farooq and Bhatkal planned the bombing in Tumkur in Karnataka, Siddiqui and Jamal joined them from Delhi and Bihar via Mumbai to strike on the cricket ground.

Delhi Police sources are saying that there are at least four more modules each armed with a plan to wreak havoc in an Indian metro.

Delhi Police produced all six suspected IM cadres-Mohammed Qateel Siddiqui, Gauhar Aziz Khomani, Gayur Ahmed Jamali, Mohammed Adil alias Ajmal, Abdur Rehman, and Mohammed Irshad Khan-in court, from where they were remanded to 10 more days' Police custody.

December 1: A project, codenamed 'Karachi Project', undertaken by the Pakistani spy agency, ISI to spread terror in India using local recruits through LeT network will soon find its place in the charge sheet to be filed by the NIA against American-Pakistani terrorist David Coleman Headley and his accomplices, including Pakistani serving and retired Army officials, in the Mumbai terror attack case (November 26, 2008, *aka* 26/11).

November 30: Delhi Police investigators announced the neutralization of a terrorist cell that they claimed was responsible for a string of nationwide attacks in the year 2010.

July 22: Indian security agencies believe that the mastermind of the recent Mumbai blast (July 13, 2011), Abdullah Khan of the IM is hiding in Bangladesh.

July 18: Investigations into the Mumbai serial blasts (July 13, 2011) were focusing heavily on suspects in Gujarat, with the Maharashtra ATS reportedly getting major leads pointing to the involvement of the IM.

July 16: On being alerted by the Intelligence Bureau, the Bihar Police conducted raids at Barchaundhi village under Mahuakhali Police station in Kisanganj District and arrested a suspected cadre of the militant outfit HuJI Times of India, however, reported that the two arrestees had links with SIMI.

July 5: NIA is exploring the possibility of taking over investigations into the murder of two college students in Karnataka (between June 8-12) following the alleged involvement of members of an organisation known as the Karnataka Forum for Dignity (KFD), considered to be a new front of the SIMI, in the crime.

June 25: Madhya Pradesh Police arrested a former cadre of the SIMI at the Cochin International Airport in Kochi town of Kerala.

June 13: Police arrested 10 cadres of the banned SIMI from a house in Khandwa in Madhya Pradesh.

June 8: According to highly placed sources in the Indian intelligence agencies, the SIMI and the CPI-Maoist have recently conducted a secret meeting in Kottayam District of Kerala.

June 5: The Madhya Pradesh ATS arrested eight suspected militants belonging to the Indian Mujahideen (IM) and the banned outfit SIMI in Bhopal.

February 25: A local court in Mumbai granted four days' transit remand to Mohammed Asad Siddiqui, a SIMI cadre and an accused in the August 14, 2000 Kanpur blast case, arrested in a joint operation by the Maharashtra Anti-Terrorism Squad (ATS) and Uttar Pradesh ATS in Mumbai. "He is one of the nine accused in the Kanpur blast. One Kashmiri accused is under arrest, another died in an encounter a few years ago. Siddiqui was around 15 when he committed the crime. He has been on the run since then. There was an award of Rs. 15,000 declared on him. The court granted his transit custody till March 2," said an Uttar Pradesh ATS official. He said that Siddiqui was staying under an assumed name in the Nalasopara area of Mumbai and ran a web-designing shop. "He is an active member of SIMI," the official said.

2010

December 30: The National Investigation Agency (NIA) filed a chargesheet against 18 cadres of the banned outfit SIMI, in a Kerala court for allegedly conspiring to advocate, incite and abet unlawful activities for secession of Kashmir from India.

December 14: The Centre prepared a list of 31 absconding terror suspects, including 19 from the Indian Mujahideen (IM), and asked all the States and Union Territories to locate and arrest them. The suspects at large also include 12 members of an outfit called Jam-I-yyathul Ansarul Muslimeen (JIAM), which is suspected to be a joint front of LeT and SIMI.

December 13: Slain Mumbai Anti Terrorism Squad (ATS) chief Hemant Karkare was on the hit list of the Islamist militant outfit Indian Mujahideen (IM).

Cadres of banned outfit SIMI are fast regrouping under the banner of Popular Front of India (PFI), an outfit which has expanded its tentacles to north after carrying out initial recruitment in South India.

Forensic experts probing the Varanasi blast case suggested the possibility of use of plastic explosives in the terror attack, Although the experts are yet to identify the composition of the explosive, a study of the blast site suggest the possibility of a PETN (pentaerythritol trinitrate combined with nitroglycerin) being used.

December 8: The Mumbai Police said that it suspected that Bhatkal brothers, Riaz and Iqbal, founders of IM, masterminded the explosion in Varanasi in Uttar Pradesh on December 7. Police Commissioner Sanjeev Dayal also said that the blast was planned in Pakistan which sheltered the suspected militants.

December 7: A powerful bomb blast in Varanasi in Uttar Pradesh killed a two-year-old girl and injured 35 others. The explosion took place at around 7pm (IST) at the Shitla Ghat (steps on the sides of the river Ganges) when 'Ganga Aarti'(an evening religious ritual on the river side) was under way. The Indian Mujahideen (IM) reportedly claimed responsibility for the explosion.

September 23: Investigations into the email sent by the Indian Mujahideen (IM) hours after the Jama Masjid firing incident in Delhi on September 18 have revealed that a second-hand Nokia mobile handset purchased from a shop in Dongri in south Mumbai was used to send the threat mail. However, the shopkeeper has no records of the person who bought the handset. Investigators believe that the terrorist bought a second-hand mobile to reduce the chances of getting traced.

September 21: Mumbai Police detained two persons in connection with the bomb blast outside the Jama Masjid (Mosque) in Delhi. Also, the e-mail purportedly sent by the Indian Mujahideen outfit was traced to Borivali in Mumbai.

September 20: Two persons have been detained by the Delhi Police Special Cell for questioning in connection with the attack on foreign nationals in the Walled City of Delhi. According to sources, the suspects were picked up from Northeast Delhi after their antecedents raised suspicion. Preliminary investigations into the attack on the Taiwanese nationals and the fire in a car parked near the area Police station indicated to the involvement of local elements. Delhi Police Commissioner Y.S. Dadwal said that the attack on foreign nationals and the subsequent low-intensity explosion in the car are being investigated from all possible angles. He also said that while separate cases have been registered in connection with the two incidents, circumstantial evidence has indicated that they are linked. The Police also plan to send teams to various parts of western Uttar Pradesh in the lookout for leads.

Police have reportedly found that the e-mail, purportedly sent by the Indian Mujahideen outfit to an international news broadcaster a few hours after the attack, was sent from Mumbai. The authenticity of the e-mail''s contents and its source is being verified.

September 7: A Special tribunal headed by Justice Sanjiv Khanna of Delhi High Court retained the ban on the SIMI. The decision came after the tribunal's countrywide probe into the alleged affairs of SIMI. It has been reported that five e-mails, including one threatening e-mail addressed to Times of India on August 23, 2008 by the militant outfit Indian Mujahideen (IM) regarding explosions in Gujarat, were treated as clinching evidences in the investigations

August 4: A one-member Tribunal, headed by Delhi High Court Judge Sanjiv Khanna, confirmed the extension of the ban on the SIMI for two more years. The Union Home Ministry had extended the ban on the outfit for the same period in February. SIMI has been banned since 2001.With the confirmation of the extension of the ban, the outfit will remain banned till February 7, 2012.

July 26: A Special Operations Group (SOG) team in Vadodra in Gujarat arrested a SIMI cadre for his involvement in three-year-old incident when a group of protestors had displayed posters of al Qaeda chief Osama Bin Laden in Mandvi area.

July 21: Intelligence reports indicates that Pakistan's ISI has renewed efforts to set up new sleeper cells in Gujarat and elsewhere in the country. For the last six months, the ISI has been trying to create new sleeper cells in the State to replace those of the SIMI that were neutralised by the Gujarat Police. Sources in the State intelligence said SIMI's sleeper cells had provided key support to the terrorists who had carried out the bomb blasts in Ahmedabad in 2008. Though SIMI is now banned, investigation into the activities of its suspected members has continued. The Detection of Crime Branch (DCB), Ahmedabad Police, recently arrested three persons suspected of planning bomb blasts in the city.

July 19: A local court sent arrested SIMI cadre, identified as Fakraan alias Farkat alias Arshad Jamal, to Crime Branch's custody for eight days, reports Indian Express.

July 17-18: Ahmedabad city crime branch officials arrested a 36-year-old man identified as Farkat Jamal alias Arshad, who had allegedly supplied illegal firearm to arrested Students Islamic Movement of India (SIMI) cadres Hasseb Raza Saiyad, said crime branch officials. Arshad was arrested by a team of Ahmedabad city crime branch officials, in a joint operation with Bihar Police, from Chhapra District.

July 17: Ahmedabad city crime branch officials arrested a 36-year-old man identified as Farkat Jamal *alias* Arshad, who had allegedly supplied illegal firearm to arrested SIMI cadres Hasseb Raza Saiyad, said crime branch officials, reports Times of India. Arshad was arrested by a team of Ahmedabad city crime branch officials, in a joint operation with Bihar Police, from Chhapra District. "We brought Arshad to Ahmedabad on Sunday [July 18]. His name had surfaced during Saiyad's questioning. Saiyad was found in possession of a country-made revolver and 17 cartridges. Arshad had supplied the weapon to him. We are probing his Guajrat footprint and connection with other SIMI members at the moment," said a senior crime branch official. According to investigators, Arshad is former state president of SIMI and was in proximity with a number of senior leaders and operatives. Earlier, officials had arrested Abu Fakir Siddiqi, 34, and Hasseb Raza Saiyad, 43, both residents of Faridabad Society, Jantanagar, Ramol, on July 11 when they were riding by on a bike.

July 14: The Delhi Police claimed before a court that the IM had allegedly carried out September 13, 2008 serial blasts in Delhi at the instance of its founder, now Pakistan-based Amir Raza Khan. The prosecutor claimed the Police had in its possession emails records, disclosure statements of accused, besides intelligence inputs, to establish links between LeT and HuJI with SIMI and IM.

The Judge put off its order for two weeks on the application of the Bangalore Police seeking custody of two suspected IM militants Salman and Shahzad on the ground that the matter at the court in Delhi was at a crucial stage and handing over their custody would disrupt the proceedings. Bangalore Police wanted the custody of the duo to investigate their alleged role in connection with M. Chinnaswamy Stadium blasts in April 2010.

July 12: The Ahmedabad Police arrested two alleged cadres of the SIMI, identified as Hasibraza alias Samim Firdosarza Saiyed (34) and Abufakir Abdulwali Abuali Siddique (43), at Prem Darwaza and claimed to have recovered an air gun, a country-made revolver and live cartridges from them.

June 24: An alleged absconding SIMI cadre identified as Khalid Naeem was arrested by the Special Task Force (STF) of Madhya Pradesh Police from Bhopal.

June 4: The Union Government declared the Indian Mujahideen (IM), suspected to be a shadow outfit of the banned SIMI and Pakistan-based LeT, a terrorist outfit.

February 24: The SIMI and the IM have claimed responsibility for the Pune bomb blast, Police Commissioner Satyapal Singh said.

February 5: The Union Government has extended the ban on the SIMI for another two years, beginning on February 8. The outfit has been facing a ban since September 2001. Sources in the MHA said that the ban on SIMI will now continue till February 7, 2012.

2009

November 28: A motorcycle-borne youth suspected to be a SIMI cadre shot dead three persons, including one ATS personnel, in the Teen Pulia area of Khandwa District of Madhya Pradesh.

The assailant first shot at ATS constable Sitaram Batham in the Teen Pulia area, city SP S. K. Nashine said.

November 3: Four cadres of the banned SIMI outfit were arrested near a graveyard in the Madra Tekri locality of Jabalpur by personnel of the Madhya Pradesh Police.

October 30: Seven persons were arrested from different parts of the Indore District in Madhya Pradesh over the last seven days and booked under section 188 of IPC on charges of providing shelter to five SIMI cadres, Police said. Referring to the activities of SIMI in the State, Director General of Police S. K. Rout told reporters that so far Police have arrested 13 top SIMI leaders and 63 suspected cadres of the group.

October 20: Five SIMI cadres were arrested from Indore city in Madhya Pradesh. Two of the arrested cadres, identified as Mohammad Shafiq and Mohammad Yunus, belonged to Ujjain District, and were wanted by the Police to stand trial for serial bomb blasts in Ahmedabad (Gujarat) on July 26, 2008.

October 6: Three SIMI cadres, including its former chief Imran Ansari, were sentenced to two-year rigorous imprisonment and fined INR 2000 each by a local court in Madhya Pradesh for spreading religious enmity. Besides Ansari, the sentence was also awarded to Afzal Abdul Rashid and Shahjad Abdul Rashid, the prosecution said.

July 21: Two militants of the proscribed SIMI, identified as Mohammed Rafiq Abdul Rehman and Abdul Ahad, were arrested from the Vidarbha region in Maharashtra, Police said. While Abdul Rehman was arrested from Mana village in Akola District on July 19, Abdul Ahad (68) was arrested in Amaravati District in the night of July 20. Earlier, the Police had arrested three more SIMI cadres when they were on their way after attending a meeting at Mana village in Mutizapur administrative division. "During the interrogation of the arrested accused, it was revealed that they wanted to come together on one platform. That's the reason why they held a meeting in Mana village," District Superintendent of Police, Pravin Padwal said.

July 20: The Maharashtra Police arrested four SIMI militants from Mana village in the Akola District. The cadres were arrested while trying to flee in an Indica car, before they were intercepted. After receiving an initial tip off from intelligence inputs, the Police neutralized a secret SIMI meeting, which was taking place with 35 cadres present at the meeting. However, the Police managed to arrest only four of them while the others managed to escape.

June 12: June 12: A militant of the outlawed SIMI, Abu Bashar, who was implicated by the Gujarat Police for the July 26, 2008 Ahmedabad serial bomb blasts, is reported to have confessed about the presence of training camps in the coastal areas.

February 27: Two suspected SIMI cadres, identified as Shibili and Hafeez Hussain, who were arrested for reportedly attending a secret training camp held by the outfit in 2007, were remanded to a 15-day judicial custody. About 40 cases were pending against the duo in various parts of the country, including in Gujarat, Indore in Madhya Pradesh, Karnataka and Malegaon in Maharashtra. Nearly 40 SIMI cadres had participated in the camp for about three days, the Police mentioned, adding that till date, ten cadres were arrested in this connection.

February 9: A SIMI cadre, identified as Amil Parvesh, a native of Ujjain in Madhya Pradesh, who was arrested by the Kerala Police from Indore in Madhya Pradesh in connection with his suspected role in the training camp of the outfit held in the Vagamon hills, was remanded by the Kanjirapally First Class Magistrate Court in Kottayam to 15 days Police custody.

2008

December 27: A trial court in Jabalpur in Madhya Pradesh convicted nine cadres of the banned Students Islamic Movement of India (SIMI) to two years imprisonment and imposed a fine of INR 500 on each for promoting communal hatred. Police had arrested them in July 2006 for their alleged links with the SIMI and booked them under various sections of the India Penal Code, mostly dealing with treason.

December 20: The Maharashtra Anti-Terrorist Squad (ATS) arrested a SIMI cadre, identified as Amir Talha from Azamgarh in Uttar Pradesh, from platform number three at Nagpur station.

One.32mm pistol and five bullets were recovered from his possession. Talha is the son of Amir Rashidi Madni, who heads an *ulema* council in Azamgarh, and is also believed to have been arrested in connection with SIMI activities in the past. Talha, who was reportedly in close touch with the Indian Mujahideen (IM) that executed the serial blasts in New Delhi on September 13, was produced before a Nagpur court and has been remanded in Police custody till January 3, 2009.

November 10: Gujrat Police said that the Madhya Pradesh Police have arrested the main conspirators of the July 26 Ahmedabad serial blasts, identified as Qayamuddin Kapadia, from an unspecified place in Madhya Pradesh. Qayamuddin Kapadia allegedly planted cycle bombs in the Ahmedabad as well as bombs in different parts of Surat and was also responsible for purchase of cycles on which the bombs were planted and kept in different parts of the city, said Joint Commissioner of Police of Ahmedabad city crime branch, Ashish Bhatia. He was also an expert in using explosives, and reportedly present during various SIMI terror training camps in Waghamon in Kerala and Halol near Vadodara and was instrumental in training the participants.

October 23: An unidentified SIMI cadre was arrested from the Nagda District of Madhya Pradesh in connection with the July 26 serial blasts in Ahmedabad, Gujarat Police said on October 24, reports *The Hindu*.

October 21: A special squad of the Thrissur District Police arrested two SIMI cadres from Kodungallur. The two cadres, identified as Nisar and Asghar, reportedly participated in a SIMI camp at Panayikulam on August 15, 2006.

October 14: The special investigation team looking into the case relating to "clandestine meeting of activists of the Students Islamic Movement of India (SIMI)" at Panayikulam in the Ernakulam District on August 15, 2006, has taken one more person, Nissar of Idukki, into custody. Nissar was among the 13 persons who were let off after the Police stopped the meeting and arrested five persons.

October 13: The Supreme Court ruled that the Union Government's plea against a tribunal's ruling lifting the ban on the

Students Islamic Movement of India will be heard by a larger bench of the Court, even as the ban is to continue. The bench of Justice S.B. Sinha and Justice Cyriac Joseph referred the matter to Chief Justice K.G. Balakrishnan saying the Government's suit be listed before "an appropriate and larger bench". The bench also said the ban on SIMI would continue till further orders.

October 6: Kerala Police arrested two persons for their suspected links with the SIMI. Abdul Hakeem (22) from Azheekal in Guruvayur and Shameer (29) from Karukapadathu in Thrissur were arrested on information that the duo attended a clandestine meeting of SIMI activists at Panayikulam on August 15, 2006. The Police had taken 18 persons into custody. Five of them were arrested and the others released for lack of evidence. Shibili and Ansar, who were among those arrested from Panayikulam and later released on bail, were again arrested from Indore in Madhya Pradesh with firearms in their possession. They were produced before the Paravoor Judicial First Class Magistrate who remanded them to judicial custody till October 21.

September 27: The Anti-Terrorist Squad (ATS) in Nagpur arrested a SIMI cadre in the IODC colony of Washim. Mohammed Khaleel Mohammed Ismail Chauhan (32) was working for SIMI since year 2000 and was based in Khandwa (Madhya Pradesh). He had taken shelter at his younger brother Aqueel Mohammed Ismail Yusuf Chauhan''s (also a SIMI cadre) place in IODC colony. Police sources said that Aqueel was involved in spreading communal violence in small cities. Khaleel has four offences of rioting and forgery registered against him in Khandwa.

September 25: A SIMI cadre was arrested in connection with the serial blasts in Bangalore on July 25. Police said that Mohammad Samee Bagewadi *alias* Mohammad Samee attended most of the important camps organised by SIMI at Castle Rock near Hubli in Karnataka, Vagamon in Kerala and other places and also underwent training in these camps. Bagewadi, a resident of Bijapur, was allegedly influenced by SIMI''s ideology, and was closely associated with its leaders such as Safdar Hussain Nagori, Hafeez Hussain *alias* Adnan, Shibly, Tauqeer, Shahbaaz, Abu Bashar and others, Police sources said.

September 24: Mumbai Police arrested five suspected members of the Indian Mujahideen. While Afzal Mutalib Usmani (32) was arrested from Uttar Pradesh, Mohammed Saddik Shaikh (31), Mohammed Arif Shaikh (38), Mohammed Zakir Shaikh (28) and Mohammed Ansar Shaikh were arrested from their Mumbai residences on September 23-night. All the accused, originally from Azamgarh District in Uttar Pradesh, have worked with the banned SIMI, Joint Commissioner (Crime), Rakesh Maria, told journalists. "They broke away from SIMI to form the radical group of Indian Mujahideen. Saddik was one of the co-founders of the outfit along with Atiq, killed in the Delhi encounter, and Roshan Khan, who is yet to be traced. The Police are on the lookout for Khan", Maria added. The Police have booked the arrested terrorists under the Explosives Act, Arms Act, various sections of the Indian Penal Code and for criminal conspiracy. The recovered items from the arrested terrorists include 10 kilograms of gelatin or ammonium nitrate, 15 detonators, eight kilograms of ball bearings, four fully active electronic circuits, one sub-machine carbine, two.38 revolvers and 30 cartridges of 9 mm carbine and eight cartridges of.38 revolver.

September 13: 30 persons were killed and 100 more injured in a series of five bomb blasts in the busy market places of national capital New Delhi, reports. The first explosion took place at Karol Bagh at 6.10 pm. The next explosion took place at 6.35 pm near the Metro Station at Barakhamba Road. Five minutes later, another explosion took place at the Central Park in Cannaught Place. Two more explosions took place in the M-block market of the Greater Kailash area at 6.30 pm and 6.40 pm. Initial investigations revealed that the improvised explosive devices were configured using ammonium nitrate. Four live bombs were recovered and diffused. While one bomb was found outside the Regal Cinema in Cannaught Place, two more bombs were diffused in the Central Park at Cannaught Place and at India Gate. In an e-mail to the media, the Indian Mujahideen claimed responsibility for the explosions.

September 11: The Supreme Court further extended its interim order continuing the ban on SIMI till the 2nd week of October, 2008. This is the second time the apex court has extended the ban.

The Union Government had filed a petition challenging the decision of a Special Tribunal to lift curbs imposed on the organisation. The Court has asked the Centre to place before it the synopsis of arguments and other documents in support of its stand to ban SIMI. The ruling came after the Government petitioned for more time for probe.

September 7: Two youths, identified as Mohammad Sohail and Azam, detained in Jodhpur were arrested by the SIT on charges of involvement in the May 13, 2008 Jaipur serial blasts case. During investigation, it was found that both had links with the banned SIMI and the main accused of the Jaipur serial blasts, including Sajid, Karimudeen and Taukir. They had allegedly arranged hotel rooms for the meetings of Sajid and his accomplices. The SIT sources claimed, "Sajid and his associates like Taukir, Karimudeen and others had visited Jodhpur many times and generated funds from there. It was found that Sohail and Azam had also gathered Zakat (charity) for them". With these two arrests, the total number of people arrested in connection with the Jaipur serial blasts went up to 14.

September 4: Four suspected cadres of the SIMI were arrested in connection with the July 26 Ahmedabad bomb blasts from Ahmedabad and Bhuj towns. An Ahmedabad police spokesman said that while Naved Kadri, Aiyyaz Sayed and Zaved Ahmed were arrested from Ahmedabad, Abbas Asmeja was arrested from Bhuj. The arrests took place following confessions made by the 10 main accused SIMI cadres. Aiyyaz was among those who had actually placed some of the bombs. Naved Kadri was present at the final planning meeting held in Juhapura. Zaved Ahmed had procured a gas cylinder from Kalupur area, which was used in the car bomb placed at the trauma centre in the civil hospital. Asmeja had secured a house, under a false name on behalf of the SIMI, under rehabilitation projects for the people hit by the 2001 Kutch earthquake. The house was sold recently to part-finance the blasts.

September 1: The Hyderabad Police arrested a person identified as Jaber from the Hyderabad city for suspected links with the SIMI. Hyderabad City Commissioner of Police B. Prasada Rao said, "Jaber has been arrested for his alleged links with the banned SIMI and sharing material with SIMI head Safdar Nagori." Jaber, son of Moulana Naseeruddin, is a Hyderabad resident. Naseeruddin is an accused in the assassination of former Gujarat Home Minister Haren Pandya and is now in Sabarmati jail in Gujarat.

August 26: Gujarat Police arrested Tanveer Pathan alias Sameer, a suspected SIMI member, from the Mira road area in Mumbai for his alleged involvement in the planting of bombs in Surat. Police sources said Pathan's name was revealed during the interrogation of Sajid Mansuri, an accused arrested in connection with the Ahmedabad serial blasts case. An unidentified police officer told, "Pathan was in touch with several SIMI activists in Pune and we passed on this information to the Gujarat Police. After Pathan's name emerged in the investigation, a team from the Gujarat Police arrived in Mumbai. With the help of the ATS, the Gujarat team caught Pathan."

August 25: The Supreme Court extended its stay of a tribunal order quashing the Union Government's February 7, 2008 notification, which banned the SIMI by six weeks. A bench, consisting of Chief Justice K.G. Balakrishnan and Justice P. Sathasivam, said, "The matter is important. We are ready to hear it. What we are concerned [with] are the documents and records relevant on the date of the ban notification."

August 23: The 'Indian Mujahideen', which had claimed responsibility for the recent serial explosions in Gujarat, sent a mail to TV channels with photographs of cars claimed to have been used in the attacks on two hospitals in Ahmedabad. Claiming that not a single Indian Mujahideen cadre involved in the blasts have been arrested so far the outfit threatened to widen the arc of its attacks. "The Indian Mujahideen on its full authority declares that by the Grace of Allah not even a single mujahid from our ranks who played even a minute role in the blasts, have been arrested to date. We are completely safe", the mail said.

August 21: The Anti-terrorism Squad (ATS) of the Mumbai Police arrested Feroz Mehboob Pathan (32), a suspected to SIMI member and part of the recently neutralised sleeper module of the outfit, from the Ghorpade Peth area of Pune. Two others were detained but not arrested.

August 20: The Union Government filed a fresh affidavit in the Supreme Court, citing the involvement of SIMI cadres in the July 26 serial bomb blasts in Ahmedabad in Gujarat. In its affidavit, the Government said investigations revealed that the accused in the bomb blasts in Ahmedabad and Surat on July 26 were members of the SIMI. Annexing the depositions made by witnesses, the Government further said intelligence sources and secret surveillance by the police made it clear that the accused had nexus with international terrorist outfits. Further, these persons were persistently involved in more than one offence or other unlawful activities and the nature of activities indulged in by the outfit would show secessionist tendencies and the potential damage to the secular fabric of society.

Replying to the debate in the Uttar Pradesh State Legislative Assembly on terrorist activities and the role of the SIMI in the recent serial bomb blasts, the State Parliamentary Affairs Minister, Lalji Verma, said that since 2003 no activity of SIMI has been witnessed in Uttar Pradesh. He further said between 1998 and 2003, 65 cases had been registered against SIMI activists in the State. Rejecting the charge of Bharatiya Janata Party (BJP) that the UP police and its security and intelligence agencies were inefficient in containing the menace, Minister Verma said the security and intelligence units in 34 sensitive districts and on the State's border have been upgraded.

Following leads given by arrested SIMI cadre Usman Agarbattiwala, the Ahmedabad Crime Branch recovered two pistols, a pipe bomb, balloons and 19 CDs and DVDs containing speeches of Osama bin Laden and other Al Qaeda leaders, laptops and hard drives from different places in the city. Usman Agarbattiwala was one of the ten SIMI members arrested for their alleged involvement in the Ahmedabad blasts.

August 19: A team of the Gujarat Anti Terrorism Squad arrested dentist Mohammed Salim Honali (31) from Bijapur in Karnataka. Honali used to work with the MA Rangoonwala College of Dental Sciences and Research Centre at the Azam Campus in Pune till

May 2008 before he was laid off. ATS officials suspect that Honali not only had a significant role in the July 26, 2008 Ahmedabad blasts but was also brainwashing other youth to bring them into the radical fold. ATS officials said jihadi literature was recovered from all four suspects.

August 17: Three persons were arrested in Bharuch in Gujarat for renting a house to the SIMI activist Sajid Mansuri, who allegedly played a key role in the July 26 Ahmedabad serial blasts. Mansuri had taken the house on rent from Saeed Hayat at Lukman society in Bharuch. Hayat had the power of attorney over the house that belonged to a London-based non-resident Indian. Two persons, Yusuf Patel and Maqbul Patel, had recommended the name of Sajid Mansuri to Saeed Hayat.

Police in Indore in Madhya Pradesh arrested a suspected SIMI activist in connection with the serial blasts in Ahmedabad on July 26. The arrest followed a tip off provided by the Gujarat Police. Nine persons arrested by the Gujarat Police on August 16 for their alleged involvement in the blasts had disclosed that the explosives used in the blasts were sent from Madhya Pradesh.

Police sources in Gujarat claimed that SIMI leader Abul Bashar Qasmi who was arrested from Uttar Pradesh on August 16 for his involvement in the serial blasts in Ahmedabad has "confessed" to his and his team's involvement in the terror attack. According to Abhay Chudasma, Joint Commissioner, Ahmedabad Crime Branch police, Qasmi also confirmed the role of Sajid Mansuri, another arrested senior SIMI member in the blasts. "We are questioning him on the details of other locals involved in the terror attack", Chudasma said. Police also suspected Qasmi and Sajid's involvement in the Jaipur blasts. "We are still questioning Qasmi on the Jaipur link", Chudasma added. The police said Qasmi had taken over charge of the SIMI national network after the arrest of its leader Safdar Nagori and his brother Karimuddin Nagori in Indore in Madhya Pradesh in March. Safdar and Karimuddin had originally planned the execution of the Ahmedabad blasts and to carry out bombings in Surat too.

August 16: The Gujarat Police announced the arrest of SIMI leader Abul Bashar Qasmi, who allegedly was the mastermind behind the July 26 Ahmedabad serial bomb blasts. Gujarat Director-General of Police P.C. Pandey said Qasmi was arrested from a village in Azamgarh in Uttar Pradesh (UP) by a joint team of the UP and Gujarat Police. The Gujarat police also said with this arrest they had unravelled the conspiracy that led to the bombings. Before Qasmi's arrest, nine SIMI cadres were arrested from Ahmedabad and Vadodara. "We now have the entire details of how and where the plans for the Ahmedabad blasts were chalked out, who were the people involved and how the entire plan was operationalised," the DGP said. He also claimed that the same group was involved in planting bombs in Surat.

August 14: A SIMI activist was arrested in Bharuch in Gujarat in connection with the serial blasts in Ahmedabad on July 26. The arrested SIMI cadre Mohammad Sajid Mansori is suspected to have been part of the conspiracy to carry out the nine blasts across the Gujarat capital.

August 8: The All India Minority Front said it had evidence that the SIMI had links with terror outfits in Pakistan. The Front national president S.M. Asif told reporters, "We have evidence of SIMI's links with Pakistani terror outfits and are ready to provide it to the central government provided we are assured security." "We have spoken to various Muslim people who have proof in this regard but they fear for their lives", he added. He further said, "We want SIMI should be banned and punished. The minorities in the country are opposed to all sorts of militancy. Even then Muslims suffer whenever there is any terror attack in the country."

August 6: The Supreme Court stayed the order by the Special Tribunal quashing the Union Government's February 7, 2008 notification declaring the SIMI an unlawful organisation. A Bench of the Supreme Court stayed the order on a mention made by Additional Solicitor-General Gopal Subramaniam about the Union Government filing a special leave petition against the lifting of the ban. The Bench, consisting of Chief Justice K.G. Balakrishnan and Justice A.K. Mathur, ordered notice to the SIMI seeking its response in three weeks.

The MHA asked the Uttar Pradesh Government to send details of the criminal cases pending against the SIMI and its activists.

Police headquarters in State capital Lucknow said that it has received a letter in this regard. The Office of the Director General of Police (DGP) has, consequently, started compiling the details of the recent cases against the SIMI.

August 5: The Anti-Terrorist Cell (ATC) attached to the Belgaum district Police Department in Karnataka arrested three suspected SIMI cadres. They were identified as Naveed Khaji and Ansar Nizami, both from Malmaruti area, and Sadiq Mulla of Azad Nagar. The arrest took place on the basis of information given by suspected SIMI cadres Tanveer Mulla and Iqbal Jakati, who were arrested recently. With the arrest of these three, the number of arrested suspected SIMI activists in the district rose to 11.

A specially-designated tribunal lifted the ban imposed by the Union Government on the activities of the SIMI. Justice Geeta Mittal of the Delhi High Court, who headed the tribunal, held that there was no new evidence submitted by the Government against the SIMI to justify the extension of the ban. A senior law officer said that the Government only came out with the evidence of the Malegaon blasts in Maharashtra in 2006 to show the complicity of the organisation in unlawful activities which was not sufficient to come out with the notification to ban it.

August 2: Immigration officials at the Mumbai International Airport detained a passenger in connection with a blast in the Judicial Magistrate First Class court in Hubli in Karnataka in May 2008. The passenger Iqbal Shaukat Ali is alleged to be a SIMI activist. A resident of Belgaum in Karnataka, Ali had fled to Sharjah soon after his name emerged as one of the major suspects in the blast. Subsequently, he was remanded to four days of police custody.

July 27: The Ahmedabad Joint Police Commissioner Asish Bhatia said an activist of the banned SIMI, Abdul Halim, who was wanted in connection with the 2002 Gujarat riots, was arrested during the combing operation in the city following the July 26 serial explosions in Ahmedabad (Gujarat).

July 15: Police arrested Mohammed Muqeemuddin Yaser, a former SIMI member, from his residence in the Saidabad area of Hyderabad, capital of Andhra Pradesh. Yaser, who is a MBA student, is also the eldest son of Maulana Naseeruddin, the founder president of Tehreek-e-Tahaffuz-e-Shaan-e-Islam (TTSI) and is presently lodged at the Sabarmati jail in Ahmedabad for his alleged role in the assassination of the former Gujarat home minister Haren Pandya. Yaser's younger brother Raziuddin Naser, a suspect in the twin blast cases in Hyderabad in August 2007, was arrested by the Karnataka Police in January 2008 for planning terrorist attacks in Karnataka and Goa. SIT sources said "Yaser was an active member of SIMI. Now, he along with some other former SIMI activists of the city has formed a group which downloads jihadi material and religious killing videos from the internet and distributes disks to extremist religious groups in the country."

June 8: Supporting continuation of the ban on the SIMI, the Karnataka Government in its affidavit submitted to the Unlawful Activities (Prevention) Tribunal contended that some of the SIMI members had been in contact with militant outfits. The Tribunal, set up by the Union Government to review the ban on SIMI concluded its two-day sitting on June 8 in Bangalore.

June 1: The Kerala Government represented its case in favour of continuing the proscription on the SIMI. The Unlawful Activities (Prevention) Tribunal appointed by the Union Government to review the ban on SIMI began a two-day sitting in capital Trivandrum. Representing the State Government, Inspector General of Police (Internal Security), N. C. Asthana, filed an affidavit before the tribunal stating that the SIMI was still carrying out unlawful activities in Kerala and hence the ban imposed on it shall be continued.

May 27: Police arrested a SIMI cadre, identified as Nasir Liyaqat Ali Patel, from Belgaum for allegedly spreading messages of hatred. Police also recovered the hard disc from his computer.

May 17: The special investigative team conducted raids across the State targeting activists of the SIMI. A SIMI cadre, Mohammad Shajid, was detained for questioning. Raids were conducted at Jaipur, Ajmer, Fatehpur, Godhpur, Tonk and Sikar on the basis of Intelligence inputs. A senior police officer said, "Raids were conducted, but it seems most of the activists have gone underground fearing arrests."

May 8: Three suspected SIMI activists were arrested from the New Housing Board colony area of Morena in Madhya Pradesh. Fake currency worth INR 80,000 and four mobile phones were recovered from them. Police sources said that one of the arrested Naajmia belongs to Kayamganj in Uttar Pradesh, while the other two, Pappu alias Sudhir Jadaun and Rajbir Gurjar, were from Morena.

April 23: The Union Minister of State for Home, Sriprakash Jaiswal, in a written reply to a question in the *Rajya Sabha* (upper house of Parliament) said that despite the ban, the SIMI has been carrying out its activities clandestinely including holding of organizational meetings and circulation of literature. The Minister said that more than 70 male SIMI cadres have been arrested during the last one year as per reports from Madhya Pradesh, Maharashtra, Andhra Pradesh, Delhi and Karnataka. No foreign national is among those arrested, he said. The Minister added that activities of the SIMI have been noticed in Madhya Pradesh, Karnataka, Andhra Pradesh, Maharashtra, Gujarat, Rajasthan and Uttar Pradesh.

April 22: The Union Minister of State for Home Affairs, Sriprakash Jaiswal, replying to questions in the *Lok Sabha* (lower house of Parliament) said that the banned Students Islamic Movement of India (SIMI) has links with terrorist groups, including the Lashkar-e-Toiba (LeT). He said that the links have been revealed in investigations into a number of cases. The minister further said that 181 SIMI cadres have been arrested in various States since 2006 and arms, ammunition, incriminating literature and other items were recovered from them. Of them, 128 were arrested in Madhya Pradesh.

April 10: The Mumbai Police arrested two SIMI cadres from the Thane district. The duo, identified as Irshad Salim Khan and Israr Ahmed Abdul Hamid Tailor, are believed to be close to the arrested secretary-general of the outfit, Safdar Nagori. Khan is a civil engineer by profession and was the former president of the outfit while Israr Ahmed is a computer professional. Joint Commissioner of Police (Crime) Rakesh Maria said, "Both are wanted in a case registered under Unlawful Activities (Prevention)

Act here on July 28, 2006, in which train blasts accused Ehtesham Siddqui was earlier arrested."

The Madhya Pradesh Police arrested a SIMI cadre from the Rishala area of Indore city. The arrested cadre, identified as Hafiz Yusuf, has been an active worker of the outfit and played a significant role in collecting funds for the outfit, police sources said. He was working in a mobile shop in Indore.

April 7: Six SIMI cadres were arrested by the Madhya Pradesh police. While five SIMI cadres were arrested from Guna, a suspected SIMI cadre, identified as Naved Irfan was arrested in Indore's Muslim-dominated Khajrana area for allegedly indulging in illegal activities and aiding anti-national elements, a senior police officer said.

The Jabalpur Police in Madhya Pradesh announced a reward of INR 5,000 to those who help trace two absconding SIMI activists Mohammad Ali and Mohammad Shakil.

April 5: Three SIMI activists were arrested from Narsinghgarh town in the Rajgarh district. The Rajgarh Superintendent of Police D. K. Arya said that the SIMI cadres, identified as Irfan, Faizal and Shakir, were arrested on charges of aiding anti-national elements and indulging in illegal activities. An unspecified quantity of objectionable material, video cassettes and CDs were recovered from the house where the arrests occurred.

April 4: Three persons, including a woman, were arrested for allegedly renting their premises to SIMI leaders in Indore and Khargone. A house in the Shyam Nagar locality of Indore was rented to SIMI's Andhra Pradesh unit chief Qamaruddin Nagori from where police arrested top 13 leaders of the outfit on March 27. The house rented to the SIMI by Gaffar Khan Bakerywale was registered in the name of his daughter-in-law Shahnaz Bi. Police arrested both Khan and Shahnaz for not providing information to the police about giving their house on rent.

Separately, in Khargone, another person, identified as Shahzad Hussein, was arrested for allegedly providing his farmhouse to the SIMI for running training camps.

April 2: Madhya Pradesh Police neutralised a SIMI training camp in Choral, a popular holiday spot, 35-kilometres from the State capital Bhopal. Police claimed that interrogation of the 13 arrested SIMI cadres led to the information on the existence of the camp. The Superintendent of Police Chanchal Shekhar told, "We were told the camp trained SIMI activists from Jharkhand, Kerala, Karnataka and a few other states. Each training camp would train around 20 SIMI members. We have information of five such camps in the past one-and-half years, which would mean about a hundred SIMI activists trained in Choral." He said that the trainees were made to climb the surrounding mountains and swim across the river daily. The police also found evidence of a firing range and exploded bits of petrol bombs.

Separately, Police recovered 122 super-explosive gelatine sticks, 100 detonators and switchboards buried underground in the Gawali village under Balwara police station area of Khargaon district.

April 1: The Assam Government told the Legislative Assembly that SIMI was active in Assam, but clarified that no member of the group had been arrested so far in the State. "While the Government had banned SIMI in 2001, there is information that the group is still active in Assam," Minister Rockybul Hussain told the Assembly.

March 31: A team of Madhya Pradesh Police arrested seven SIMI cadres from an unspecified location. The investigators interrogating the 13 SIMI leaders arrested in Indore on March 27 claimed that the banned outfit were planning to kill top leaders of the Bharatiya Janata Party (BJP), including the Leader of Opposition L. K. Advani, and Gujarat Chief Minister Narendra Modi. The investigators further claimed that the SIMI was even running training camps for militants to carry out terrorist attacks in the country.

March 27: 13 SIMI leaders, including the outfit's General Secretary Safdar Nagori and his brother Kamruddin Nagori, were arrested following several raids in Indore by the Madhya Pradesh Police. Police described the arrested persons as active members of the outfit hailing from Kerala, Karnataka, Uttar Pradesh, Haryana, Maharashtra and Madhya Pradesh. The arrested persons included

SIMI's Karnataka unit chief Hafiz Hussain and Shivli, who is the mainstay of the group's operations in Kerala. Pistols, cartridges, nine mobile phones, INR 45,000 in cash, 15 masks, 22 pairs of surgical gloves and surgical instruments, SIMI literature were recovered from the arrested persons.

Police raided the house of SIMI leader Shiblyin a village in Kottayam district. Two computers were recovered from the houses of Shibli and his brother, Shaduli.

March 18: The Union Minister of State for Home, Sriprakash Jaiswal, said in a written reply in the Lok Sabha (lower house of parliament) that the SIMI and its associates were planning to commit serial blasts and other serious offences in the country. "While there was no present input indicating any specific plans of SIMI to attack important installation,...One arrested person disclosed that he along with his SIMI associates were planning to commit serial blasts and other serious offences," Jaiswal said.

March 11: A former Bihar unit chief of the SIMI, Arif Abrar, who had surrendered before a lower court in Nagpur in January 2008, was reportedly granted bail by the 10th Ad hoc Sessions Judge. Abrar who was lodged in the Nagpur central jail after police interrogation is expected to be released shortly. Defence lawyer A.M. Rizway stated that court found no incriminating evidence against him.

February 21: The Corps of Detectives arrested a software engineer for suspected links with the banned SIMI from Guruappanapalya under Mico Layout police station limits in Bangalore, capital of Karnataka. However, four of his alleged accomplices escaped during the police operation. Yahya Khan is a native of Kerala and was working in a leading multinational information technology company in the city and he was reportedly under watch by the Bangalore Police for the past few days. Police sources said that the arrest followed information given by Mohammad Asif, a final-year MBBS student, and another SIMI activist, who was arrested in Hubli recently.

February 12: The Corps of Detectives, which is investigating a terrorist module unearthed by the Davangere police in Karnataka, arrested an electrician from Dharwad for his alleged links with the banned SIMI. The arrested identified as Shakeel, a resident of Koppadakeri in the Dharwad district, had helped the SIMI activists to hold two meetings, one near the Mastansab Darga on Saudatti Road and the other at the Halligere forests on Haliyal Road in Hubli in November 2007. Shakeel reportedly participated in these meetings where some 25 SIMI activists from Karnataka, Uttar Pradesh and Kerala allegedly discussed plans to carry out acts of sabotage. These activists had held another meeting near Dandeli in May 2007.

February 12: Firoz Sanadi, the former deputy mayor of Belgaum city in Karnataka, and nine medical students were detained for alleged links with the SIMI and suspected militant Mohammed Asif who is in police custody.

Former Bihar unit chief of the SIMI, Dr Abrar Arif, who had surrendered before the Nagpur court recently, was sent to jail after he was produced before the lower court 2 by Sadar police.

February 10: The Islamic Students Association (ISA) is functioning transparently and it has no links with the banned SIMI, said ISA ad-hoc committee secretary E K Noufal in Kozhikode in Kerala.

February 7: The Union Government decided to continue the ban on the Students Islamic Movement of India (SIMI) for another two years. "The decision to re-impose the ban for two years has been taken in view of the fact that the group continues to indulge in unlawful activities," said the home ministry spokesperson Onkar Kedia.

February 6: Police arrested four activists of the Islamic Students Association (ISA), while trying to stick wall posters in the early hours at Edavamgal near Bekal in the Kasargod district of Kerala. The four activists of the newly-floated ISA, which seemed to be a front organisation of the banned SIMI, said the police.

January 31: Mohammad Abrar Arif Mohammad Kasim, a key SIMI leader, surrendered before a court in Nagpur after remaining at large for 18 months.

January 22: A report in *The Hindu* stated that the SIMI is believed to be operating under the cover of at least 12 organisations in Kerala. SIMI organisers periodically change the name of their front organisations to shake off police surveillance. Intelligence officials believe that SIMI activists in Kerala had developed links with the Lashkar-e-Toiba in 2006. They said that SIMI activists are operating under the cover of religious study centres, rural development and research centres and institutions for developing "personal effectiveness." Some of these organisations were spreading "extremist religious ideals" among a section of impressionable youth by acting as "counselling and guidance centres working for behavioural change". In the past 10 years, the police have registered 17 cases against suspected SIMI activists.

2007

October 23: Daily News & Analysis reported that the role of a splinter group of the SIMI is being examined by the internal security agencies for its alleged linkages with some rural non-government organisations (NGOs) in Maharashtra. An unidentified intelligence official said cadres belonging to the SIMI splinter, Tehereek Taifooz Sher-e-Islam, could have established linkages with a section of Muslim functionaries in these NGOs. Central intelligence agencies and the State Intelligence Department reportedly have been investigating the way these NGOs are managed.

September 6: The Supreme Court asked the SIMI to serve a fresh notice to the government on its plea for transferring the petition relating to the ban imposed on the organisation from the Delhi High Court to the apex court. SIMI had sought transfer of the petition filed by it in the High Court challenging the ban imposed in September 2003 for its alleged anti-national activities. Two other petitions filed by SIMI challenging the ban in September 2001 and February 2006 are pending in the apex court and hence it has sought transfer of the 2003 petition so that all the three petitions could be decided by the apex court.

July 5: Four persons, including two Hizb-ul-Mujahideen (HM) militants, were convicted by a court in New Delhi for possessing explosives and conspiring to wage war against the country. The other two persons, held guilty under various provisions of the Indian Penal Code (IPC) and Explosive Substances Act, are members of the outlawed Students Islamic Movement of India (SIMI). Gulzar Ahmed Wani and Mohiuddin, the HM militants from Baramulla in Jammu and Kashmir, and Feroz Rafi and Mumtaz, the SIMI activists from Uttar Pradesh, were arrested at New Delhi Railway Station on July 30, 2001.

Police had then seized a huge haul of RDX, grenades, launchers, detonators and other explosives from them. The Hizb militants had reportedly come to Delhi to deliver the explosives to the SIMI activists. With their arrest, police had claimed to have solved six bomb blast cases, including the 2001 Sena Bhavan blast. However, the court on February 23 acquitted them in all these cases for lack of evidence.

Times Now reported that the SIMI has stepped up efforts to strengthen its base in the northeastern region along the India-Myanmar border. SIMI has been trying to tie up with Manipur-based outfits and especially the Peoples' United Liberation Front (PULF), an organization of indigenous Muslims of Manipur called Pangals. The report further indicated that SIMI's presence in the north-eastern region could pose a grave threat since several *jihadi* outfits with similar ideologies are already active on both sides of the border.

March 9: Police in Patna (Bihar) arrested Mohd Haseeb Raza, an activist of the SIMI, from his Phulwari residence. Police sources said that Raza was the state secretary of the outfit and was wanted in a case lodged in 2001 as a prime accused for planning subversive activities in the country.

February 15: The Supreme Court described the proscribed Students Islamic Movement of India (SIMI) as a "secessionist movement". A bench of Justice S. B. Sinha and Markandeya Katju observed while dealing with the Special Leave Petition filed by the SIMI challenging the ban imposed on it, "You are a secessionist movement. You have not stopped your activities." The Bench refused to agree with the submissions put forth by Kamini Jaiswal, counsel for the SIMI, that there was no evidence to link SIMI to any anti-national activity after 2003. In the petition, the SIMI had challenged the judgment of the Unlawful Activities (Prevention) Act Tribunal headed by Justice B. N. Chaturvedi of the Delhi High

Court, which confirmed the ban imposed on the organisation by the Union Government on February 8, 2006.

January 22: Police have beefed up security in the Cuttack city amidst intelligence reports indicating that the Jaish-e-Mohammed (JeM), Lashkar-e-Toiba (LeT) and Students Islamic Movement of India (SIMI) cadres are planning to orchestrate a terrorist attack during the India-West Indies one-day Cricket Match at the Barabati Stadium on January 24.

2006

December 21: The Anti-Terrorist Squad (ATS) of the Maharashtra Police filed the charge sheet in the September 8 Malegaon serial blasts case. The charge sheet stated that nine SIMI cadres had hatched and executed the conspiracy with the help of two Pakistani nationals in the textile town to "infuriate the entire Muslim community and trigger communal riots". 40 persons died and 312 were injured in four blasts.

December 4: The Uttar Pradesh Government said that it had not received any direction from the Union Government to proscribe the SIMI. In a written reply to a question in the State Legislative Assembly, Chief Minister Mulayam Singh Yadav said that no instructions had been received from the Centre to ban SIMI. The State Government had recently successfully moved an application in a district court in Baharaich seeking withdrawal of cases against SIMI chief Shahid Badar Falah.

November 7: According to IANS, the SIMI is contemplating changing its name to evade attention it receives for its association with the terrorists. Quoting unidentified sources, the report said that SIMI may emerge under a new name such as Teharik-e-Millat or Awaz-e-Sura, with a view to expand its activities in Madhya Pradesh.

November 5: Six SIMI cadres are arrested in Indore. Police said that the six had met a detained senior SIMI operative, Imran Ansari, at a local restaurant while he was being escorted for a court hearing on November 1.

October 30: Maharashtra Police arrests Noorul Hooda

Shamshul Hooda, a SIMI activist, in connection with the Malegaon serial bomb blasts of September 8, 2006.

October 8: A suspected SIMI cadre, Nurullah Samsudoha, is arrested from the Jaffar Nagar area of Malegaon town in Maharashtra.

September 6: The Bahraich District court in Uttar Pradesh grants permission to withdraw a treason case against the banned SIMI chief Shahid Badar Falah and 11 other members of the outfit.

August 23: Two suspects in the October 2005 Delhi serial bomb blasts are remanded to the custody of Mumbai Police till August 28 by a local court in Mumbai. Firoz Abdul Latif Ghaswala and Mohammed Ali Chippa, who were lodged in a jail in Delhi, were brought to Mumbai on August 23 and produced before a local court. Both, suspected to be linked to the SIMI, have allegedly visited Pakistan clandestinely to undergo training in arms and explosives handling at the Lashkar-e-Toiba (LeT) camps.

Speaking in the State Legislative Assembly, the Uttar Pradesh Chief Minister Mulayam Singh Yadav ruled out the involvement of the Students Islamic Movement of India in recent terrorist attacks in the State.

August 22: Faizal Ataur Rehman Sheikh, allegedly Lashkar-e-Toiba's Mumbai chief, and younger brother Muzamil, a software programmer, were booked in the Bandra blast case and remanded to police custody till September 4. In its remand plea, the Anti-Terrorist Squad said the brothers were active members of the proscribed SIMI and had been to Pakistan for military training.

August 18: SIMI activists, Waqar Baig Yusuf Baig and Jitaullah Rehman Mehmood Khan, are arrested from Kazipur in the textile township of Hinganghat in Wardha district of Maharashtra.

August 16: Five suspected SIMI activists, identified as Saduli, Abdul Aziz, Shammi, all from Kottayam district, and Anzar and Nizammudin, both from Aluva, arrested in Kerala.

August 15: Kerala Police arrested 18 suspected SIMI activists from Binamipuram in the Kochi district.

August 13: Two SIMI activists, Irfan Sayeed and Najib Bakali, are arrested by Mumbai Police personnel investigating the July 11 blasts.

August 8: Three SIMI cadres, Shakil Warsi, Shakir Ahmed Nasi and Mohammad Rehan Khan, are arrested in connection with the July 11 Mumbai serial blasts from Nagpur in Maharashtra.

August 7: The tribunal, constituted to examine the ban imposed on SIMI by the Union Government, holds it "legal and valid".

July 29: SIMI activist, Ehtashan Siddiqui, is arrested from his Mira Road residence on the outskirts of Mumbai for alleged links to the 7/11 blasts.

July 21: Bhopal Police arrests a SIMI activist, Imran, wanted in two cases, one registered at Surat in the State of Gujarat and the other at Khandwa in Madhya Pradesh. He is said to be an organising SIMI activities at the national level.

July 13: Uttar Pradesh Chief Minister Mulayam Singh Yadav says in Lucknow that the SIMI is not active in the State and there is no evidence of its involvement in any unlawful activity during his regime. He further said that as far as its existence in Uttar Pradesh is concerned, it will be improper to initiate action without evidence.

July 6: The Supreme Court upheld the ban on the SIMI rejecting a petition that claimed that the organisation had not been found to engage in any terrorist activities.

June 2: According to the Government of Kerala, the SIMI is operating under the cover of at least 12 organisations in the State. At least two organizations linked to the SIMI are operating in the capital city of Thiruvananthapuram.

April 25: Mohammad Aamir, the chief of SIMI's Uttar Pradesh State unit and the prime accused in the Kanpur riots of March 16, 2006, surrenders before a metropolitan magistrate in Kanpur.

April 21: The Union Government declares the SIMI an unlawful association under the Unlawful Activities (Prevention) Act, 1967. It also constitutes a Tribunal, comprising Justice B.N. Chaturvedi of the Delhi High Court, for adjudicating whether or not there is sufficient cause for declaring SIMI as an unlawful association.

2005

July 11: Police in Uttar Pradesh arrest six persons, including four of a family, from Faizabad in connection with the July 5-attack on the disputed complex in Ayodhya. The arrested family members were associated with the banned Students Islamic Movement of India, according to official sources.

June 11: All eight accused in the Ghatkopar blast case, allegedly cadres of the SIMI, are acquitted by a POTA court in Mumbai due to lack of evidence.

March 8: Delhi Police arrests a SIMI member, Mohammad Iftikar Ehsan Malick, from Dehradun, the capital city of Uttaranchal.

2004

November 1: Maulana Nasiruddin, president of the Tahaffuz Shari'at-e Islam (Protection of Islamic Sharia) and allegedly linked to the SIMI, is arrested from Hyderabad in connection with his suspected links to the murder former Gujarat Home Minister Haren Pandya.

2003

November 11: A court in New Delhi acquits SIMI president Shahid Badar Falah in a case of sedition, which was filed against him in September 2001.

September 12: Five persons, including two SIMI activists, are arrested for the removal of railway sleeper clips from the tracks in Kumardubi-Barakar section in West Bengal.

July 21: POTA court in New Delhi sentences two SIMI activists to a five-year imprisonment under POTA for their membership of the proscribed organization and seven years imprisonment for sedition.

July 16: A POTA Court in Delhi convicts two SIMI activists for their active involvement with the banned outfit.

May 26: Mumbai Police arrest two suspected activists of the SIMI in the Ghatkopar bomb blast case and remand them to police custody till June 5.

May 14: Mumbai Police arrest three persons from Padgah

village and foil a plan that envisaged a series of explosions in Mumbai and Kerala, which was allegedly hatched by the SIMI and Lashkar-e-Toiba. The accused were identified as Muzzamal Ansari, Mohammed Nadir Palob and Arif Hussain.

May 11: Mumbai Police detains SIMI activist Anwar Ali, a lecturer of the National Defence Academy in Khadakvasla, Maharashtra, for his suspected involvement in the March 13-Mulund train bomb explosion case.

May 3: Mumbai Police arrests six SIMI activists with links to the LeT and also seizes lethal chemicals and some arms and ammunition from their possession.

April 25: Mumbai Police arrests two suspected SIMI activists for their alleged involvement in the March 13-Mulund-bomb blast case from the Padgha village of Thane district.

April 21: Mumbai Police arrests Ghulam Akbar Khotal, an alleged SIMI activist from Ratnagiri in Maharashtra, in connection with March 13 Mulund blast.

April 10: Saquib Nachan, a SIMI activist, surrenders before the Mumbai High Court. He is subsequently arrested by the Mumbai Police and booked under POTA for his alleged involvement in the Mulund blast. Saquib was arrested from Gujarat in October 1992 under the Terrorist and Disruptive Activities (Prevention) Act (TADA) for his subversive activities and sentenced to life imprisonment, which was later commuted to 10 years by the Supreme Court. He was released from the Sabarmati jail in April 2001.

March 12: Noman Badar alias Falahi, one of the top leaders of SIMI, is brought on transit remand to Delhi from Lucknow, Uttar Pradesh. A case against him is pending in a Court in Delhi for his involvement in unlawful activities, including publishing objectionable using inflammatory language.

February 24: Police arrest two persons allegedly connected with the SIMI at Rabodi in Thane District of Maharashtra and seize incriminating documents from their possession.

January 29: Mumbai Police suspects the LeT and SIMI for the twin blasts near Vile Parle railway station in Mumbai on January

27 and January 28. United Arab Emirates (UAE) based LeT terrorist Abu Hamza is suspected to be the masterminded behind the first explosion, in which a women was killed and 25 more injured.

January 27: Uttar Pradesh Police arrests three SIMI activists from Lucknow and recover certain incriminating documents from them.

January 26: Dubai authorities deport Mohammed Altaf, an activist of the SIMI and main accused in the December 2, 2002, bomb blast at Ghatkopar.

January 9: Madhya Pradesh Police arrests Bhopal district unit former president of the SIMI Khalid Naeem. He was later released on bail.

January 3: Mumbai Police invokes POTA against four SIMI activists— Abdul Mattin, Sayed Khwaja, Muzzamil Ahmed and Zahir Shaikh—for allegedly setting off a blast inside a bus in Ghatkopar on December 2, 2002, in which three persons were killed.

2002

December 21: A Delhi court discharges SIMI leader Mohammed Javed Iqbal in a sedition and unlawful activities case and also drops sedition charges against its president Shahid Badar and three others. While discharging Iqbal, the court granted bail to Badar and four others in the case. The court also dropped sedition charge against Badar in another case and granted him bail on a personal bond of Rs 5,000 and one surety.

October 7: Supreme Court issues notices to Union Government and eight States on a petition filed by the SIMI challenging the Union Home Ministry's order declaring the organization as unlawful and the subsequent order of a Tribunal upholding the same. States to which notices were issued are: Kerala, Maharashtra, Madhya Pradesh, Tamil Nadu, West Bengal, Gujarat, Rajasthan and Andhra Pradesh.

May 27: Two SIMI activists are arrested in Delhi.

May 5: Uttar Pradesh unit SIMI chief Noman Badar is arrested in Lucknow.

March 18: SIMI activist Hasib Raja is arrested in Kolkata, West Bengal, and half a kilogram of RDX is seized from him. He was allegedly planning to blow up the Howrah Bridge.

January 28: Police arrest eight SIMI activists from Vadodara in Gujarat.

2001

December 28: Police in Surat, Gujarat, arrest 123 persons for their alleged links with SIMI and also recover certain incriminating documents from their possession.

October 24: Maharashtra Police files charge sheet in a Jalgaon Court against 11 SIMI activists arrested for suspected terrorist activities.

October 8: Police arrest the Tamil Nadu State vice-president of SIMI, Abdul Qudoos, from Madurai.

October 5: Maharashtra Police arrest three SIMI activists from Ahmednagar.

October 1: Police arrest nine SIMI activists in Madhya Pradesh and one in Delhi.

September 29: After the ban on SIMI, the Police arrest another 122 of its cadres across the country.

September 28: Delhi Police seals SIMI headquarters at Zakir Nagar and arrests four senior members of the organisation, including its national president Dr Shahid Badr Falah. Shahid Badr was subsequently charged with sedition and inciting communal disharmony in Uttar Pradesh.

September 27: Union Government imposes a ban on the SIMI under section 3(1) of the Unlawful Activities (Prevention) Act. Following the ban, 241 SIMI activists were arrested across the country and authorities seal many of its regional offices.

September 21: Uttar Pradesh Police arrests three SIMI activists in Bahraich for alleged anti-India activities. Five more SIMI cadres were arrested in the same town a day earlier.

August 8: The Uttar Pradesh Police says SIMI activists arrested in Kanpur earlier have revealed that the ISI had asked one of its agents to supply explosive material for subversive activities in northern India.

August 6: Police in Kanpur register cases against 12 SIMI activists on charges of waging war and sedition.

May 9: Police arrest 13 SIMI activists, including zonal President Irshad Khan, in Kurla and Vikhroli in Maharashtra for allegedly possessing weapons and several incriminating documents.

April 10: Ilyas Gausn, main accused in the Pune communal violence, surrenders before a judicial magistrate in the city.

March 16: Six persons, including an Additional District Magistrate, are killed in a clash between SIMI activists and police in Kanpur, Uttar Pradesh.

March 11: Police arrest Sajid Sundke, city unit chief of SIMI, and four of his associates in Pune for their suspected involvement in the communal riots in Ganj Peth and Ghorpade Peth areas of the city.

2000

March 12: Deputy Chief Minister of Maharashtra, Chhagan Bhujbal, discloses in the State Legislative Assembly that Pakistan-based underworld don Chhota Shakeel, in league with the SIMI, is inciting communal riots in some parts of the State.

August 15: Uttar Pradesh Police arrest Mohammad Aquil, a former student of Aligarh Muslim University and an active SIMI member, in connection with a bomb blast in the Sabarmati Express train near Faizabad.

4

Indian Mujahideen: Evolving Challenge

Revelations made by Indian Mujahideen (IM) 'India operations chief' Yasin Bhatkal *aka* Mohammad Ahmed Siddibappa Zarrar *aka* Imran *aka* Asif *aka* Shahrukh, and his associate Asadullah Akhtar*alias* Haddi, during their ongoing interrogations by several agencies have brought to the fore some new facts. The duo also reconfirmed much that was already known about IM. The revelations in their totality outline the emerging challenges that Indian security agencies are going to face in the foreseeable future. Bhatkal and Haddi were arrested from Indo-Nepal border on August 28, 2013.

In the most startling of revelations so far, Yasin Bhatkal is reported to have told security agencies that the "IM is trying to turn into an al Qaeda-like terror network". An unnamed official noted, further, "Two options were on the table-either the IM would turn an assisting outfit of Qaeda in India or merge with it to work directly under the command of Zawahiri [al Qaeda 'chief' Ayman al-Zawahiri]."

Yasin Bhatkal has also claimed that there has been a split within IM ranks. According to interrogation reports, the IM structure changed after the Batla House (New Delhi) encounter of September 19, 2008. The entire organization split into two factions — Azamgarh and Bhatkal. While the Azamgarh Unit was led by Amir Reza Khan, with Shahnawaz Alam as his lieutenant, Riyaz Bhatkal headed the Bhatkal Unit. Some reports, however, suggest that Yasin Bhatkal has also spoken about another unit led by Mohammad Sajid *alias* Bada Sajid and Mirza Shadab Beg. Significantly, these names also appeared in the National Investigation Agency's (NIA) First Information Report (FIR) on allegations related to terrorist activities of members of IM and conspiracy for waging war against the Government of India, dated September 10, 2012, along with seven other IM cadres.

Indeed, an unnamed security official observed, "Our initial assessment was that the group has weakened with (the) arrest of so many cadres and there is division. But the IM... has grown many folds. Each group has its men and logistics in India."

These two developments, if found to be correct, are ominous.

The growing links with al Qaeda are a very real threat, suggesting that the global *Jihad* has started focusing increasingly on India, bringing new and more dangerous strategies, tactics and resources to this theatre. Indeed, current al Qaeda leader Ayman al-Zawahiri in his first specific *Jihad* guidelines, endorsed the right of Islamist militants to fight "Indians in Kashmir", as reported on September 17, 2013. Further, an al Qaeda statement released on September 30, 2012, indicates that the terror group is evolving its strategy on the Myanmar-Assam region. In the statement, Ustad Ahmad Farooq, who was appointed as al Qaeda's head of the 'preaching and media department' for Pakistan in 2009, warned that the recent killings of Muslims in Myanmar and Assam "provide impetus for us to hasten our advance towards Delhi." June 2013 reports indicated that Maulana Asim Umar, a senior al Qaeda ideologue, released a video titled "Why There Is No Storm in Your Ocean?", exhorting Indian Muslims to join the global *Jihad*. IM and al Qaeda are believed to have discussed attacks on foreign nationals based in India, most notably Jews. Significantly, in September this year, New Delhi asked all Mumbai-based Jewish establishments to step up security measures in the face of an impending terrorist threat. India's Union Home Ministry has also briefed Israel about a possible IM attack on Israeli nationals visiting Rajasthan, especially in the tourist centre of Pushkar, Jaisalmer and Jodhpur.

In this context, the four individuals of Indian origin, who have participated in global terror activities, offer a vital pre-text. They are Dhiren Barot (aka Abu Musa al-Hindi), a British citizen of Indian origin who plotted bomb attacks against the New York Stock Exchange, International Monetary Fund and World Bank; Haroon Rashid Aswat, another Indian with a British passport, was a self-proclaimed hitman for Osama bin Laden and allegedly a key figure in the July 2005 attacks in London; Bangalore-born Kafeel Ahmed, who was involved in the June 2007 attack on Glasgow International Airport, and a known follower of al Qaeda; and finally, Mohammad Niaz Raseed, a cadre of the Students' Islamic Movement of India (SIMI), the parent organization of the IM, who was recently sentenced to eight years in prison by the Paris Criminal Court for plotting a series of terrorist attacks. These important examples demonstrate an escalating threat potential not only in India, but of a terrorist mobilisation within this country that could have international ramifications.

On the home front, IM's link or efforts to establish linkages with other groups have also been reconfirmed. Disclosures during interrogations of Yasin Bhatkal and Asadullah Akhtar indicate that IM was in touch with the Communist Party of India-Maoist (CPI-Maoist), discussing a possible tie-up with the outfit to procure explosives and ammunition for use in terror attacks in India. Sources claim IM offered 'handsome payments' to the Maoists for supply of weapons and explosives. Yasin Bhatkal also revealed that he had met CPI-Maoist leaders in Nepal before the serial blasts that rocked Bodh Gaya in Gaya District of Bihar on July 7, 2013. Bhatkal had reportedly surveyed the area around the Mahabodhi temple a year before the blasts took place. The explosive devices used in the blasts resemble the bombs used by Maoists. Similarly, close connections with the National Development Front (NDF) in Kerala and the Karnataka Forum for Dignity (KFD) also came to the fore.

Counter-intuitively, the alleged splits within IM may actually result in a deeper percolation of terrorist networks and activities in India, with multiple and overlapping structures of operation, and increasing specialization. Indeed, Beg's Unit, which is reported to have the backing of al Qaeda and Taliban, is believed to be focusing only on *fidayeen* (suicide squad) attacks on prominent people in India. Akhtar revealed that, during an online chat in July 2013, Beg told him that 15 people from five Indian States had been called to Pakistan earlier in the year, to discuss IM's future operations in India. Sources indicate that these persons underwent intensive training in Afghanistan to carry out *fidayeen* attacks.

Disclosures during interrogations also indicate that IM is planning to target political leaders. Yasin Bhatkal admitted, "The funds flow from our international sympathisers will increase many times if we manage to reach Narendra Modi. Modi is one to 10 in the list of targets. The rest of the targets figure much below him."

IM is also planning a series of bomb blasts across the country. Significantly, agencies have recovered a whopping 90 Improvised Explosive Devices (IEDs) from Zephyr Heights in Mangalore and Abdullapur in Hyderabad, among other IM hideouts. In what can be considered further evidence of the plan, all these devices were almost ready for use, and had been developed at the instance of Yasin Bhatkal and his aide, Akhtar.

A top intelligence officer disclosed to the media, "Only the circuitry was not connected to the IEDs, otherwise these bombs were ready to use." Several unattached timers, batteries, detonators and shrapnel were also recovered from various hideouts. Yasin Bhatkal is learnt to have told interrogators that IM was experimenting with the manufacture of hydrogen peroxide-based IEDs. On the 'ideological' front, Yasin Bhatkal is reported to have reconfirmed that IM's main objective was to establish *Shariah* in India, as in Afghanistan and Somalia.

IM is clearly undergoing dynamic transformations under the direction and guidance of the Inter Service Intelligence (ISI) which has provided the top leaders of the group safe haven and resources in Pakistan, and facilitated deepening linkages with regional and global *jihadi* groups. With a progressive international outreach, vertical splits and increasingly specialization, the group and its successors are likely to evolve more lethal capabilities that would certainly be manifested in India, but are likely to have reverberations across the world as well.

PAKISTAN

At least seven persons, including two women-one civilian and one Police constable-were killed and another 16 were injured when militants triggered an Improvised Explosive Device (IED) explosion targeting the Jaffar Express train in the Notal area of Naseerabad District in Balochistan Province on October 21, 2013. Reports indicated that the train, which runs between Rawalpindi in Punjab Province and Quetta in Balochistan, was carrying hundreds of passengers. The passengers were returning from Punjab to Balochistan after *Eid al-Adha* (festival of sacrifice) holidays. Meanwhile, claiming responsibility for the attack, the Baloch Republican Army (BRA) claimed that the train was carrying Security Force (SF) personnel who were returning to Balochistan after celebrating *Eid* in Punjab.

Earlier, on August 16, 2013, the same Jaffar Express had come under rocket attack by militants in the Dozan area of Mach in Bolan District (Balochistan). At least three civilians had been killed and another 32 persons had sustained injuries. The Baloch Liberation Army (BLA) had claimed responsibility for that attack. On this occasion, the train was going to Rawalpindi. Later that day, SFs killed at least eight BLA militants during a search operation in the mountains of Mach and Kolpur.

On January 5, 2013, five passengers had been killed and another 10 had sustained injuries when militants had opened fire on passengers travelling in the Jaffar Express near the Kohsar area of Kachhi in Bolan District, while it was travelling to Quetta from Rawalpindi.

While the Jaffar Express has been targeted repeatedly, the wider Rail network across Pakistan has also come under recurring attack. According to partial data compiled by the *South Asia Terrorism Portal* (SATP), the Railways in Pakistan have been attacked on at least 109 occasions since March 2000 (data till October 27, 2013). Of these, 105 attacks have been recorded in just two Provinces: Sindh (56) and Balochistan (49). 56 fatalities have been recorded in the total of 109 attacks, with 30 killed in Balochistan and 20 in Sindh.

SATP data indicates an escalation in such incidents and fatalities since 2011, with a succession of major attacks (each involving three or more fatalities) targeting the Railways. Of these, in addition to the incidents mentioned above, the most significant included:

June 27, 2012: At least seven persons were killed and another 30 were injured when a remote-controlled bomb went off at the Sibi Railway Station in Sibi District, Balochistan.

April 24, 2012: At least three people, including a Railway Police official, died and around 45 received injuries, when a bomb exploded at the Lahore Railway Station, Lahore District, Punjab.

August 28, 2011: Three persons were killed and 19 were injured in firing and rocket attacks on the Peshawar-bound Quetta Express in the Mach area of Bolan District, Balochistan.

However, in terms of fatalities in such attacks, the year 2000 remains the deadliest, with 18 killed in two incidents in that year. On July 17, 2000, ten persons were killed in a train blast in Hyderabad city, Sindh. Earlier, on February 5, 2000, a bomb exploded in a train in Hyderabad, killing eight persons and injuring more than 40.

The concentration of attacks on the Railways in two provinces – Balochistan and Sindh – is the result of separatists operating there, and engaging in different patterns of economic subversions. Attacking the Railways is one of several such tactics. Significantly, most of the attacks on Railways-as is also the case with attacks on gas pipelines -are non-lethal. Reports indicate that Pakistan Railway has suffered a loss of PKR 132 billion over just the last four years. Though the reasons for this have not been specified, it is certain that the series of attacks on the Rail infrastructure will aggravate the financial crisis of the Railways, which constitute the backbone of an already depleted Pakistan economy.

While Baloch nationalist groupings like BLA and BRA have been engaged in attacks on Railways inside Balochistan, it is the relatively little known Sindhi groups like the Sindhu Desh Liberation Army (SDLA), a banned separatist formation, which is fighting for the establishment of an independent Sindhu Desh, that have led the attacks inside Sindh.

Despite the evident hike in the frequency of such attacks, security agencies have failed to meet the challenge because of enveloping shortcomings. Crucially, Pakistan Railways has a network of 11,755 kilometers of track with 558 stations. During the year 2011-2012, the Pakistan Railways carried 41,097,192 passengers, covering a total of 16,093,350,581 passenger-kilometers. Just about 20,000 ill equipped and ill trained personnel are there to provide safety to this vast complex. The Pakistan Railways Police (PRP), like other wings of the Police in Pakistan, has been facing acute shortages of arms and communication system for decades. Available data indicates, for instance, that PRP has just 1,625 walkie-talkie systems, 102 VHF mobile stations, 86 VHF base sets, 30 HF base sets and 300 head phones. Document available with the media in April 2012 indicated that *the*Railways had just 40 G-3A3 rifles for its eight Divisions; no such rifles were available at Lahore and Multan. Similarly, against the total of 10 Light Machine Guns (LMGs) in the PRP armoury, there were no LMGs at the Lahore, Peshawar, Rawalpindi, Multan, Sukkur and Quetta Divisions. The Railways Police also have small numbers of few revolvers, pistols, shot guns and Henry Martin rifles. There is also a severe and persistent shortage of anti-riot equipment, from helmet to walkthrough gates. The entire availability is just 1,721 helmets, 2,727 polo sticks (canes), 103 tear gas guns, 350 tear gas masks, 746 anti-riot jackets, 10 statures, 10 mega phones, 530 material detectors and three explosive detectors (with just one available at Lahore). Police also have 22 walkthrough gates and eight mine detecting sets.

The Department is, moreover, facing an acute shortage of funds for purchasing security equipment. Even the meager allocation of PKR 20 million in 2012, though approved by then Prime Minister Yousuf Raza Gilani, has not been released by the Finance Division under the grounds of monetary constraints.

Much of the Railways security infrastructure, moreover, is dysfunctional. Investigations after the April 24, 2012, attack at Lahore Railway Station, for instance, revealed that the CCTV cameras at the station were not working. Furthermore, the CCTV cameras installed at the Railway Stations across the country lack the feature of night-vision recording, and are of little use after dark, though activity on the Rail network continues round the clock.

Some ineffectual measures have, of course, been initiated to 'counter' attacks on the rail system. On May 15, 2012, the Federal Ministry of Interior cancelled licenses and No Objection Certificates (NOCs) for transportation of arms and ammunition aboard trains. "All the NOCs and permissions issued for allowing carriage of arms, weapons and ammunition through railway carriers stand cancelled until further orders, and those found violating this order will be dealt with according to the law," then Federal Minister of Interior Rehman Malik wrote in a letter to Provincial Home Departments, the Railways Inspector General and Pakistan Railways Divisional Superintendents. Recently, PRP Inspector General (IG) Ibne Hussain on October 13, 2013, disclosed that the 'latest communication and tracking system' was being installed to monitor Railway tracks and trains across the country. He added that PRP had been assigned the responsibility of operating the new tracking system, while it was the IT department that had previously monitored it. He added, further, that the latest weapons, including sniper guns, G-3 7.62 mm rifles, telescopic-sighted rifles, night vision telescopes and other weapons of various calibre, were being purchased from the Pakistan Ordinance Factory, and that PKR 21 million had already been approved for the plan-though it is not clear whether the funds have been, or will be, released. IG Hussain, however, insisted that, "The weapons will be received within two to three months." He also stated that 13 railway stations – including Lahore, Peshawar, Rawalpindi, Quetta, Karachi, Multan, Sukkur and Gujranwala – had been declared 'high security zones'.

Other measures have also been promised. The Minister for Railways, Khawaja Saad Rafique, on August 29, 2013, pointed out that no anti-terrorist training had been provided to PRP personnel, despite the increased security threats prevailing across the country, and claimed that Pakistan Railways was planning an anti-terrorist training programme for PRP. In its first phase, he added, Pakistan Railways would nominate 100 Police personnel for the training. He also disclosed that satellite devices would also be acquired with the help of the Ministry of Information Technology, along with CCTV cameras and multiple scanning machines. The Minister also stated that an additional 600 constables would be recruited to PRP, for which special permission would be sought from the Federal Government. Even on the face of it, however, these proposals appear far too modest to impact significantly on the prevailing situation.

Worse, given the track record of the security establishment as well as that of the leadership at the helm in Pakistan's political spectrum, it remains highly unlikely that even these limited proposals are going to be implemented in full. On the other hand, discontent among the separatists can only grow, given Islamabad's flawed approach to the Provinces. Under the circumstances, attacks on soft targets like the Railways with widely dispersed and vulnerable infrastructure can only be expected to increase.

BANGLADESH

Nine persons killed in street violence across the country during the week: At least seven people were killed in street violence across the country on October 25. Several hundred people were also injured in violence as the opposition and the ruling alliance tried to hold rallies at same places or tried to violate bans on gathering that had been ordered by way of Section 144 of the Code of Criminal Procedure.

One person was killed and 116 others injured when scores of crude bombs exploded in at least 50 places including the houses of a Supreme Court judge, law minister, environment minister and chief election commissioner, and the offices of a Police high-up, a Police station, and Ekattor TV in Dhaka city on October 26. 71 people were arrested from different areas of the city.

In Rajshahi District, Rashedul Islam (30), treasurer of Motihar unit of Islami Chhatra Shibir (ICS), the student wing of Jamaat-e-Islami (JeI), was killed, and over 30 people including seven Policemen and a ward councillor were injured as Bangladesh Nationalist Party (BNP), JeI and ICS cadres clashed with Police and hurled around 15 homemade bombs in Rajshahi city on October 26. *Daily Star; New Age*, October 21-28, 2013.

INDIA

Sevnen persons including one militant killed in serial explosions in Bihar : At least seven persons, including one militant were killed, and 100 others were injured in eight serial bomb blasts near Gandhi Maidan, the venue of Bharatiya Janata Party (BJP) Prime Ministerial candidate Narendra Modi's rally in Patna on October 27 minutes before he reached there to address a huge gathering,. Eight explosive devices with timers went off between 9.30am and 12.25pm as part of a serial bomb attacks suspected to be the handiwork of Indian Mujahideen (IM). *Times of India*, October 27-28, 2013.

Meanwhile, four alleged operatives of the IM have been arrested, one of whom is in critical condition after being caught in a blast. "A suspected accused (who was) seriously injured in bomb explosion while fitting a timer at Patna railway junction died on late Sunday night," Patna Senior Superintendent of Police (SSP) Manu Maharaj said. During interrogation, they reportedly told the Police that they had staged the attack in retaliation for the Muzaffarnagar riots. They are also said to have named the IM module involved in the Bodh Gaya blasts. The names of the four detained are Imtiaz Ansari, Ainul, Akhtar and Kaleem. Ansari, a resident of Ranchi, was apprehended at the railway station just after the first two bombs went off. He was apparently planning to plant some more bombs but panicked when he saw the Police and bomb disposal squad. On being challenged, he tried to flee but was arrested..

254 infiltration bids in first nine months of 2013 in Jammu and Kashmir, says report: Infiltration attempts in Jammu & Kashmir (J&K) in 2013 have breached the levels witnessed during the last couple of years, with 254 instances being recorded until September 30 as against 233 during the corresponding period of last year and 247 during 2011. The Security Forces (SFs), however, have managed to contain the number of cases where the terrorists could successfully sneak into Indian Territory. *Times of India*, October 22, 2013.

IM might attack Israeli nationals visiting Rajasthan, says report: Israel was briefed in September about a possible Indian Mujahideen

(IM) attack against the country's nationals visiting Rajasthan, said Union Ministry of Home Affairs and Israeli sources. The Israeli Embassy was briefed by Indian counterterrorism officials, but did not issue a warning to tourists "beyond the normal." *Hindustan Times*October 25, 2013.

LeT 'chief' Hafiz Muhammad Saeed training terrorists along borders, says Union Minister of Home Affairs, Sushilkumar Shinde: Union Minister of Home Affairs Sushilkumar Shinde on October 22 said that Lashkar-e-Toiba (LeT) 'chief' Hafiz Muhammad Saeed is training terrorists along borders. "As per our information, it is possible that he (Hafiz) must be giving training to terrorists on the other side of the border at various launchings pad and unless Pakistan hands him to us, there would be a problem…Infiltration attempts from across the border have increased this year and it is a matter of concern".*Times of India,* October 25, 2013.

Over 15 IM modules have taken shelter in Pakistan, reveals Yasin Bhatkal: Arrested Indian Mujahideen (IM) 'India operation chief' Yasin Bhatkal's interrogation has revealed that more than 15 active IM modules have taken shelter in Pakistan. The interrogation has also given conclusive evidence to the security agencies in India on pro-active involvement of Pakistan's Inter-Services Intelligence (ISI) in formation and operations of the IM. *Asian Age*, October 21, 2013.

Terror emanating from 'our neighbourhood' affects India and China, says Indian Prime Minister Manmohan Singh: Prime Minister Manmohan Singh on October 24 warned that terrorism and radicalism emanating from "our neighbourhood" had directly affected both India and China and could lead to instability across Asia. He said, "If we look carefully, many of our challenges are common. Terrorism, extremism and radicalism emanating from our neighbourhood affect both of us directly and can create instability across Asia". *Times of India,* October 25, 2013.

PAKISTAN

Seven persons killed in IED explosion on train in Balochistan: At least seven persons, including two women-one civilian and one Police constable-were killed and another 16 were injured when militants triggered an Improvised Explosive Device (IED) explosion targeting the Jaffar Express train in the Notal area of Naseerabad District in Balochistan Province on October 21, 2013. Reports indicated that the train, which runs between Rawalpindi in Punjab Province and Quetta in Balochistan, was carrying hundreds of passengers. *Dawn*, October 22, 2013.

27 polio workers killed since 2012, reveals Prime Minister's Special Cell on polio report:According to an October 24 report by the Prime Minister's Special Cell on polio, militant attacks on Pakistan's polio workers have killed 27 vaccinators and Police guards during the past year and a half. The report, released in connection with World Polio Day (October 24, 2013), said 16 of those killed were from Khyber Pakhtunkhwa. Central Asia Online, October 25, 2013.

THE INCEPTION OF THE INDIAN MUJAHIDEEN (IM)

A study of the modus operandi of the IM has shown that the role of educated and technologically advanced youth in masterminding and executing terror attacks is of utmost importance. Such subversive elements have been indoctrinated with assorted ideologies like the Wahhabi and Deobandi schools of thought, to give legitimacy to their version of terror in the name of Islam. Drawing their own interpretations of the Quran, there has been a rapid spread of 'radical' teaching in the mushrooming *madrasas*. During the recent times there has been a sudden surge in the formation of such destructive organisations throughout India. One such organisation is the Students Islamic Movement of India (SIMI), which gave birth to the IM.

SIMI was founded with 250 members on April 15, 1977, by Mohammed Ahmedullah Siddiqui, as the students' wing of the Jamaat-e-Islami Hind (JIH).v JIH was the first organised Islamic reformist movement in India formed in Lahore on August 26, 1941, under the leadership of Sayyid Abul Ala Mawdudi.vi However, the alliance between the JIH and SIMI lasted only till 1981, when radical student members of SIMI protested against Yasser Arafat's visit to India, while the senior JIH leaders saw him as a champion. The rift in ideologies led JIH to abandon SIMI and float a new students' wing, the Students Islamic Organisation, while SIMI continued as a separate hard-line Islamic organisation.

After breaking away from JIH, SIMI underwent radicalisation, and its fanatical position was dictated entirely by geo-political events taking place in the world, which were interpreted as direct attacks on Islam and Muslims. Events, both domestic and international, which led to a shift in SIMI's philosophy, were:

- The Soviet invasion of Afghanistan and toppling of the Shah of Iran by Ayatollah Khomeini.
- The imposition of harsh Shariah laws in Pakistan by General Zia-ul-Haq in 1980.
- The demolition of the Babri Masjid in Ayodhya in December 1992.
- The militancy in the Kashmir Valley since 1989.

Provoked by the Godhra carnage of 2002, the divide, assisted by the ISI, LeT and HuJI, eventually led to the creation of a new militant organisation of SIMI called the Indian Mujahideen. It was co-founded by Riyaz Shahbandri and Abdul Subhan Qureshi. The IM, at this point in time, consisted of students, most of them Kashmiris, studying in Deobandi madrasas in South Gujarat, Andhra Pradesh, Karnataka and Maharashtra. The Indian Mujahideen was, thus, born, taught by its masters to spread jihadist doctrines in India, through homegrown militants, aided, abetted and calibrated from across the borders.

The Ideology

The name Indian Mujahideen is apparently drawn from a book on a *Jihad* waged by two Islamic warriors in north-west India around 1831 in Balakot, now in Pakistan-occupied Kashmir (POK), and which suited the terror mission devised by the Students Islamic Movement of India.x The IM ideology primarily draws inspiration from the Wahhabi philosophy of the Deobandi School, which practises a rigid, puritanical version of Islam. All the arrested members of the IM and SIMI, so far, have been students of Deobandi *madrasas* from Bharuch, Ujjain, Azamgarh and Saharanpur.

The Deobandi Wahhabis advocate that a Muslim's first loyalty is to his religion and only then to his country. Secondly, Muslims should recognise only the religious frontiers of their *ummah* (community) and not national frontiers. Thirdly, they have a sacred right and obligation to go to any country to wage *Jihad* to protect the Muslims of that country.xi The Deobandi and Ahle-e-Hadith schools were revived in India through funding by Saudi charities, when oil prices skyrocketed in the 1970s. Significantly, a majority of terror groups like the JeM, HuJI, LeT, HuA and now the IM owe 'allegiance' to the Deobandi *madrasas* and the Mawdudi school of thought. Thus, the Deobandi school of thought and Wahhabism combined to form an extremist version of radical Islam, which advocates the prominence of *Jihad* for Islamisation.

The Leadership

The leadership of the IM can primarily be traced to a man from Mumbai named Abdul Subhan Usman Qureshi, code name "Kasim" or "al-arbi" who has signed the e-mail manifestos sent by the IM before and after the multiple blasts of 2008. It has been reported that he may have escaped into Bangladesh recently. Interestingly, Qureshi's background refutes the theory that most IM cadres come from deprived backgrounds or are schooled in radical *madrasas*.

Qureshi studied at the Antonio DeSouza High School ran by a Christian missionary in Byculla, Mumbai, and came from an economically priviledged background. In 1995, he obtained a diploma in industrial electronics and in 1996, a specialised software maintenance qualification from the CMS Institute in Marol.

After obtaining these degrees, he joined various software and computer firms. However, somewhere during this period, Qureshi was also harbouring radical ideologies and in 2001, he left his job at the firm stating in his resignation letter that "I have decided to devote one complete year to pursue religious and spiritual matters."

According to Mumbai police intelligence, by 1998, Qureshi was one of the most committed SIMI activists to edit one of SIMI's house-magazines, *Islamic Voice,* from New Delhi. By then, SIMI's growing links with global Islamic movements like the Egyptian Brotherhood and Hamas were clear. Links with Bangladesh based

HuJI and Pakistan based LeT were also coming to the fore. Since 2007, Qureshi succeeded in training hundreds of SIMI-IM cadres and was the mastermind of the Delhi blasts undertaken by Mohammad Bashir, Mohammad Fakruddin and Saif Ahmad in September 2008.

According to a UP based IM cadre, Sadiq Shaikh, hailing from Azamgarh district and who was arrested on September 23, 2008, IM modules exist in Uttar Pradesh, Karnataka, Pune and Mumbai. Most arrested IM cadres are computer professionals and bomb makers.

Among those arrested are Pune based Mohammed Mansoor Asgar Peerbhoy and Mubin Kadar Shaikh, who jointly designed the IM logo and hacked into unsecured Wi-fi connections. Another significant intelligence input from the UP police indicates that UP based IM cadre Fahim Arshad Ansari who was arrested in UP in February 2008 was in direct contact with the LeT in masterminding the Mumbai attacks of November 2008.

Ansari studied at the Malad Municipal Secondary School in Mumbai, from where he graduated in 1989 but later on went onto Dubai. In 2005, another Hyderabadi, Sami Ahmad who was arrested by the police in 2006 revealed that he had had agreed to put Ansari in touch with the LeT.

Conclusion

At present the Gujarat Police suspect that the same absconding Indian Mujahideen (IM) terrorists wanted for the 2008 serial bombings in Ahmedabad could be behind the December 7, 2010, blast in Varanasi. The IM, which claimed responsibility for the Ahmedabad blasts by sending emails to media houses, reportedly owned up the Varanasi blasts in a similar fashion.

The two mails bore striking similarities in both language and content, a senior ATS officer said.xvi Fifty-nine people were killed and over 200 injured in the Ahmedabad blasts. "The two mails have great similarities. Both mention the Godhra riots, both mention the name of (Chief Minister) Narendra Modi and state in a similar way how he had presided over the massacre of Muslims in his state but is still free. Both mails also say the motive was to avenge the Godhra riots," the officer said.xvii ATS sources said there were strong indications that two top IM men, Riyaz and Iqbal Bhatkal – believed to be holed up in Pakistan and wanted for the Ahmedabad blasts – were involved in the Varanasi bombing. According to them, there were inputs suggesting that Riyaz had supported Dr Shahnawaz, a top IM operative suspected to have overseen the planning and execution of the blast in Varanasi.

A senior ATS officer added: "Riyaz and Iqbal are remote-running the banned SIMI outfit in the name of IM. They adopted the method of low-intensity blasts in Varanasi, just like the Ahmedabad bombings.

Even the mail in which their outfit claims responsibility for the blast is strikingly similar to the one they sent out after the Ahmedabad blasts."xviii It is thus beyond doubt that terror groups have established a pan-Islamic network, with a large number of sleeper sells in the hinterland, with extreme linkages with J&K, the global terrorists, and the ISI. In the recent past, a number of terrorist modules have been broken up in all metropolitan cities, and hitherto unaffected areas in the country. It remains to be seen as to whether such horrific carnage as meted out in Varanasi will follow in the near future or effective counter terrorism measures would be successful in annihilating the menace of domestic terrorism from within the heartland of India.

THE ORIGINS AND FORMATION OF THE INDIAN MUJAHIDIN

Information on the early years of the Indian Mujahidin has been drawn from Sadiq Israr Sheikh, the only founding member of the group in custody. Like Riyaz and Iqbal, Sheikh was born in a family that had migrated to Mumbai. Beginning in 1996, he began attending SIMI meetings near his home in Mumbai's Cheeta Camp area. Perhaps drawn by the sense of purpose, SIMI appeared to provide many young Muslims in Mumbai a calling when the relationship between Hindus and Muslims became increasingly strained due to communal violence. According to police, Sheikh grew tired of SIMI's polemics and was in search of a more effective medium to turn his beliefs into action.

In April 2001, a relative of Sheikh set forth a process where Sheikh would eventually meet Asif Raza Khan. Riyaz and Sheikh had known each other from their days as SIMI activists in Mumbai; however, they came together as partners in the Indian Mujahidin project through Asif Khan. After reportedly receiving training at an LT camp in Pakistan, Sheikh, on instruction from Amir Raza Khan, began to recruit cadre in Azamgarh, starting in late 2002. Key among them were Atif Amin, who was killed in an October 2008 shootout with New Delhi police, Arif Badar, and Mohammad Shahnawaz.

By 2005, after the gathering at Jolly Beach, the multiple Indian Mujahidin network components had fallen into place. Prosecution documentation filed in New Delhi suggests Atif Amin's Azamgarh cell was responsible for providing manpower for the attacks. Sadiq Sheikh liaised between the Azamgarh cell and the Indian Mujahidin's Mumbai-based senior leadership. Iqbal Shahbandri raised operatives for a specialist computer-services cell. Riyaz Shahbandri and his cell sourced explosives and bomb components that were assembled into usable devices. Abdul Subhan Qureshi traveled nationwide, finding SIMI sympathizers to assist with cells.

During this period, parallel jihadist groups led by figures who knew the Indian Mujahidin leadership from their time in SIMI proliferated as well. For example, Rahil Sheikh formed cadre who attempted to stage an abortive attack on Gujarat in 2006—an operation the Maharashtra police claim involved assault rifles and grenades packed into computer cases and shipped across the Indian Ocean by the LT. Nevertheless, the leadership of each separate jihadist network appears to have maintained operational secrecy, despite their common political past.

Little is known about the precise state of play between the Indian Mujahidin and the Karachi Project, but it is clear that the Indian Mujahidin network itself is just part of a larger jihadist project across India. The 2008 bombings in Bangalore, for example, were carried out by a jihadist cell that had supplied explosives to Riyaz, but had no knowledge of his operations. In the Bangalore case, LT-linked SIMI operative Sarfaraz Nawaz funded a Kerala-based jihadist cell run by long-time Islamist activist Tandiyantavide Nasir that trained recruits to carry out bombings on a ginger plantation in the forests around Kodagu, in southern India. Nawaz, who had worked closely with Qureshi in SIMI, does not appear to have known of his role in the Indian Mujahidin.

The central point is that the jihadist networks in India remain extremely fluid and consist of small groups of individuals who are loosely allied together. In this sense, they bear little resemblance to the large, hierarchically-structured Pakistan-based jihadist groups such as the LT or Jaysh-i-Muhammad—although even in the Pakistani cases there appear to have been some recent splintering.

Conclusion

Riyaz Shahbandri's story is evidence that substantial political problems are driving jihadist mobilization within India. It also makes clear, however, that the LT's infrastructure in Pakistan is critical to these networks' reach and lethality. Key leaders such as Riyaz Shahbandri and Sadiq Israr Sheikh trained in Pakistan. Indian investigations into the Indian Mujahidin's bombings have not reached closure because figures central to the network's functioning have sought safe haven in Pakistan.

Many in India's intelligence services fear that the recent bombings in Pune in February 2010, Bangalore in April 2010, as well as the abortive attack in Deloitte in Hyderabad in May 2010 herald the coming of a renewed wave of jihadist violence intended to undermine the country's economic progress and status in the run-up to the high-profile Commonwealth Games, which will be held in New Delhi in October 2010. Whether or not Riyaz Shahbandri's so-called Karachi Project is a new endeavor or simply a name for ongoing jihadist activity directed at India, the country clearly faces a growing problem from Indian Muslims who have become radicalized and are able to seek assistance from Pakistan-based militants.

Praveen Swami is Associate Editor of the Hindu, one of India's largest English-language newspapers, and reports on terrorism and low intensity conflicts in India. His most recent book, India,

Pakistan and the Secret Jihad: The Covert War in Jammu and Kashmir, 1947-2002, was published by Routledge in 2007.

The book was written while he was a Jennings Randolph senior fellow at the United States Institute of Peace in Washington, D.C., in 2004-2005. His scholarly work includes a 1999 book, The Kargil War, chapters in several edited volumes, and papers in journals including The India Review and Faultlines. Mr. Swami has won several major awards for his work, including the Indian Express-Ramnath Goenka Print Journalist of the Year prize, 2006.

5

The Indian Mujahideen: The New Face of Jihadist Consolidation

On 29 February 2000, a one-page note, scribbled on a piece of paper, arrived at a newspaper office in Hyderabad, in India's southern state of Andhra Pradesh. The "Indian Muslim Mohammadi Mujahideen (IMMM) has been formed," it announced. According to the note, the organization was "committed to eradicate the western culture from India" and, as a first part of this campaign, had bombed cinemas that ran pornographic films.

The note ended law enforcement agencies' search for the perpetrators of a number of incidents that had taken place a month earlier. These included a bomb blast at a sweets shop owned by a sympathizer of the Rashtriya Swayamsevak Sangh, a Hindu right-wing organization with a pan-Indian presence; two unexploded devices recovered from a movie theater and a location near the high-security Defence Research and Development Organisation laboratory; and explosions at two movie theaters, one in Andhra Pradesh and the other in the neighbouring state of Maharashtra. All of the recovered and exploded bombs had been devised from the same substances: potassium nitrate, potassium permanganate, aluminum powder, and sugar.

Less than two months after the note's appearance, the IMMM's chief, Azam Ghauri—who was also a top leader of the Pakistan-based Lashkar-e-Taiba (LeT)—was killed in an encounter with police, and the threat from the IMMM was thought to be over. The IMMM, however, was only one of many offshoots of a larger organization, the Students Islamic Movement of India (SIMI), that set about implementing SIMI president Shahid Badr Falahi's 1992 pledge: "Muslims organise themselves and stand up to defend the community." Security agencies were able to swiftly neutralize organizations like the IMMM and the Mujahideen Islam e-Hind (MIH), another SIMI offshoot, mostly because the groups sought instant publicity for their actions, which exposed them to the security establishment. Law enforcement agencies' experience with the Indian Mujahideen (IM) has proved to be different, however.

In the following three sections, we analyze the unique operational dynamics of the IM, which, we argue, are responsible for its cohesion as well as its success as a terrorist organization. On the basis of some recent findings, we examine the IM's cadre recruitment, explosives manufacturing, external and internal linkages, attack patterns, and attempts to transform itself from a guardian of wronged Muslims in India to an avenger of ill-treated Muslims worldwide. We argue that the IM's future and its success in carrying out attacks are critically linked to India's internal efforts to target the IM's unique strengths and neutralize the support that the IM receives from external sources.

THE IM'S DEVELOPING IDEOLOGY: THREE DISTINCT PHASES

On 17 July 2013, the National Investigation Agency (NIA), the organization that New Delhi set up after the 2008 Mumbai terrorist attacks as the primary agency to investigate all terrorist incidents in India, stated in its charge sheet that the IM "was formed in 2003 after ultra-radicalised Muslim youth segregated from the Students Islamic Movement of India." Similar to the IMMM and the MIH, the IM has its roots in the avowed need to radicalize the SIMI's plan of action even further. In 2001 and 2002, a rebellion of sorts was brewing within the SIMI. A faction broke away from the less-radical parent organization and sought new cadres who were already sufficiently radicalized; their extremism was further boosted by contact with external militants such as the LeT. This new faction became the IM. The IM, in a way, was also a result of the LeT's "Karachi Project," which had sought to raise a new network of jihadists. In its 17 July 2013 charge sheet, the NIA added that the IM cadres "do not believe in India's Constitution and IM's members nurse communal hatred against the Hindu community."

Since the IM had been formed on an agenda of waging a violent war against Hindu India, no spell of moderate militancy separated the IM's birth from its first act of violence. Within a relatively short time period, however, the IM underwent three distinct phases of ideological expansion: traversing from a narrow India-centric ideology to revenge-seeking and eventually embracing the concerns of Muslims in other countries. This is not to suggest that the IM abandoned or progressed beyond any of the causes that it initially championed. Rather, it acquired new additional causes to fight for. In effect, the IM's successes in the Indian theater and its constant ideological oscillation demonstrated the IM's widening profile and proclivity for becoming an integral part of the global Jihad. Such a broadening of ideology was important, for it fit in well with the amplification of jihadist terrorism in South Asia, especially boosted by the prospects of instability in post-2014 Afghanistan.

Guardian of Wronged Muslims in India

According to an estimate by an intelligence agency,

By 2005, the IM had firmly established a complete terror outfit, with different sections in charge of providing manpower and sourcing explosives and bomb components. A specialist computer-services cell was already in place. Different leaders were already travelling countrywide, liaising between cells.

The IM's war on Hindu India began in 2005 with a string of urban attacks, which included serial explosions in the national capital, Delhi—two bombs exploded at busy marketplaces and a third exploded inside a Delhi Transport Corporation bus, killing 62 people. There was some question about who had carried out the attacks. The LeT was initially suspected. A Delhi Police special cell team also claimed to have killed the mastermind of the blasts in an operation in the Indian state of Jammu and Kashmir in 2007.

In 2006, the IM carried out serial bombings in the Hindu pilgrimage town of Varanasi, in the state of Uttar Pradesh. Three explosions, one in a crowded temple and two in a railway station, killed 21 people and injured 62 others. In 2013, an arrested IM cadre who had participated in the 2006 bombings told his interrogators that the timers and improvised explosive devices (IEDs) used in the Varanasi blasts were similar to the ones used in the 2005 Delhi blasts. Since the formation of the IM had remained unannounced, these attacks were thought to have been perpetrated by Pakistan-based outfits, like the LeT, and the Bangladesh-based Harkat-ul Jihad-al-Islami. The fact that the LeT was still perpetrating large-scale attacks, like the July 2006 explosions that targeted the train systems in Mumbai and killed 200 people, made the task of looking for another perpetrator seem unnecessary. Indian security personnel felt comfortable in the assumption that because the LeT was still active within India, the LeT must be behind the Varanasi attacks.

The IM's first-ever ideological affirmation came in the form of its first manifesto, which the group released in 2007 after it had bombed court complexes in Lucknow, Varanasi, and Faizabad. The manifesto claimed that the blasts were intended to "punish local lawyers" who had physically attacked some suspects who were being held for an abortive kidnap plot against politician Rahul Gandhi by the terrorist group Jaish-e-Muhammad (JeM). The manifesto, however, spoke broadly of "wounds given by the idol worshippers to the Indian Muslims" and the demolition of the Babri Masjid, a disputed mosque in the state of Uttar Pradesh that Hindu radicals had demolished in 1992 following violent countrywide communal riots. Emphasizing the miserable condition of the Muslims in the country, the manifesto concluded, "If you want to be a successful person in India, then you should be an idol worshipper and kill Muslims."

The IM released two other manifestos in 2008 and 2010, following more bombings in Delhi and Varanasi, respectively. Both documents pointed at the role of "the Supreme Court, the high courts, the lower courts and all the commissions" for failing the Muslims in India. The 2008 manifesto, running nearly 14 pages and titled The Rise of Jihad, indicated that the bombings were carried out to avenge the 2002 anti-Muslim violence in Gujarat. "In the light of the injustice and wrongs on the Muslims of Gujarat, we advance our Jihad and call all our brethren under it to unite and answer these irresolute kafireen [infidels] of India," it said. The 2010 manifesto, titled Let's Feel the Pain Together, said that the attack in 2010 served as a reminder to Hindus that the IM had "resolved that none of your mandirs [temples] will remain safe until and unless all our occupied Masjids [mosques] throughout India are returned back to the Muslims."

When the IM targeted the Indian judiciary in explosions outside the Delhi high court in 2011, its attacks had already spanned the entire country and were being carried out in almost all of the major urban centers, including New Delhi and the country's FINANCIAL capital, Mumbai. Attacks in Ahmedabad and Pune in the west, Hyderabad and Bangalore in the south, Patna and Bodh Gaya in the east, and Delhi in the north made the IM look like a pan-Indian outfit capable of taking its activities to almost any corner of the country. Among these attacks was a 2010 incident in which two bikers fired on tourists gathered at the gate of the Jama Masjid in the Old Delhi area. The drive-by shooting, the only attack of this nature carried out by the IM so far, was to be followed by an explosion, but the explosive, which was fitted into a car parked in the area, did not go off due to faulty circuitry. This attack was carried out on 19 September 2010, days before the opening of the Commonwealth Games in the national capital. Two Taiwanese nationals sustained bullet wounds.

By the time of the Jama Masjid attack in 2010, the IM had stopped mailing its usual manifestos claiming responsibility for its attacks, so investigative agencies had to rely on interrogations of arrested IM cadres to unravel the intentions behind the explosions. The IM had also diversified its target selection, demonstrating that it was indeed willing to go after almost any target, with the sole intention of maximizing fatalities. Revenge against Hindus and the institutions facilitating the dominance of Hinduism over the Muslims remained the proclaimed raison d'être of the IM—at least for awhile.

Avenging the Deaths of Its Cadres

Over a period of time, the IM began perpetrating terror attacks even to avenge the deaths of its cadres, representing a drastic climbdown from its larger goal of fighting on behalf of the Muslim community. According to interrogation reports, the explosions in Pune, Maharashtra, on 1 August 2012 were intended to avenge the killing of imprisoned IM cadre Qateel Siddique by his cell mates in a Pune prison a couple of months earlier. The attack included five coordinated low-intensity explosions on a busy road in the heart of Pune, injuring one person. Another live IED was later recovered from the area.

Within a year of the Pune attack, the IM had expanded its worldview, aiming to take up the causes of persecuted Muslims outside of India. Blasts that targeted the Buddhist shrine in Bodh Gaya, Bihar, in July 2013 were said to have been in response to violence against the Rohingyas, a Muslim population in Myanmar, by members of the ethnic Buddhist majority. Arrested IM cadre Umair Siddiqui told his interrogators that he had been approached by another IM cadre, Haider Ali, about the Rohingyas' situation, and both had finalized the plan to carry out the attack at the Buddhist shrine. Earlier, arrested LeT cadre Abdul Karim Tunda revealed that the LeT had also been part of the Bodh Gaya attack; during his interrogation, Tunda detailed the LeT's plan, in collaboration with the IM, to recruit Rohingyas and carry out the attack.

On 27 October 2013, explosions in Patna, Bihar, were reportedly carried out to protest communal riots in Muzaffarnagar, in the neighbouring state of Uttar Pradesh. The recovery of a large amount of explosives at Ranchi, Jharkhand, on 4 November 2013 demonstrated the IM's plan to maintain the momentum in its violent campaign. Similarly, the recovery of documents from an IM safe house in Ranchi, including handwritten notes from IM members detailing future action plans, pointed to the possibility that the IM would carry out future attacks on Buddhist shrines, foreign tourists, and public installations in the state of Chhattisgarh.

The IM's wide array of unconnected objectives underscores the fact that, instead of remaining a purely ideology-based organization with both local and global aspirations, the IM could be willing to carry out attacks for almost any cause that suits its convenience. Believed to be controlled by external forces (including the JeM, the LeT, and the Pakistani external intelligence agency known as Inter-Services Intelligence [ISI]), and to nurture the aspiration of making common cause with al Qaeda, IM leaders could be looking well beyond the traditional outfit that was triggering explosions only on behalf of wronged Indian Muslims. Although the IM is largely defined as an indigenous or homegrown terror organization within India, its leadership does not appear to be averse to eventually transforming the outfit into a pan-Islamist terrorist operation.

INDIAN MUJAHIDEEN AND ITS DUBIOUS ORIGIN

For all the claims, the probing and prosecuting agencies have not come out with one individual who has a proven association with this so-called nationwide organization supposedly working at the behest of Lashkar e Toiba, Hizbul Mujahideen, Taliban and you name who, so how do we know IM really exists or is merely the figment of imagination of the IB/Saffron brigade happily lapped up by an already biased media?

But let us just glean through the official explanation. Wikipedia says, "Investigators believe that Indian Mujahideen is one of many groups composed of lower-tier SIMI members. According to the Indian Intelligence Bureau, SIMI took new titles because the top leadership of SIMI have been detained and would be available for interrogation.

The change in name is believed to signal a change in tactics as SIMI affiliated militants attempt to garner more support from India's Muslim community rather than be seen as a group consisting of foreigners. Two days after the 13 May 2008 Jaipur bombings, the extremist group sent an e-mail to Indian media in which they claimed responsibility for the attacks and said they would "demolish the faiths (all religions apart from Islam) of the infidels of India". The biggest and boldest attack to date by the group was the 2008 Ahmedabad serial blasts, where it gained national notoriety with a casualty count towards 50."

Now who banned SIMI and when was it banned and on what grounds? First came the terror attack on the Indian Parliament on December 13, 2001, which is a grey area because of the apprehension of the whole exercise sponsored by the then NDA-led government and specifically the Union Home ministry under the then Home Minister LK Advani. Soon thereafter Narendra Modi led Gujarat government patronized the pogrom of Muslims ostensibly to avenge the burning down of kar sevaks in coach number S-6, in the Sabarmati Express on February 27, 2002, just two months after the Parliament attack. Those who don't suffer from a memory loss remember the whole charged atmosphere created by Advani-Modi and Jaitley combine against the Muslim youth in preparation of bringing in POTA and to justify POTA SIMI was banned just a little before POTA was conceived. While announcing the ban Advani held a press conference in North Block and distributed to the media some SIMI posters in Urdu, none of which carried any seditious material. All these were expressions of anger and frustration over the Gujarat pogrom and the inability of anyone to counter Modi.

So what is wrong in saying that IM is an outcome of Gujarat pogrom? When did IM come into prominence and how? The official version says, "Two days after the 13 May 2008 Jaipur bombings, IM sent an e-mail to the Indian media in which they claimed responsibility for the attacks and said they would "demolish the faiths of the infidels of India". The biggest and boldest attack to date by the group was the 2008 Ahmedabad serial blasts, where it gained national notoriety when 56 people were killed in those serial blasts." This is the official version.

Who according to the official version are prominent leaders of IM:

1. Abdus Subhan Qureshi, alias Ali Tauqeeer a Gujarati software engineer from Mumbai
2. Safdar Nagori from Indore
3. Qayamuddin Kapadia, a TRADER from Vadodra
4. Usman Agarbattiwala, a PG diploma holder from Vadodra
5. Alazeb Afridi, a jobless youth from Ahmedabad

6. Abdul Razzzak Mansuri, an embroidery unit owner from Gujarat
7. Mujib Shaikh, a stone polishing artisan from Gujarat
8. Zahid Sheikh, a mobile repair owner from Ahmedabad
9. Amil Parvaiz, a native of Ujjain. These were the original IM men according to the IB along with just one Mufti Abu Bashir from Azamgarh. Later after the Batla House incident of Delhi, according to the investigative agencies it had also spread its tentacles in UP as well, and in particular in Azamgarh district.

But then stating the obvious becomes a crime and the BJP cries hoarse attacking poor Shakeel Ahmad while the Congress always lacking spunk, hurriedly withdraws what with the Heir Apparent in the ruling party advising everyone not to irritate BJP/Modi too much and so poor Shakeel has to shut up.

A FORMULA FOR SUCCESS: THREE OPERATIONAL PATTERNS OF THE IM

In this chapter, we show that, apart from its emergence as an alleged protector of Muslims' interests, the IM's success as a terrorist formation is based on three distinct operational patterns: its external support base and linkages, its unique and secretive recruitment drives, and its manufacture of explosives.

External Support Base and Linkages

As explained earlier, the IM is by no means the first-ever homegrown Islamist outfit to wage a war within India. It has several predecessors—the SIMI, the IMMM, the MIH, and the Al Ummah, an organization born in the early 1990s with the intent to radicalize Muslim youth in the southern Indian state of Tamil Nadu. However, the way that the IM carries on with its shadowy bombing campaign, over a large swath of the country's territory, makes it a completely different, and far superior, entity than its predecessors in its organizational capacities and its ability to withstand the kinetic measures of the state.

Indian officials' assessments have routinely pointed at the IM's connections with Pakistan, contending that without the continuing assistance that IM leaders receive from India's western neighbor, the outfit's potency would have been far more limited. Home Minister Sushil Kumar Shinde's description of the IM says that it draws "motivation and sustenance from inimical forces operating from across the Western border." India claims that two of the IM's founders, brothers Riyaz Bhatkal and Iqbal Bhatkal, are based in Pakistan under the protection of state agencies including the ISI. Indeed, both Bhatkal brothers, along with top IM leaders such as Abdul Subhan Qureshi and Sadiq Israr Sheikh, have undergone training in the LeT camps in Pakistan. Their names are regularly included in the list of persons, both Indian and Pakistani nationals, whom India wants Islamabad to deport from Pakistani territory. Interrogations of arrested IM cadres have revealed that several persons within Pakistan have extensive connections with the IM outfit. The Indian home minister has claimed that a number of IM cadres "were sent to Pakistan for training in weapon and explosives" and investigations "will throw valuable light on the role played by elements based in Pakistan in fomenting acts of terrorism in India."

Pakistani nationals have taken a direct part in a few of the IM's operations in India. Among the six IM cadres arrested in the 2010 Jama Masjid attack in Delhi was a Pakistani operative. Zia-ur-Rehman (alias Mohammad Waqas), who served as the principal explosive assembler for the IM and was arrested in the Indian state of Rajasthan on 21 March 2014, also is from Pakistan. Inversely, the IM's Pakistani connection is a natural corollary of the fact that its leaders are based in Pakistan and their actions are believed to be directed by the state and by allied non-state agencies like the LeT. According to a report, the LeT and the ISI could have influenced individuals and modules within the IM, even to the point of promoting specific attacks. However, whether such nexus, safe haven, and ad hoc support translates into "strict command and control over the entire IM network, which is significantly decentralised," as the report claims, remains a matter of debate.

Contrary to the definitive official assertions linking the IM to its Pakistani sponsors, some recent accounts have pointed to a significant level of autonomy and self-sufficiency in the IM ranks and to the outfit's ability to carry out attacks without any external help. Stephen Tankel's extensive 2014 report on the IM suggested that this jihadist movement constitutes "an internal security issue with an external dimension." Indian media reports have also underlined that the IM "works on its own and recent attacks have shown that they have carried out blasts with no support from Pakistan." Theories about the functional independence and self-sufficiency of the IM explain, to an extent, the IM's unique operational dynamics and success.

At the same time, however, none of the reports and theories points to a severing of ties between the IM and its Pakistani mentors. On the contrary, the IM's achievement of a level of self-sufficiency indicates the fruition of the LeT/ISI strategy to portray the IM as a wholly homegrown terror formation—a key ingredient of Pakistan's clandestine destabilization project, known to Indian officials as the Karachi Project.

In the words of an unnamed intelligence official, "While it would not be right to say that there is no Pakistan patronage any more, the fact is that Inter Services Intelligence, the Pakistani spy agency, and the Lashkar-e-Tayiba have ensured that the IM becomes self-sufficient." IM cofounder and senior leader Syed Mohammed Ahmed Zarar Sidibapa (alias Yasin Bhatkal, hailing from the same village as the two Bhatkal brothers), following his arrest on 29 August 2013, revealed that the IM wished to become a part of the global Jihad. The realization of such an arguably pretentious and grandiose dream can only be facilitated by the LeT.

Cadre Recruitment, Modules, and Linkages

Key to the functional efficiency of the IM is its somewhat unique, personalized recruitment campaign targeting small, Muslimmajority towns and villages in different parts of India. Available data suggest that select senior leaders of the IM were assigned to be at the centre of highly personalized and closely guarded micro recruitment drives that targeted technically savvy and educated youth, who were to function as attack planners, and petty criminals and the less educated, who would function as the more dispensable logistics providers and explosive planters.

Available listings of IM cadres include men as young as 18 years of age and middle-aged men past 50 years.

IM modules comprising both tech-savvy and illiterate individuals sprang up in many of the medium-size and smaller cities of India. Each module is based on a formula: keep the cadre profile small and maintain a mixture of new and energetic as well as experienced individuals. The modules' cadres come from rural as well as urban areas, such as Azamgarh in the state of Uttar Pradesh, which is known to have contributed a large number of jihadists to the Indian theaters of conflict, and Seethio, a nondescript village in Jharkhand state that is far away from the radar of the Indian intelligence agencies. The IM had set up a module in Ranchi, Jharkhand, code-named *Machhli-5 (Fish-5)*, to assassinate Narendra Modi, the prime ministerial candidate of the right-wing Bharatiya Janata Party (BJP). According to intelligence sources, a module had also been planned in Nepal.

Each IM module replicates the model popularized by al Qaeda: it is functionally independent, although finances are centrally disbursed by the IM's top leadership. Such functional independence maintains a regime of insularity between the modules, protecting the other modules and the IM in the event that a particular module is compromised.

The IM's seemingly uncomplicated organizational model, however, achieved some degree of complexity with reports of a three-way split within the IM in late 2008. On 14 May 2008, a day after the IM executed serial explosions in the city of Jaipur, killing 80 people and injuring 216 others, an e-mail sent to the media claimed that the IM now had three wings: "the Shahbuddin Ghouri group to attack southern India, the Mahmood Ghaznavi group operating in north India, and the Shaheed Al Zarqawi group that executed suicide attacks." The IM's identification of the three groups, which were named after historical Muslim invaders and al Qaeda leaders, was mostly a propaganda exercise. Later in 2008, however, the IM is known to have split into three factions in actuality.

Following the Batla House encounter in New Delhi in September 2008, in which two IM cadres were killed and two others arrested, IM founding members Riyaz Bhatkal and Iqbal Bhatkal, based in Pakistan, are believed to have tried to gain complete control over the IM's operations. This initiative, which was accompanied by allegations of improper spending of FUNDS by Iqbal, created a rift between the Bhatkal brothers and senior member Amir Reza Khan.

Khan decided to operate separately with his own set of people and formed the second IM faction. The third faction of the IM is headed by Mirza Shadaab Beg and Mohammad Sajid, both hailing from Azamgarh. Beg and Sajid are part of the first IM module that executed blasts from 2006 onward at various places, including in Uttar Pradesh, Jaipur, Mumbai, and Delhi. Beg is also accused of having participated in the 2007 blasts in Gorakhpur and Varanasi. Despite the divisions among the IM factions, available evidence suggests that the factions' top leaders maintain their independence while remaining in constant communication with one another, seeking advice and assistance.

Although the SIMI effectively disbanded itself in 2001, following its official proscription in India and subsequent governmental actions targeting SIMI cadres and facilities, it continued to provide significant support to the IM cadres. According to an estimate, by 2000, roughly three years before the IM's creation, the SIMI had some 400 ansars (full-time workers) and 20,000 ikhwans (sympathizers) in addition to a cell for young children aged seven to 11, called the Shahin Force. This significant mass of people comprised lower-middle-and middle-class families who were energized by the message of Islam's preeminence over the decadent and immoral West and a polytheistic Hinduism. It would be correct to assume that by the time the IM achieved some influence in 2005, most of the SIMI cadres who had not become foot soldiers of the IM became its ikhwans. The SIMI cadres continue to provide shelter and gathering space for IM cadres who are attempting to evade security forces following an operation. Among the many examples of this collaboration between the two groups is an episode in which four IM operatives involved in the Patna explosions in October 2013 were hidden in Chhattisgarh for a fortnight by a group of erstwhile SIMI activists. According to intelligence sources, certain IM cadres are responsible for maintaining a steady linkage with the SIMI. These include Hyder Ali, who is wanted in connection with the Patna explosions, and Abu Faisal, who is suspected of devising a plot to kill three judges because they handed down an allegedly pro-Hindu judgment in the Babri Masjid bombing.

Tools of Terror

Aside from the lone drive-by shooting incident at Jama Masjid in Delhi in 2010, the IM's modus operandi has involved planting explosives in crowded places and is geared toward two objectives: maintaining the bomb planter's anonymity and maximizing casualties. Within this tightly defined mode of operation, the IM has benefited from its highly diversified, flexible, and cost-effective explosives manufacturing process.

To begin with, the IM's mode of manufacturing explosives involves a central bomb-making expert, believed to be Mohammad Waqas, the IM Pakistani national. Waqas was described as suffering from a facial paralysis that necessitated frequent visits to doctors within India, a story that allowed Waqas, over time, to pass on his techniques to a select band of Indian IM recruits during his stays in the country. This group included Yasin Bhatkal, one of the IM's founding members. To carry out explosions on an array of targets while maximizing fatalities, the IM requires a large number of IED assemblers to fulfill the needs of its different modules. After his explosives training with Waqas, Bhatkal in turn went on to train other IM cadres in the techniques.

The strategy of having an array of explosives assemblers, however, backfired to some extent. Starting in 2010, three of the IM's bombing campaigns—at the Jama Masjid, Pune, and Bodh Gaya—were largely unsuccessful. Many of the planted explosives either could not be detonated or were ineffective in their impact. Forensic experts who examined the unexploded bombs identified problems in the circuitry of the devices, among other issues. It is probable that the learning process for IED assembly in these cases was somewhat incomplete.

On many occasions, senior leaders like Yasin Bhatkal also doubled as planters of explosives, indicating that the IM is indeed non-hierarchical and fully geared toward achieving its objectives. This further upholds the organization's operational principle of keeping its module strength small and maximizing the output of every member.

The IM has also experimented with establishing central manufacturing units for explosives. Indian officials raided at least four such facilities: one on the fringes of the Bhadra forests near Chikmagalur, Karnataka, in 2008; another in the Meer Vihar area of Nangloi on the outskirts of New Delhi in 2011; and two more in 2013, in the southern coastal city of Mangalore, Karnataka, and in Hyderabad, the capital of Andhra Pradesh. As many as 90 ready-to-use IEDs were recovered from the raided facilities in Mangalore and Hyderabad. Also recovered from the Mangalore facilities were 50 magnets. Interrogation of Yasin Bhatkal revealed that the IM had planned to develop sticky IEDs and use them on freight trains that carried petroleum products, in an attempt to turn the entire train into a mega bomb.

The IM has manufactured its explosives predominantly using locally available chemicals. As a result, its IEDs contain less research department explosive (known as RDX), which has to be imported from foreign countries and is thus both harder to procure and more easily traceable than local products. Ammonium nitrate, which continues to be available in the Indian MARKETS even after a 2011 sale ban by the government, has remained a primary component in the IM's explosives throughout the group's bomb-making career. On some occasions, nitro-gelatin sourced from private suppliers has also been used in IM explosives. Police sources reveal that the IM may be using stolen industrial explosives as well for manufacturing its IEDs. While the explosive content of the IM's IEDs has remained more or less the same, the IM has attempted to bring sophistication to the manufacturing process by experimenting with a variety of timers.

SOME SHORTCOMINGS OF INDIAN LAW ENFORCEMENT AGENCIES

Unlike the conflict-affected regions in India's northeast, the disputed territory of Jammu and Kashmir, and the states affected by left-wing extremism, where New Delhi uses a mix of force and development-centric approaches for conflict resolution, there isn't an official Indian policy toward violence perpetrated by the Islamists. Some of the key elements of the investigative agencies' anti-IM policy include pursuing IM cadres who are involved in particular attacks and targeting their networks, FINANCIAL channels, and explosives manufacturing. Strengthening intelligence, hardening targets, and recruiting security-force personnel have also been key strategies to neutralize the IM game plan. This largely reactive approach has appeared successful in the event of a terrorist arrest, seizure of explosives, or raid of a module, but looks far less successful when the IM has managed to carry out its bombings.

Apart from India's inability to pursue the IM leadership based in Pakistan and the largely unresponsive attitude of Islamabad toward antiterrorism, Indian law enforcement agencies' overall policy suffers from three interlinked primary shortcomings: limited knowledge of the IM, increasing sectarian polarization in Indian politics with regard to the IM, and the Indian culture's apathy toward in-depth research on counterterrorism.

Limited Knowledge of the IM

Although hundreds of IM and SIMI cadres have been arrested since 2008 in connection with the bombings, including many who provided logistical assistance to the bombers and IM leaders, there is little indication that the agencies have developed any significant understanding of the IM's modus operandi, recruitment patterns, and FUNDING. Only part of the problem has been addressed since the NIA came into existence in 2009 and was assigned to investigate the IM attacks. The NIA has struggled to gain adequate cooperation from the state police departments, and has been handicapped by botched investigations conducted by state counterterror units into a number of IM attacks prior to the NIA's formation. The unique and highly diversified operational tactics of the IM have created additional roadblocks for the NIA, even as NIA agents pursue leads generated from arrests of individual cadres.

The 29 August 2013 arrest of IM cofounder/leader Yasin Bhatkal has been the biggest achievement so far for the NIA vis-a-vis the IM. According to a statement issued by India's home minister, Bhatkal was arrested along with his associate Asadullah Akhtar (alias Tabrez) while "planning to meet in East Champaran area (near Raxaul), Bihar to plan/execute some terrorist acts." Other media reports, however, indicated that both of these terrorists were arrested in Nepal and deported to India. The Nepalese government has denied that the arrests occurred on its soil, while at the same time asserting that no anti-India activity would be allowed in Nepal. The confusion around the exact location of the arrest notwithstanding, Bhatkal's arrest provided the intelligence agencies with some new inputs regarding the operational dynamics of the IM organization. The NIA nevertheless has struggled to transform those inputs into tactical advantages against the outfit. It is not clear whether the huge workload of the NIA, which is in charge of a large number of terror incidents in addition to the IM's activities, is taking a toll on the agency's capacities.

Increasing Polarization with Regard to the IM

The IM's activities have increased the polarization of Indian politics along sectarian lines, with Muslim groups doubting the existence of the IM and Hindu groups calling for strict action against it. This political polarization has, to an extent, forced the security agencies to scale down the intensity of their investigations into the IM's activities.

The Urdu-language newspapers of India, some prominent Muslim organizations, and even some Indian national ministers continue to insist that there is no such thing as the IM. For example, an article in the October 2012 *Milli Gazette*, a Muslim magazine, said that the IM "is a fictitious organisation most possibly created by the Indian Intelligence Bureau to justify the repression and terrorisation of the Indian Muslim community in the name of fighting terror." In October 2013, a number of Urdu newspapers and periodicals rejected reported linkages between the Muzaffarnagar riots and the explosions in Patna. Dismissing the conclusion that the IM could have been responsible for the explosion, one of these publications noted, "Political link of these blasts cannot be ruled out. In the past too, several blasts which were thought to have been perpetrated by Indian Mujahideen mercenaries were actually the handiwork of Hindutva terror groups. This fact must be kept in mind while investigating Patna blasts."

In July 2013, the Jamaat-e-Islami Hind (JIH), an Islamic organization in India, sent a letter to the general secretary of the ruling Congress Party insisting that Muslims of the country, particularly its educated class, feel that no organization by the name of " 'Indian Mujahedeen' exists in the country." In the same month, K. Rahman Khan, the union minister for minority affairs, went on record to say that he's skeptical that the IM exists because "nobody knows what it is, where it was formed, and who runs it." "The Muslim community," he continued, "is not buying its existence." The political implications of such statements could have had a significant impact on the official policy of the Indian government.

Indian Culture's Apathy toward Counterterrorism Research

Although the Indian Ministry of Home Affairs and the intelligence agencies are largely insular institutions and fairly impervious to interventions from outside the country, the efforts they have made to delve deeper into the IM's operations have been thwarted by a general cultural disinterest in strategic research. Research institutions and think tanks in India have often shied away from research on terrorism.

In the absence of primary, field-based research—a dearth reflected by the fact that one lone book on the IM has been published so far—the ill-informed news media have dominated reporting on security issues. Known mostly to publish what the intelligence agencies feed them on a regular basis, the Indian media's pervasive lack of knowledge on the IM has been illustrated by news headlines that speculate on the future of the IM's activities. Attributed to police sources, these headlines have ranged from the grand to the benign and include plans to detonate a "small nuclear bomb," hijack an aircraft, abduct politicians, and hire sharpshooters to kill BJP leader Narendra Modi. Some outlets have even published grandiloquent articles speculating that the IM might carry out a "9/11 type of attack."

The Prognosis

The threat from the IM could easily transform into a much larger menace if this terrorist juggernaut remains unaddressed both inside India and in countries like Pakistan, where key IM leaders are based. While arrests of IM cadres within India may provide temporary setbacks for the IM's plan of action, its expanded presence in multiple Indian states makes it elimination-proof. Terrorist groups like the LeT are willing to play a supporting role to the IM, as long as the latter continues to inflame the Muslim-Hindu divide in India and batter the country with its hate and bombing campaigns. The year 2014 and beyond could prove to be important for the IM's future, especially if instability in Afghanistan continues to fuel the capacities of Pakistan-based terrorist groups as well as the IM.

The IM will maintain its status as the lead jihadist outfit in India in the time to come, unless India can focus on strengthening its current weak points: the NIA's knowledge gap regarding the operational dynamics of the IM, political polarization regarding the IM, and a lack of in-depth research on the evolving threat of Islamist groups.

6

India's Security and Internal Armed Conflict

INDIA'S SECURITY CHOICES

As we consider India's rise to power, there are two main scenarios that come to mind. According to the first and most commonly held, India's current trajectory will continue in a 'straight line'. Exponents of this view hold that India's underlying growth rate of 7-9 per cent and growing military capability mean that by 2030 it will join China and Japan as one of Asia's three great powers.

By 2030, India will have the world's largest population. It will have the world's third largest economy in purchasing power parity terms (PPP) after China and the US. It is likely to remain democratic and will have enormous 'soft' power potential, resulting from its large English speaking population, vociferous free press, innovative IT industries, vibrant civil society and widely influential Bollywood film industry. Its navy will be able to range at will over the Indian Ocean and beyond. It will have a fleet of nuclear submarines and an independent nuclear deterrent capable of deterring even China. It will be a major power in space, with the capacity to 'neutralise' enemy satellites.

According to the second and more pessimistic analysis, this new superpower will be expected to rise out of one of the most-troubled sub-regions of the globe – South Asia. South Asia will continue to have more people living in poverty than any other region in the world for the foreseeable future. It will be awash with economic and political refugees. Its great rivers and ground water will be under severe stress. Its regional association, the South Asian Association for Regional Cooperation (SAARC), will still be struggling to provide a viable forum, according to which all in the region can 'rise on the same tide' through enhanced trade, security, travel and cultural exchange. Pakistan, India's neighbour of 166 million and a long-term adversary, will have added another 85 million mouths to feed and jobs to find. It will be subjected to extreme environmental stress. Hundreds of thousands of its young men will have been educated in madrassas that provide inadequate modern education and extremely narrow interpretations of Islam. Bangladesh – another neighbour which has already despatched an estimated 10 million illegal immigrants to India – may well be struggling to accommodate the estimated 10-15 millions of its population currently living on and farming low lying areas, subject to ever-increasing inundation resulting from climate change.

Trapped within this region (or so this pessimistic scenario goes), India will confront its own demons. It will be ever more dependent on costly imported energy. Its mega cities will be struggling to provide sufficient fresh water, accommodation and sanitation. Riots over distribution of drinking water – as witnessed in 2009 in Mumbai – will be frequent events. Antiquated infrastructure and restrictive labour laws will constrain labour-intensive manufacturing that could provide jobs for the massive rural population seeking a better life. Corruption will continue to be a major burden on governance, as democratisation spreads to new classes who are hungry for its benefits but impatient with its norms. Maoists will continue to recruit those in the poorest states suffering from corruption and poor governance. Maoist-generated unrest will jeopardise India's extractive industries, which happen to lie within the regions most seriously affected. Criminality will continue to flourish under a creaking legal system that provides near impunity to the wealthy and powerful and no rapid legal punishment for the guilty. Criminals, corruption and terrorism together will continue to erode the security of citizens and tarnish India's investment reputation.

In many states, the massive police service, which today totals 1.5 million for India as a whole (not including paramilitary forces and un-filled police positions), will remain an ineffective, repressive, colonial-era relic, incapable of investigating crime, providing security to communities, supporting human rights or lifting intelligence from the grassroots to the strategic level. India's 150 million Muslims – 75 per cent of whom belong to underprivileged groups and occupations – will still not have the benefits of the Constitution provided for Dalits and tribals. As the community sinks further in comparative terms, its members will provide more people willing to engage in violent, home-grown Jihad, assisted from across the border in Pakistan.

According to this sombre view of the future, these difficulties in India's polity will continue to resonate across borders in South Asia, just as the domestic difficulties of India's large neighbours will resonate in India. They will be transmitted by a brand of democratic politics, which seeks to blame the neighbour for local ills, by refugees and economic migrants, by sharpening religious misunderstanding as the region's traditional syncretic values erode in a world of globalisation and by ever-deepening cross-border environmental problems, particularly relating to the sharing of the diminishing river waters upon which hundreds of millions depend. Thus, South Asia will continue to be caught in a vicious circle of local and national troubles that wash back and forward across borders like so much political 'flotsam and jetsam'.

These two scenarios are at the outer extremes of what is likely to occur. Reality will likely be somewhat closer to the middle. But it will nevertheless veer towards one end or the other of the spectrum. Governments of the region will make choices that will have a role in shaping reality. This is particularly true of Indian governments – India being the giant of the region and having greater capability of influencing outcomes.

This chapter is especially concerned with Indian choices around the problem of security. The concept of security can range from the traditional, realist idea of security as constituting freedom from threats to the existence of the nation state, to the concept of 'comprehensive' or 'human' security. The latter involves a focus on the security of individuals within the state and surrounding countries, rather than on the existential security of an individual state. It includes all aspects of the welfare of individuals, including their human rights, gender rights, environmental rights, health, nutrition, education, employment, security from violence (whether from state or non-state actors), and so on.

In this chapter, we will be concerned with security from existential threats to the nation (as an important basis for the security of individuals within the nation) along with threats of physical violence and property threats to governments and individuals. Such threats can come from other nations, state actors such as security personnel and police, corrupt politicians and officials, terrorists, criminals and insurgents. We will not be considering directly some of the broader aspects of human security, encompassed by issues such as lack of water or food or work, environmental problems, or pandemic diseases – serious though they may be. But we do consider such factors indirectly because of their role in triggering violence, terrorism, insurgency and social dislocation. This relationship between deprivation and security is present throughout India, but is most noticeable as it applies to the tribal, Maoist-affected belt that covers east-central India. Here, environmental degradation, poor governance, poverty, human rights abuses and corruption have each played major roles in triggering the discontent that lies at the heart of the Maoist revolt.

Our primary concern is to demonstrate that there is a 'seamless web' between security of communities at the grassroots and security of nations and sub-regions (in this case India and South Asia). Such a line of analysis requires linking mechanisms between lower and higher order security issues. It needs to be explained, for example, why an attack on a police contingent in Chhattisgarh can be relevant to India's higher order security and even to its rise as a power. It is this linking process, we argue, which means that it is as important for governments successfully to address lower order security issues as it is to tackle higher order issues.

This approach to security is by no means unique or new: many recent Indian commentaries have covered similar ground. This chapter does, however, bring the added perspective of an Australian security analyst. Australia, as a Westminster-style democracy with a federal structure similar to India's, has experienced similar difficulties with establishing its internal security architecture. Australia's experience with internal security and terrorism is, however, obviously of a much less intensive nature than India's. And as a small, resource-rich nation, it also has many more available resources with which to deal with the problem.

SECURITY LINKAGES IN INDIA AND SOUTH ASIA

The line of analysis that posits a 'seamless web' between grassroots and grand security issues necessarily requires a 'transfer mechanism' both from the grassroots to the national, sub-regional and global levels and vice versa. Thomas Homer-Dixon and his associates describe the transfer process in the context of the 'upward' transfer of environmental problems into national and sub-regional security issues. According to this process, both the local level environmental problems themselves and the instability they produce amongst the affected populace further lead to provincial and state-level violence and decay, as competition for scarce resources increases and people are forced to become economic or actual refugees (both nationally and internationally) and internal tension undermines governance, even sometimes leading to civil war. States undergoing such crisis tend to make worse neighbours, with economic and political refugees from such states also damaging the polity in neighbouring states.

Specific transmitters of this instability from local to national levels include forced migration of economic, environmental and political refugees. An example is the mass migration from Bangladesh to India. Since the beginning of the 20 century, people have been forced to migrate from the poor, relatively dry Meymensingh province of what is now Bangladesh into the lush plains and the dangerous, but fertile, char lands of Assam in India. Today, Bangladeshis are still being forced across the border by economic circumstances. While many drift into Assam and other neighbouring provinces, such as Bengal, many more end up in far away Mumbai and Delhi. About 10 million Bangladeshis are now said to be living in India illegally, but the actual figure may be far more. They have upset the ethnic and religious balance in Assam and are often resented by the local people. This resentment has sometimes spilled over into attacks on people of Bangladeshi origin and has fuelled the separatist movement in Assam and elsewhere in the North-East.

The issue of Bangladeshi illegal migration has also been taken up by the central wing of the Bharatiya Janata Party (BJP) and other elements on the so-called 'Hindu right', who either have genuine concerns about the national character of India or wish to exploit such tensions in order to extend the influence of the party beyond the so-called Hindi heartland. The BJP also asserts that border controls and laws have remained inadequate in order to allow for the influx of Muslim Bangladeshis and garner vote banks in Assam for the Congress Party. Because of these local and national political ramifications, the migrations – essentially generated by local issues of governance and the environment in Bangladesh and facilitated by poor border control on both sides – have developed as a troubling, negative factor in India-Bangladesh relations. 'Securitisation' of such problems – that is, when they are considered to constitute an existential threat to the receiving state – has contributed significantly to the international ramifications of the problems themselves.

States caught up in this type of endemic crisis also often blame the resultant political instability on their neighbour. For example, many in Nepal tended to blame the breakdown of the Maoist government on Indian 'interference', despite the fact that Nepal has been caught in a spiralling political, economic and social crisis for at least a decade. Where two contiguous states are in crises of this nature, a vicious circle of violence and counter-violence can be set in motion, in which the complexities of intra-state relations interact negatively both within and between the states in question. Often, communal relations within India are thus regarded as a manifestation of Pakistani interference. Indira Gandhi, for example, was fond of referring to the 'foreign hand' as political metaphor for machinations by the Pakistani Inter-Services Intelligence Division (ISI) and the US Central Intelligence Agency (CIA) to explain a range of troubles in India. Similarly, Pakistan today blames its troubles in Balochistan and elsewhere on Indian interference. While such accusations can in some instances have a measure of truth (which makes them all the more plausible), in part also such tensions arise from pre-existing sets of difficulties that are locally generated and that cannot wholly be attributed to a neighbour.

Although the type of environmental crisis of interest to Homer-Dixon is certainly part of the process of transferring troubles upward, a more complex analytical framework is required. Explanations should include not only environmental factors in themselves, but also how they are caused and exacerbated by other factors, such as law and order problems and socio-economic and related political conditions. For example, the case study of Pakistan, in the volume edited by Homer-Dixon cited above, highlights the fact that unequal distribution of land and other problems arising from Pakistan's feudal structure play a major role in exacerbating environmental factors. A more recent study of the situation in Pakistani Punjab, sponsored by the Asian Development Bank (ADB), points to the role of poor governance over water resources as a factor in the severe diminution of ground water. (A similar fall in ground water resources has also occurred in Indian Punjab). The problem in Pakistani Punjab is widely perceived by affected farmers to be the result of the upper riparian power, India, using more than its fair share of the waters that originate in India and flow into Pakistan. The degree to which this accusation is true is unclear – but what is clear is that the two sets of problems (the riparian and water governance problems) have become entangled in the discourse and have severely stressed an already very difficult relationship.

In India, poor governance has played a significant role in the deforestation and loss of lands to mining companies in tribal areas in states such as Chhattisgarh, Jharkhand, Bihar and Orissa. These factors have, in turn, played a major role in radicalising tribal populations and driving them into the arms of the Maoists. As the

Indian Ministry of Home Affairs states in its 2008-09 Annual Report, "Naxalites operate in the vacuum created by functioning inadequacies of field level governance structures ..." Indeed, the issues of governance and law enforcement go well beyond environmental crisis and become problematic in their own right.

Due to poor governance, moreover, the mechanisms of the state intended to provide for the welfare of the people are often rendered inadequate or totally ineffective by corruption and incompetence. Again referring to the tribal, Maoist-affected areas of India, many schools have no teachers, health clinics no doctors or nurses and the National Rural Employment Guarantee Act (NREGA) has no funds to distribute to those in genuine need. The police, rather than providing for the security of the population, are widely seen as corrupt agents of the powerful and as part of the problem. In states like Bihar, this nexus between corrupt and criminalised politicians and the police has become particularly acute. Although matters have recently improved, in the past in Bihar, 33 per cent of contesting politicians had some kind of criminal charge pending against them.

These essentially local problems can have a multiplier effect that results in serious problems at the national and international levels. Thus, if we consider the Maoist-affected areas of India, the worst affected areas also happen to be co-extensive with India's principal mining provinces. Mining enterprises are subject to occasional attack and more frequent pressure to finance Maoist groups through the levy of so-called 'revolutionary taxes'. Mining employees have also been kidnapped. Corrupt governments (as possibly indicated by the allegations against former Jharkhand Chief Minister Madhu Koda) levy their share of pain on private and state enterprises operating in the area. In these activities, they are often protected by the close political and financial relationships that exist between the police and politicians. The net result is that Indian investment, direct foreign investment (DFI), technology, raw materials and foreign exchange are denied in Maoist-affected areas and India as a whole in this vital extractive area. The overall climate for DFI is adversely affected due to the perception of violence and instability thus portrayed. Similarly, the focus of violent jihadis on key commercial centres, such as Mumbai, Hyderabad and Bengaluru (formerly Bangalore), could also potentially affect the wider Indian economy and the international perception of India as a rising economic power and safe place to invest.

The instability generated by flawed systems of law and order and poor governance is not just a 'one-way street' from the local to the national and international: negative effects often flow the other way. Centrally initiated agendas and problems can have pernicious local repercussions. This occurred when the BJP at the central level initiated events that led to the destruction of the Babri Masjid at Ayodhya in Uttar Pradesh in December 1992. The fact that a BJP-led government was in power in the state in which Ayodhya is located meant that the normal mechanisms of control were not in place to prevent the demolition. This local event, initiated by a central political party, impacted in Mumbai in Maharashtra in the form of rioting in which up to 1,000 people, mostly Muslims, were killed. In turn, this precipitated a classic attack-revenge cycle – the serial terrorist attacks perpetrated by the Dawood Ibrahim-led 'D Company' in March 1993, in which 257 were killed and 700 injured. It is worth noting that the destruction of the Babri Masjid also spread upwards and had international repercussions. In Bangladesh, the event was followed by widespread destruction of Hindu temples and killing of Hindus. Similar events occurred in Pakistan, although on a lesser scale.

In the modern, globalised setting, 24x7 reporting afforded by light video cameras and other technologies, has provided a crucial transfer mechanism, both upward and downward. (But equally, it can also provide a mechanism for greater transparency). The riots in Gujarat in 2002 – in which up to 1,000 people, mostly Muslim, were reportedly killed – have since had a wider impact on Muslim sensibilities through the advent of 24x7 TV news reporting of the riots themselves, recordings of the atrocities on video and digital film image, and their subsequent circulation amongst Muslims, both in India and abroad. There is considerable evidence that the riots themselves and the way they were widely transmitted were a significant factor in recruitment and revenge attacks by jihadi terrorist groups in the following years. Indian Mujahideen (IM) operatives allegedly repeatedly showed footage of the riots to motivate young recruits to seek revenge. It is a well-publicised fact that the attackers of 26/11 referred to Gujarat as a reason for their violent revenge.

Local-level unrest has complex roots. The ability of governments to deal with such unrest is severely constrained by poor governance, which both exacerbates the problem and also constrains preventive measures, both of the law and order kind and also of the mitigation kind. In these circumstances, local unrest can quickly translate as state and central unrest through transfer mechanisms, such as the effect of local unrest on the national economy (the failure fully to develop India's crucial minerals and energy provinces), the role of modern media in publicising potentially inflammatory events and flows of economic and environmental refugees, who can have a destabilising political effect. Similarly, centrally and internationally generated problems are also transferred downward and can have negative impact at the local level.

The mechanisms of governance, law and policing fulfil an important – indeed crucial – role in either helping to stabilise this situation and knitting a fractious nation together, or else in actually producing 'trouble' that can be transferred either upward through the system or downward. Moreover, if these mechanisms are not functioning well, the instruments at the disposal of the state to contain and mitigate such dissonance are limited. In some circumstances, the law enforcement authorities can even be part of the problem rather than the solution. We now explore this role of law enforcement a little further in the Indian context.

POLICING AND GOVERNANCE IN INDIAN SECURITY

As with any large country, India's security mechanisms are required to meet multiple needs. They must defend the nation against attack by another country. They need to defend against terrorist attacks. They have to deal with insurgencies. They are supposed to investigate corruption and ensure the probity of government at all levels. A fundamental requirement is that they protect an individual from criminal attack. And they need to maintain order nationally and at the street level. In each one of these roles, and at each level of activity (national, state or local), security authorities and governance mechanisms can either be a part of the problem or the solution. Often, they act in different ways and are driven by different political imperatives at different levels.

Although security agencies have clear national goals, at the state and local levels, they can tend to become biased in favour of the government of the day through the political and economic nexus that develops between security authorities and politicians at the local level. There is nothing new about such bias. At the time of the assassination of Indira Gandhi in 1984, the Congress (I) authorities were accused of doing nothing to protect Sikhs in New Delhi from attack or in subsequently prosecuting alleged attackers. Similar allegations were levelled against the BJP government in Gujarat in relation to the anti-Muslim riots of 2002. The allegations against the Gujarat police and courts have several dimensions. One level of complaint does not involve government connivance as such, but rather the fact that the police simply reflected wider community anger over the killing of 58 Hindu activists at Godhra and therefore failed to control the anti-Muslim backlash that followed. This idea that the police can be 'biased' is reflected in The Sachar Committee Report (2006).

The committee found that in India as a whole, Muslims are under-represented in the police, constituting only 6-7 per cent of constables, whereas they constitute 13.4 per cent of the population. The situation is even worse for the Indian Police Service (IPS), where the committee reportedly found only 4 per cent Muslim officers. But arising from the Gujarat riots, there were also more troubling accusations of actual police connivance in supporting the riots at the behest of a biased political class. Although reports of police and political connivance are contested, the Special Investigations Team (SIT), established by the Supreme Court to inquire into the riots, has demanded the arrest of at least one senior policeman for complicity in the riots. And finally, there is the view that the Supreme Court of India was required to intercede in a justice system that was not affording justice to the victims at the level of the Gujarat High Court. In short, this case provides a ready example of the differing influences and perspectives at play in the different levels of India's justice system.

The justice system can be a part of the problem, but there are also many recent instances where strong, neutral political leadership has mitigated any supposed bias within the police. Although the Srikrishna Commission report implicated the government and police in the Mumbai riots of 1992-93, in recent years, strong action by the Government of Maharashtra has resulted in several potentially inflammable communal situations being contained. Despite two terrorist attacks on the communal 'tinderbox' of Malegoan, and despite the attacks of 26/11, careful handling by the Maharashtra government and the police managed to defeat the obvious purpose of such attacks – to trigger communal rioting and consequent polarisation of communities towards extremists. All too often, however, the reverse is the case: politicians have a leading role in manipulating the police for negative, rather than positive, purposes or at least they turn a 'blind eye' to police inactivity in the face of disorder.

Given the many different levels of performance of the Indian justice system, one of the challenges in a paper such as this is to obtain a reasonable measure of the state of internal security. The debate about internal security in India can be conducted in the 'glass half empty or half full' framework, depending on one's emphasis. In India, one can find the best and worst of policing at any one time. But the assessment of the extent of the reform process needed depends on the assessment of the degree of the problem involved, so an over-arching assessment is required.

The level of violence against individual citizens is one measure, even if a crude one, of the effectiveness of law enforcement and governance in India. On the one hand, those of us who follow security issues in India are assaulted on a daily basis by accounts of seemingly high levels of violence. On any given day, we can come across an account of a terrorist attack in a major Indian city in which dozens are killed and many more wounded and maimed; in which police fire on unruly mobs; in which Indian Maoists attack and kill whole contingents of police; in which women are set alight in so-called dowry deaths; or in which criminals or police are killed in major shoot-outs. Against this, those who travel through India are often struck by the way in which optimism and good prevail amidst extreme poverty and in which syncretic values persist and different religions and communities live in harmony and close proximity. Again, the booming economic data do not indicate that violence, dissonance and unrest in India are sufficient to dampen the economy in any significant way. But these are subjective views and the question still remains: how violent, corrupt and dysfunctional is India in comparative terms? This is a difficult issue. The data are hard to extract not only for India but also for other, possibly more violent, regions and sub-regions, such as Africa and parts of Central and South America.

In terms of violence, judged according to the statistics of violent deaths, India at first appears to be a dangerous place. Up to 2007, the US State Department continued to collect comparative data, but its findings are limited to the category 'terrorism'. Besides definitional problems with that term, in itself it does not cover the full spectrum of violence. Nevertheless, the 2007 report recorded 2,300 lives lost due to 'terrorism' in India (no comprehensive data were available in the 2008 report). According to data provided by the South Asia Terrorism Portal (SATP), India has lost 22,789 people to extremist violence between September 2001 and now. Even allowing for a flexible view of terrorism that includes all forms of extremist violence and taking account of India's population of 1.1 billion, this appears at first sight to be an alarming problem.

Measures such as the Global Peace Index are equally flawed as an absolute measure of violence. The index includes factors such as 'democracy' and excludes important areas such as 'domestic violence'. But nevertheless, the large South Asian countries rank relatively low (poorly) on the index (Pakistan 127; Sri Lanka 125; India 107; Bangladesh a surprisingly good 86).

Other data, however, paint a less alarming picture of the situation in India. The murder rate in India (which presumably also reflects deaths in terrorism and political violence) has somewhat fallen since Independence – from 3.7 per 100,000 in

1951 to 3.4 per 100,000 in 2007. Others put India's murder rate, at 3.8 per 100,000, still well below that of the US at 5.5 per 100,000, but well above many western European countries and the UK. China, perhaps a more valid comparison given its vast population, has a rate of 2.4 per 100,000. But China is a more homogeneous country and is more tightly controlled by its undemocratic political system. In terms of general crime rates, the officially recorded statistics are also reasonably positive. They report a declining rate for crimes under the Indian Penal Code (IPC – which fall towards the more serious end of the scale) in relation to population growth rate over the decade prior to 2007.

It would seem then that in per capita terms, India is not especially violent by world standards and is becoming less violent and crime-affected. While political violence, including terrorism, is concentrated in some cities and sub-regions, it does not, on the whole, stifle the daily lives and economic transactions of the majority of people.

Although India is in statistical terms not an especially violent place, there are nevertheless worrying signs that in some parts a destructive cycle of violence can intensify, possibly leading to a classic downward spiral of terrorism (or other forms of violence), excessive state response and further violence triggered by such response. Such was the pattern, indeed, that led to the inter-generational civil war in Sri Lanka. It would be particularly worrying if such trends were to emerge in key economic centres, such as Mumbai, Hyderabad and Bengaluru. As mentioned, another key area in terms of India's economic performance is the Maoist-affected regions. Violent separatism in Kashmir and India's North-East also has worrying strategic implications.

Moreover, crime statistics in India do not tell the whole story concerning governance, crime and violence. There is evidence that India's crime problem is seriously under-reported, and worse, that this under-reporting occurs in part due to a loss of faith in policing. It is impossible to know the extent of under-reporting of crime in any country, but there are ways we can explore the data to give an indication of the dimension of the problem. Crime victim surveys are a useful tool in this regard, but are not sufficiently developed in the Indian context to enable us to draw country-wide conclusions. One survey of four major cities in Tamil Nadu (notably a state with more effective policing than many others) found that "many crimes occurring in India are not reported and that police (crime) figures are only the tip of the iceberg". A victimisation survey of Rajasthan conducted by Massachusetts Institute of Technology on behalf of the Rajasthan Police reportedly found that only 29 per cent of crimes were ever reported, and that of those that were, only 72 per cent received a First Information Report (FIR – the vehicle for setting the legal process in motion). Nevertheless, we need to note that the more serious the crime (such as murder), the more likely it is to be reported.

Serious under-reporting is also likely true of drugs crime. It is worth exploring this problem in a little detail, because serious drugs crime is usually associated with high levels of organised crime and corruption. Drugs crime and associated criminality, in turn, typically mount major, long-term challenges to legal structures, particularly when they become entangled with the so-called problem of 'narco-terrorism'.

The Indian Narcotics Control Bureau (NCB) reports a virtually flat pattern of opiates seizures (at about one tonne of heroin annually and two tonnes of opium), suggesting India's trafficking in and use of this class of drugs is not rising markedly, or that interdiction has fallen markedly. The United Nations Office of Drugs and Crime (UNODC), however, has another view. In a survey of India, the UNODC found that "in 2004, the number of chronic substance-dependent individuals were as follows: 10 million (alcohol), 2.3 million (cannabis) and 0.5 million (opiates)." The report continued: "The survey not only points to the problem of India's population having twice the global (and Asian) average prevalence of illicit opiate consumption, but also shows that the treatment resources available are not commensurate with the burden of work (number of dependent drug users) requiring immediate treatment". A national 'habit' of half a million chronic (highly addicted) users is indicative of consumption of massive quantities of illicit drugs, even allowing for the presumed lower levels of purity in India. This is, in turn, indicative of high levels of criminality.

The US State Department in its 2007 report also designated India as a major hub for illicit drugs. The State Department was concerned at the possibility of diversion of India's substantial licit opiate production and noted the sudden surge in discoveries in illicit growing in 2007. The NCB notes: "It was decided to conduct an intensive survey of the probable areas (of cultivation) involving NCB, state authorities and other central authorities." Eight thousand hectares of illicit poppy were destroyed in that year compared with 218 hectares in 2006 and 623 hectares in 2008. Illicit harvesting of at least 8,000 hectares (the amount discovered and destroyed) suggests major criminal involvement in the purchase, consolidation and processing of the opium gum. For example, this area (which would be by no means the total area illicitly grown) constitutes nearly one-third of the estimated total illicit cultivation in Myanmar in the same year.

The concerns of the US State Department were reflected by findings of the Australian Crime Commission (ACC). Australia has reported an increasing quantity of South West Asian origin heroin (mainly from Afghanistan), with India supplying in the 2007-08 reporting year "the largest number of detections (as a global source of origin) over 500 grams." This indicates that India is a major source of heroin transhipment from the Golden Crescent – reporting that is simply not consonant with the Indian Government's view of its illicit drug problem and the criminality involved with it. Just recently, a gang of Nigerians allegedly transhipping heroin from India to Australia was interdicted in Chennai.

US authorities also express grave concern about India's capacity to deal with money laundering. Although India passed legislation in 2009 that strengthens its anti-money laundering regime, the US Bureau of International Narcotics and Law Enforcement Affairs said in its 2009 report (issued annually through the State Department) that India was still falling well short of the Financial Action Task Force (FATF) recommendations. The report noted that illicit hawala transfers for incoming remittances amounted to US$13-17 billion alone, leaving aside the fact that the majority of hawala dealings relate to criminality and tax evasion rather than remittances. The concern of this chapter is especially with India's counter-terrorism mechanisms; but we also assert that these in turn relate intimately to general issues of governance, corruption and policing. This relationship was recently defined on a practical level by the Minister of Home Affairs, P Chidambaram:

> If intelligence-gathering is the corner stone of fighting insurgency or insurrection or terror, the foot soldier (police man or woman) cannot work in isolation. He must be enabled to gather intelligence from the people ... It is therefore important that State Governments adopt Community Policing.

In terms of developing a more sustainable approach to internal security (and consequently, the closely-related area of external security), the police and judiciary have crucial, even primary, roles to play. The police are the 'eyes and ears' of the system. They are a massive force that, if properly trained and networked, can observe intelligence at the grassroots and pass it upward to the strategic level. They are the ones in a position to pre-empt attack and provide a first response once it occurs. (We shall not quickly forget the images of police in Mumbai attempting to do battle with Kalashnikov-armed terrorists with World War II vintage Lee Enfield.303 rifles.)

A police service capable of providing these services should be more oriented to community policing than the paramilitary structure dictated by the 1861 Police Act. Under a community policing model, the constable is an independent, well-trained and educated operative, capable of making independent, street-level decisions on individual cases, which he or she encounters, rather than deferring to higher authority and acting purely according to direction. This is the policing model conferred by the idea of the London 'bobby' patrolling the streets unarmed, as originating in the reforms of Sir Robert Peel in 1829. Under these reforms, the police were to be accountable, of un-impeachable integrity and to be at one with the public, who they were seen to serve.

Regrettably, the efforts to reform India's state police services, which still mostly operate according to acts very similar to the central government Act, which in turn dates back to the colonial legislation of 1861, have not significantly progressed. As expressed by Sanjay Patil in a recent report written under the auspices of the Commonwealth Human Rights Initiative,

When the British Empire first started wielding more control and influence on its colonies in South Asia, it modelled policing after the militaristic Irish Constabulary rather than the civilian London Metropolitan model. This was meant to subjugate very large and hostile indigenous populations with a relatively small force.

No lesser body than the Indian Planning Commission has pointed out that policing and legal structures in India are currently highly dysfunctional. Whereas the primary concern of the Commonwealth Human Rights Initiative is the rights of individuals, the Planning Commission is primarily concerned with India's economic and social performance as a nation. According to the Planning Commission, the poor performance of the legal sector is actually dragging India and its development down. In its words, "a more orderly society is the bedrock of planned development".

In 2006, the Indian Supreme Court also brought down seven requirements (six directed against the states and one against the Union) directed towards policing reform. These requirements, many of which reflected the recommendations of the Indian Police Commission, have never been implemented. The Police Commission had met eight times between 1988 and 1991. Its recommendations were wide ranging recommendations – from the establishment of proper, independent complaint mechanisms, to the replacement of the repressive and anachronistic 1861 Police Act, and to ensuring the independence of policing from the influence of the government executive. One important factor apparently preventing reform is the nexus between the police and senior politicians in some states. Obviously, such states will be reluctant to introduce reforms attacking the cosy relationships that are of mutual benefit. So far, 11 of 26 states have implemented some kind of reforms, but often such reforms fall short of providing accountability and transparency.

Much of the above is common sense and covered elsewhere. What is sometimes overlooked, however, is that the ability to conduct successful investigations is a prime tool of counter-terrorism and that the police are the key investigators in counter-terrorism. Successful investigations can break up terrorist cells and organisations and provide far-reaching intelligence leads.

For example, B. Raman has pointed out that there have been no major attacks in India in the year since 26/11. In part, he attributes this to the successful investigation of the Indian Mujahideen series of attacks that took place on major Indian cities throughout 2008 and the consequent significant erosion of IM cells. The opening up of the investigations into the IM through an 'encounter' with three IM activists in New Delhi in September 2008 and the subsequent arrest of one has opened a whole chain of cases in India that had hitherto escaped detection.

But despite the successes against the IM, there is evidence that India's capacity to investigate terrorism and crime in general is still not always what it should be. Even crime scene management in important cities like Mumbai and New Delhi is often inadequate, as evidenced by the obvious and very poor crime scene control in Mumbai in the aftermath of 26/11. (Although it must also be said that crime scene management after any massive terrorist attack such as 26/11 is bound to be difficult). In other instances, investigations have not always had early successes and have sometimes been characterised by poor practices and worse. For example, the investigations of the bombings in Hyderabad in 2007 resulted in a number of false arrests and accusations on use of torture by the police – accusations subsequently upheld in a report of the Andhra Pradesh Minorities Commission. The bombing of the Samjhauta Express train in 2006 has also not been resolved, despite a number of initial false arrests.

The attacks on the Mumbai rail system in July 2006 resulted in serious differences between agencies as to which terrorist group was responsible, with the Maharashtra Anti-Terrorism Squad (ATS) arresting Student's Islamic Movement of India (SIMI) members and the Crime Branch of the Mumbai Police arresting IM members. Eventually, the Crime Branch was forced by the courts to release its arrestees. Following the blasts, about 300 Muslims were randomly 'rounded up' by the Mumbai police and held for questioning. Even the investigation of the 26/11 attacks was mired in controversy. And a suppressed, official report of the Maharashtra government reportedly points to poor policing practices in the response to the attacks.

All too often, Indian investigations seem to involve the arrest of a suspect on grounds of inadequate evidence and subsequent administration of the so-called 'truth drug' (Sodium Pentathal). Suspects are sometimes tortured in these encounters with the police, as occurred in the Andhra Pradesh case mentioned above. These approaches seem to be based more on desperation resulting from political pressure to obtain a result rather than sound investigation practices. The otherwise cumbersome court system appears to bear out the view that the investigations process is generally poor in India. The conviction rate for IPC (more serious) crimes in India in 2007 was 42.3 per cent. This compares with a conviction rate of 80.7 per cent in the UK. It is worth noting that conviction rates are a different data set than 'clear up' rates, which would be far lower than 42.3 per cent, given the fact that in 2007,14.5 million were awaiting trial on IPC crimes alone, suggesting that, on an annualised basis, the 'clear up' rates are extremely low.

On their part, senior police in India express considerable frustration with a legal system that can take years to bring cases to judgment and that is increasingly subject to the 'purchasing of justice' by the deployment of slick lawyers capable of finding loopholes in the system on technical grounds. In these circumstances, the police are increasingly taking matters into their own hands. In less serious cases, they are giving alleged criminals a thrashing and letting them go; in more serious cases, they are sometimes killing them in so-called 'encounters'.

In one of the most serious of these, three senior policemen have been arrested in Gujarat; but this is alleged to be only one of a number of such encounter cases in that state. Even a frustrated public is increasingly resorting to so-called 'lynch law'. A video of a man in Bihar being beaten nearly to death by a mob shocked even the President, who remarked that something needed to be done to prevent ordinary citizens taking the law into their own hands, and also noted that "the realm of judicial administration is not without its own share of inadequacies and blemishes". While such methods might be seen to give temporary relief from criminality, they unfortunately also lead to grave injustices and further alienate disaffected minorities, who are often the targets of police bashings, torture and 'encounter' killings.

General crime and the police capacity to deal with it cannot be de-linked from counter-terrorism, especially in the South Asian context. In South Asia, there is a particularly close relationship between crime, corruption and terrorism. Criminal gangs like Dawood Ibrahim's 'D Company' have widespread networks for smuggling purposes, involving agents of corruption in the police and customs. Court cases show that these were heavily utilised in the Mumbai bombings of 1993. Just recently, members of a criminal gang reportedly working on behalf of D Company were arrested for issuances of false passports. Given D Company's links with terrorists, the security implications of these activities are profound. According to the US Congress Research Service (CRS), Lending his (Ibrahim's) criminal expertise and networks to such terrorist groups, he is capable of smuggling terrorists across national borders, trafficking in weapons and drugs, controlling extortion and protection rackets, and laundering ill-gotten proceeds, including through the abuse of traditional value transfer methods, like hawala.

There is also a close nexus between firearms and explosives trafficking and terrorism and insurgency, between hawala and terrorism fund transfers, between the giant web of fraudulent under-invoicing and terrorism financing, and between all areas of criminality and the raising of funds to support terrorist and insurgent organisations. Moreover, these problems are not specific to India, but are general throughout South Asia, which only goes to complicate India's situation. For example, India suffers from the fact that a major arms shipment route from South East to South Asia passes through the Bangladeshi ports of Cox's Bazaar and Chittagong. The largest-ever such interdicted case involved a shipment of 10 truckloads of arms through Chittagong, allegedly destined for the United Liberation Front of Asom (ULFA) and allegedly involving corrupt senior Bangladeshi ministers and intelligence officers. India's porous border with Nepal also often features as a source of smuggled weapons and explosives, subsequently used in terrorist attacks and other crimes.

Given this close nexus between crime, corruption and terrorism in South Asia, it would be impossible to make India safe from terrorism and insurgency without also greatly improving the performance of the police and related agencies in investigating major crimes and corruption. Policing, however, is predominantly a state government function and mainly still undertaken in India according to the authoritarian mould bequeathed by the perceived needs of the colonising power. Judging from the quotation of the Minister of Home Affairs, it is apparent that the Union government is well aware of the problems with policing in India and that the need to improve policing is integral to the counter-terrorism effort. Indeed, stimulated by the poor response evident to the attacks of 26/11, the government has commenced a major process of reform of India's counter-terrorism and security mechanisms. If implemented in full, these reforms will go a good way to meeting some of the major concerns about internal security in India. But as we shall see, they are still likely to have some serious limitations.

INDIA'S INTERNAL SECURITY REFORMS UNION GOVERNMENT CHOICES IN SECURITY REFORM

Given India's limited resources, New Delhi's increasing re-allocation of its overall security resources towards internal and border security, and 'continental' defence against near neighbours like Pakistan tends to detract from military modernisation and development of force projection capability. One way of illustrating this is to show that the share of defence spending on the 'blue water navy', the classic tool of force projection, has remained in percentage terms fairly constant over the last few decades, shifting only from 13 per cent of the defence budget in 1994 to 14.5 per cent today. This percentage share is low for a power seeking a force projection capability. For example, it compares with a percentage share for the US Navy of 26 per cent. Against this, concentration on close-in coastal defence and security has risen dramatically following 26/11.

Another way of measuring the costs of internal security is to look at the rising cost of police and paramilitary forces in relation to military forces. State police numbers have been rising at well above the rate of the population increase, from 1.37 million in 1997 to 1.75 million in 2007 (available positions – there are about 1.5 million police in situ.) This rise reflects the position of the Union Government that India is under-policed.

As well as this rise in police numbers, the Union Government's burden of expenditure on homeland security has also risen significantly. Since 9/11, the percentage share of homeland security (not including the Coast Guard or state police) in relation to defence spending has risen from 11.76 per cent in 2000-01 to 18.5 per cent in 2009-10 (budget estimate). The Union Government now supports police forces costing Rs 12,817 crore (US$2.27 billion), up from Rs 5,677 crore (US$ 1.2 billion) in 1999-2000 – or a rise of 126 per cent in nominal terms.

The data suggest that there has been a proportional shift within India's security spending between power accretion spending and internal security spending. This is not to say that conventional defence spending has not been rising handsomely, but rather that internal security has become an urgent focus of the Union Government. Internationally, however, this proportional shift has been overshadowed by the far greater global interest on India's rise as a military power.

Although there has been a shift in emphasis in favour of internal and border security spending, the focus of that shift is still in favour of 'hard' (or some might say 'repressive') use of power and against other instruments for achieving better governance outcomes. In this equation, the various paramilitary forces, the armed constabulary (numbering nearly half the state police), the Coast Guard and the various intelligence agencies might be considered as 'hard' power. 'Soft' elements, on their part, might be said to consist of the police working to protect the community from crime, the legal structure, various measures to ensure governance, justice and accountability, and approaches that seek to alleviate the lot of those with grievances, such as economic support for tribal and Muslim populations or granting greater autonomy to separatist regions. Diplomatic, economic and aid efforts designed to create a more robust regional grouping in South Asia also fall within this 'soft' category.

This chapter focuses only on India's security choices in relation to its internal security mechanisms rather than its diplomatic, trade and aid activities in the South Asian region or the needs of national defence against attack by another country. But it is worth noting that, although regional security building is an extremely difficult area of activity for India as the regional 'giant', it is a crucial activity in terms of India's wider security, not least in achieving cooperative regional outcomes against transnational terrorism and crime. Nor do we deal with the various attempts of the government to meet the needs of disaffected minorities such as tribals, Muslims or those in other areas, seeking separation or greater autonomy. Equally, these are absolutely vital areas of activity for balanced approaches to counter-terrorism and counter-insurgency. Due to the magnitude of these topics, however, they cannot be covered in this chapter.

Given the reality of India's federal structure, it will be natural to expect the Union Government to be most active in areas of its jurisdiction such as defence, federally funded paramilitary forces, the national intelligence agencies, central police and centrally administered laws. State and local level activities will tend to get a lesser emphasis, at least from the Union Government. Thus, many of the activities at the 'soft' end of the spectrum, such as policing reform and 'community policing', will not fall directly within the jurisdiction of the Union Government. As for state governments, while some may have an incentive to improve these aspects of security in their jurisdictions, others will be less active in the pursuit of reform. A state political class that has the police under its influence, for example, will be far less willing to conduct meaningful police reforms than one that is not. And it is because of this that many states have resisted efforts to reform the police, including the efforts of the Supreme Court and various police reform commissions.

It is a central tenet of this chapter that the Union Government should develop ways of providing additional focus on so-called 'lower order' issues of security, such as anti-corruption measures, the rights of individuals and modernisation of the police and judiciary, even though they fall predominantly within state government jurisdictions. Without leadership from the centre in these areas, the current drive for greater internal security – especially as it has been developed since the attacks of 26/11 – is unlikely to prove sustainable. Although the Union government is clearly restrained in the level of its activity in respect of these areas by the Constitution, there are a number of ways it can become more active and activist and these areas.

POST-26/11 SECURITY REFORMS

In common with many countries, India's internal security architecture has evolved in an ad hoc way. The National Security Guard (NSG) was founded in 1986 in the aftermath of the 1984 Operation Blue Star. The Multi-Agency Centre (MAC), an intelligence 'fusion centre' within the Intelligence Bureau (IB), was first mooted in the aftermath of the intelligence failure associated with Kargil in 1999 and re-furbished in the aftermath of the 26/11 attacks. Due to this ad hoc process and because of India's federal structure, the current security architecture is characterised, in the words of Home Minister Chidambaram, by the fact that "there is no single authority to which these organisations report and there is no single or unified command which can issue directions to these agencies and bodies." It is also plagued by 'turfdom', fragmentation and careerism.

According to its status as a Westminster-style democracy, the apex of India's security architecture is the Prime Minister and the Cabinet and various offices attached to them. The Cabinet Committee on Security (CCS) consists of ex-officio ministers (the Prime Minister, Minister of Home Affairs, Minister of Defence, Minister of External Affairs and Minister of Finance). It is supported by a National Security Council (NSC), with representatives from the above ministries and the Deputy Chairman of the Planning Commission and National Security Adviser (NSA-who answers to the Prime Minister). The NSC, in turn, is serviced by a secretariat of officials. The NSA is responsible for the Joint Intelligence

Committee (which brings together the heads of various intelligence agencies), the Aviation Research Centre (ARC) and the National Technical Research Office (NTRO). The Cabinet Secretariat is responsible for the external intelligence agency, the Research and Analysis Wing (RAW). The Ministry of Finance hosts the Financial Intelligence Unit (FIU). The Ministry of Defence hosts the Defence Intelligence Agency (DIA) and the respective arms of the defence forces host their own intelligence agencies. The Ministry of Home Affairs (MHA) hosts the major domestic security intelligence agency, the Intelligence Bureau (IB), which in turn hosts the MAC. The MHA also hosts the various central government police and paramilitary services, such as the Indian Police Service (IPS), central paramilitary forces (which in turn hosts the NSG), various border paramilitary forces such as the Border Security Force (BSF), the Central Reserve Police Force (CRPF – used to support states in crisis), the Central Bureau of Investigation (CBI), and recently formed National Investigation Agency (NIA).

The major connectivity in terms of intelligence between the Centre and states comes about through the state offices of the IB, through the fact that the Centre can insert its various agencies into the states at the request of the states, through the newly created Subsidiary Multi-Agency Centres (SMACS) and through the connectivity between the SMACS and state police Special Branches. Under the Constitution, except in the case of President's Rule, intelligence relating to national security or investigations relating to the central government's jurisdiction (such as fraud in a central government agency or those relating to the newly created NIA), these relationships all exist according to the invitations and goodwill of the states. Thus if a state does not wish to call in the central government agencies, it need not do so.

As with other federal structures, such as Australia and the US, the artificial bifurcation of intelligence between state and central authorities constitutes a major impediment to the flow of intelligence between the grassroots and the central agencies. This natural tendency of federations is greatly exacerbated in India because of the vast size of the country. Further, intelligence agencies everywhere are extremely poor at sharing intelligence, and India is no exception. They are restricted in doing so by different 'intelligence cultures', the existence of multiple agencies essentially doing the same thing ('stove-piping'), lack of trust and the natural desire to protect sensitive sources. Unfortunately, the police are particularly prone not to share intelligence for all the above reasons and because of a police culture that can often be sceptical of the intelligence function.

The hallmark of sound intelligence in the age of terrorism is the ability to fuse the intelligence gathered at the grassroots with that gathered and analysed at intermediate, national and international levels – what has become known in the US as 'connecting the dots'. Intrinsically, this demands that police and the intelligence agencies work closely together at all levels and develop the capability to share intelligence. It requires that intelligence be 'sucked up' from operations to the analytical and strategic levels. In turn, it requires a sound relationship between the police and the communities they are policing. It also involves trust, compatible data sharing arrangements and adequate security for information and intelligence. Ideally, it requires that all this happens in as near as possible to real time, which in turn implies sound data sharing and analytical systems. But however sophisticated the systems, the sharing of intelligence always Under Section 356 of the Constitution, the central government may dismiss a state government and govern the state directly if the state is deemed to exhibit a failure of the constitutional machinery. If, after six months, no workable majority has emerged, fresh elections must be held.

Since he took over the Ministry of Home Affairs portfolio in December 2008 in the aftermath of the 26/11 attacks, Mr Chidambaram has already conducted a series of reforms and has outlined further major reforms. Reforms, either anticipated or accomplished, include the following (compiled from press reporting and from Chidambaram's speech in December 2009):

Re-vitalisation of the Intelligence Agencies and Counter-Terrorism Mechanisms

- The Multi-Agency Centre (MAC), within the Intelligence Bureau (IB), has been re-furbished and strengthened. The

IB has been given an additional Rs 147 crore for the purpose. So-called 'Subsidiary Multi-Agency Centres' (SMACs) have now also been established in the states.

- The MAC and SMACs are to be linked by a dedicated, secure network. In all, 30 locations (including the MAC, the SMACs and a number of police Special Branches) are to be linked by this network.
- • A new, over-arching counter-terrorism organisation is to be created by end 2010, to be called the National Counter-Terrorism Centre (NCTC)
- To incorporate the MAC, NIA, NTRO, JIC, NCRB and National Security Guard (NSG)
- To have an operations division (presumably to include the NSG)
- And thus to minimise the current bifurcation between agencies currently controlled by the NSA and the Ministry of Home Affairs.
- To enable a more rapid response to major terror attacks than was achieved on 26/11, NSG hubs have been established in Hyderabad, Bengaluru, Chennai and Kolkata and two additional regional response groups have been located in Hyderabad and Kolkata. Each hub is staffed by 250 people.
- The Border Security Force (BSF) has been significantly upgraded and re-equipped and 29 additional battalions are to be raised. The Central Reserve Police Force (CRPF) and other central paramilitary forces have also been significantly upgraded.
- In the next 12-18 months, 21 existing, standalone databases will be networked through NATGRID. According to Chidambaram, NATGRID will provide "quick, seamless and secure access to desired information for intelligence/ enforcement agencies".
- In a recent development, the National Security Adviser has resigned, possibly opening the way for an integrated security architecture, one more fully reflecting the objectives laid out by Chidambaram.

Strengthening of Coastal and Border Defences

- Coordination has been strengthened between the Coast Guard, Navy and coastal police.
- 64 coastal police stations have been operationalised.
- 56 interceptor boats have been purchased (of 204 scheduled).
- A vessel tracking and monitoring system is being considered.
- Intensified patrolling is in place.
- ID cards are to be issued to fishermen and possibly also coastal residents.
- Following the exposure of serious gaps in the visa system by the Headley case, the Mission Mode Project (MMP) will be implemented. This will provide for online visa and foreigners' registration and tracking with the objective of creating a secure and integrated service delivery framework for facilitating legitimate travellers and strengthening security. It is estimated to cost Rs 1,011 crore and will be implemented over a period of four-and-a-half years.

Policing and Legal Reform

- The National Investigations Agency (NIA) has been established and is now staffed by a small number of investigators and analysts
- The remit of the NIA is to investigate terrorism crimes under the Unlawful Activities (Prevention) Act and other crimes, such as drug-related crimes, counterfeiting, and major organised crime and money laundering, that have international or multi-state implications.
- The Union government has assisted with funds for the recruitment of 400,000 additional state police
- It has promulgated guidelines for non-corrupt recruitment and developed an electronic system to ensure 'hands free' and non-corrupt recruitment. This system has already been implemented for central recruitment.
- The Union government is to assist with connectivity between police stations and the establishment of a system

for police called Crime and Criminal Tracking Network System (CCTNS) "to facilitate collection, storage, retrieval, analysis, transfer and sharing of data and information at the police station and between the police station and the state headquarters and the central police organisations".

- The Home Minister has admonished states to implement 'community policing'.
- He has also requested that "to organise and analyse information derived from the community, the state police Special Branches should be restructured as a specialised and self-sufficient cadre of the State police in terms of personnel, funds and equipment." To this end, on January 7, 2009, the central government circulated a proposal to restructure the Special Branch in the State police forces. The implementation of the proposal will mark the beginning of a long-haul effort to restructure the intelligence-gathering machinery at the district and state levels.
- The Union Government will assist state police to establish 24x7 command and control posts and quick response teams (QRTs), properly equipped and trained.
- States are admonished to establish (where they don't have them) antiterrorism units (ATUs) to pre-empt and investigate terrorist attacks.
- In a major legal reform, the Law Minister has conducted negotiations with chief law officers and chief ministers to enable the release of 'undertrials', who have already served a significant proportion of the sentences to which they would be convicted, if found guilty, thus releasing up to 1.25 million of India's 3.5 million inmates, 70 per cent of whom are under trial.

Analysis

The collective changes outlined above, if fully implemented, would amount to an internal security 'revolution' in India. The idea of a NCTC, to bring a number of important agencies under one umbrella, act as a 'fusion centre' for terrorist related intelligence, minimise 'stove-piping', and provide operational coordination, closely reflects changes introduced in the US following 9/11, especially the establishment of the umbrella NCTC there, under the auspices of the Director of National Intelligence (DNI). This mimicry of the US architecture in part arises from the early assistance provided by the Federal Bureau of Investigation (FBI) in the aftermath of 26/11 and a subsequent series of visits to the US by senior Indian politicians and officials, including the Home Minister and Prime Minister.

But do the changes go far enough? Do they 'press the right buttons', and are they likely to be successful in providing better governance throughout the Indian Union – a prime consideration of this chapter in its approach to counter-terrorism and counter-insurgency?

In all such architecture relating to federations like India, Australia, Canada and the US, there are five major heuristic 'gaps to be bridged':

- between overseas and domestic intelligence;
- between military and non-military intelligence;
- between central and state intelligence;
- between the intelligence agencies and police intelligence; and
- between intelligence and the operational counter-terrorism role (response), which is in turn divided into:
- investigations;
- operational coordination in event of an attack; and
- consequence management.

These five major 'gaps' are heuristic in the sense that each and every inter-agency relationship also needs to be bridged. But they represent the major conceptual divides and provide a useful point of departure for the analysis. We will now briefly critique the proposed Indian architecture in light of each of these five main areas.

OVERSEAS AND DOMESTIC INTELLIGENCE

The proposed Indian NCTC, although influenced by the US, will be architecturally somewhat different from the US model. It will be hosted by the Department of Home Affairs and not the NSA (the counterpart of the American DNI). This is a significant difference, since under the Indian model there will be no intelligence 'czar' having authority over all Union government intelligence agencies (unless the Minister of Home Affairs were deemed to fulfil that role). Thus, the domestic agencies involved with intelligence, such as the IB and NIA, will be organisationally separated from the foreign intelligence agencies and military agencies (although their intelligence may be 'fused' in the MAC, which will be within the NCTC). Depending on the effectiveness of the operations of the MAC, this potentially provides an area of weakness in the model. It also means that the 'gap' between domestic and external intelligence may not be adequately bridged in the Indian case.

MILITARY AND NON-MILITARY INTELLIGENCE

The military intelligence agencies are hosted by the MOD and the same reservations can therefore be made as regards to overseas and domestic intelligence, above. Moreover, the military-related collection agencies, such as India's SIGINT agency, are also administratively separated from the military, further cementing the military-non-military divide (but also facilitating a closer relationship with the nonmilitary agencies).

CENTRAL AND STATE INTELLIGENCE

Some additional links will have been achieved by the reforms. The IB, located within the NCTC through the MAC, will have links into the states via its state offices and the SMACS, which will in turn have links with the state police Special Branches. These links, however, will be indirect and incomplete. Most seriously, there is no indication in the counterterrorism and internal reform package to date that policing in India will be reformed. The Home Minister has simply exhorted the states to introduce what he calls "community policing" and to ensure that the intelligence so provided is linked with state police Special Branches. Special Branches are generally separated from the main body of police and their existence in Western countries has often been highly controversial. Not only have they often proved ineffective in the counter-terrorism role, but also they tend to divorce that role, and the intelligence process, from normal policing. Often too, they have resulted in embarrassing and incompetent police involvement in the political process. This danger is particularly pronounced in India, where the doctrine of the separation of powers in relation to policing is practically non-existent.

POLICE AND INTELLIGENCE AGENCIES

The main police body within the NCTC will be the NIA. The NIA is, however, a strictly limited agency that will not have the capacity according to its current legislation to provide the link between the intelligence agencies and state police. The NIA will need to be properly resourced and staffed, which is still not the case. The NIA Act is seemingly generous in providing agency officers with India-wide powers in respect of scheduled offences. The Act states at 3(3):

Any officer of the Agency of, or above, the rank of Sub-Inspector may … exercise throughout India, any of the powers of the officer-in-charge of a police station in the area in which he is present for the time being and when so exercising such powers shall, subject to any such orders [of the Central government] as aforesaid, be deemed to be an officer-in-charge of a police station discharging the functions of such an officer within the limits of his station.

The procedures for putting an investigation in motion. Unfortunately, they are somewhat ambiguous and bear some of the hallmarks of hasty drafting. For example, Section 8 allows the investigator to investigate any other offence of the 'accused' related to the original offence scheduled under the Act. It is not clear whether this can only happen after an arrest, but presumably the reference to the 'accused' signifies that this is the case. If so, then that will be a serious limiting factor in the scope of the investigations. Another limiting factor comes about through the system of notification. This stipulates that any scheduled offence reported to any police station in India will be brought to the attention of the 'state' authorities, who will bring it to the attention of the Union Government authorities, who will in turn determine if it is a subject of the Act and bring it to the NIA for investigation. The relevant words of Section 6(1) are: "On receipt of information and recording there of under section 154 of the (Criminal) Code relating to any Scheduled Offence the officer-in-charge of the police station shall forward the report to the State Government forthwith."

Offences scheduled under the Act are: terrorism, counterfeiting of currency, human trafficking, illicit drugs trafficking, organised crime, plane hijacking, violations of the Atomic Energy Act and Weapons of Mass Destruction Act. In addition, all offences alleged against the accused under these scheduled offences may also be investigated.

This seemingly unambiguous stipulation has a myriad of practical implications. The system for involving the NIA in an investigation is extremely cumbersome and could take months. Anyone who has any practical knowledge of investigations knows that it is a virtually impossible situation to be brought into an investigation in the latter stages, when one has no control over the crime scene, collection and maintenance of evidence, or early interrogation processes (which are the most crucial).

But our main issue with the NIA Act is that it does not support the intelligence collection process – which is in turn essential for prevention. It is essentially concerned with an 'offence' reported as a FIR. But intelligence is not about offences or evidence as such (although it can include evidence) but the analysed information surrounding offences and potential offences. It is this information surrounding potential offences that will need to be collected by local-level police and passed upward through the intelligence process. Thus, the NIA Act is not an ideal vehicle for either investigations or intelligence and could prove very difficult to operate. That is not to say, however, that such intelligence will not be passed between Special Branches, the SMACs and the MAC, but rather that, if it is, it will continue to be a 'hit and miss' process. Moreover, and crucially, the intelligence feed from the grassroots will only be as good as the police providing it: and as mentioned above, nothing in the present reform process indicates that the process of state-level policing will be progressed from the present paramilitary thrust under the 1861 Police Act.

INTELLIGENCE AND THE OPERATIONAL COUNTER-TERRORISM ROLE (RESPONSE)

To the extent that the MAC, the NIA, the IB and Union Government response agencies, such as the NSG, will presumably be housed within the NCTC, at least some of the connectivity concerns between intelligence and counter-terrorism operations will be met. However, the weakness in this area arises from the fact that the NSG (as a special weapons and tactics – SWAT – group) is only one small component of counterterrorism response. The other components, such as state police first response, post-facto investigations, consequence management and deradicalisation programs for those arrested, rest predominantly within the state jurisdiction. Also the intelligence effort surrounding a terrorist event will still have all the problems of coordination and data matching mentioned above. This is the exact situation faced by Australia, which has derived a number of mechanisms to try to overcome the problem.

Other Missing Elements

The Indian reform process outlined above will go some way in providing a viable counter-terrorism and counter-insurgency base if fully and effectively implemented. It has several major deficiencies, however. Some of these, such as the need to concentrate on uplifting the South Asia region as a whole and on meeting the concerns of India's disaffected minorities, are beyond the scope of this chapter. But other important concerns about policing, governance and accountability need to be addressed. They particularly need to be addressed because – as argued above – the state and grassroots levels are key elements in counterterrorism and counter-insurgency.

The closely related factors of accountability and governance lie at the heart of the state and local-level security problems. Without accountability and good governance, governments will not be able to implement any programmes to alleviate the economic and political grievances of disaffected communities, such as the otherwise commendable NREGA. And the police, far from being able to act as the eyes and ears of the community, will actually be a part of the problem in that they will alienate those very communities.

ACCOUNTABILITY AND GOVERNANCE REFORM IN INDIA

Accountability and governance mechanisms need to be addressed at all levels of government and in relation not just to policing, but also issues like corruption in general and failure of public servants such as teachers and medical workers to fulfil their duties. For the purposes of this chapter, however, we confine ourselves to the more manageable topic of policing and law enforcement accountability.

As pointed out by the Commonwealth Human Rights Initiative, continued adherence to India's 1861 Police Act lies at the heart of the accountability problem in policing. Thus, the very foundation of policing in India is the proposition that the police are subject to the dictates of the governments which they serve. Obviously, this subordination of the police to the political class is always the case to an extent, even in countries supposedly subscribing to the separation of powers doctrine.

NREGA is a job guarantee scheme enacted by legislation on August 25, 2005. The scheme provides a legal guarantee for 100 days of employment in every financial year to adult members of any rural household willing to do public work-related unskilled manual work at the statutory minimum wage of Rs 100 per day. The Central government outlay for scheme is Rs 39,100 crore ($8 billion) in FY 2009-10. Recently, it was renamed as the Mahatma Gandhi National Rural Employment Guarantee Act.

Governments hold the 'power of the purse'. As with the Australian Federal Police Act in Australia, the Minister for Home Affairs may also convey to the AFP his or her broad programme for investigations and other activities. But the key point is that in countries subscribing to the doctrine of the separation of powers, politicians cannot become involved in any individual legal case for fear of political malfeasance. In India, this is not the case at all, as was witnessed recently in Uttar Pradesh when the state government under the Chief Minister Mayawati apparently initiated a malicious prosecution of a leading Congress opposition figure – an occurrence that is, unfortunately, all too common.

Other problems with policing also follow from the continued adherence to the 1861 Act. The Indian Police Service (IPS), while an august and often useful institution, has forced 'community policing' into a 'lowest common denominator'. Under current structures, the fact that constables and senior constables are often poorly educated, trained, paid, accommodated, equipped and have no prospects for promotion means they cannot provide the backbone of a genuine community policing effort. And under current structures, it is they, rather than the IPS, which form the vast majority of Indian police.

Many of the problems with the 1861 Act were recognised and overcome in a 'model police act' written by a committee under the auspices of the MHA and published in 2006. For example, under this model act, the rank of constable was to be abolished and a police officer would be designated a 'Civil Police Officer' after three years initial training. Accountability measures would be strengthened through introduction of independent complaints mechanisms and the hold of state governments over police would be reduced by measures such as police boards (including the leader of the Opposition) and tenured, merit-based appointments for Inspectors General of Police (Commissioners). Although many states have updated their police acts, by no means all have adhered to the tenets of the model police act in doing so, fearing loss of control over the police.

Police reforms in India will not be quick or easy. Both the states and their police services will resist them. Given the size and poor condition of Indian police services and lack of resources at the state level, the task is enormous, even with the best possible circumstances that would not involve such resistance. The Union Government will need to ensure that police reforms remains a major priority in its security reform process, that it does not get pushed to one side by other seemingly easier, quick fix reforms and that it remains in focus over the long-term. India has a number of federal and state-level accountability mechanisms relevant to police and law enforcement.

One such measure that is often over-looked is the collection and maintenance of sound law enforcement and crime statistics. Statistics are fundamental to accountability in so far as citizens are given a clear insight into how their services are performing. For example, strong, inter-linked statistics between courts and the police are capable of furnishing key information about both court and police performance. It is through the linking of these statistics that they are 'turbo-charged' so that they can be far more exacting as accountability measures.

One early measure the Union Government can consider is to fund and oversight (to ensure quality) in each state periodic crime victimisation surveys designed to give longitudinal and comparative pictures of genuine crime problems. The results of these surveys can also be compared with the results of the existing Indian crime database to determine how effective current collection methods are. They should be widely available to the public, including through the Internet.

India also has a number of existing accountability institutions. At the central level, the National Human Rights Commission (NHRC) is designed to protect the rights of individuals. The commission has the powers of a civil court in respect of all Indian jurisdictions.

It may intercede in court processes in relation to human rights and visit institutions to investigate alleged human rights abuses. But its weakness is that it may only make recommendations to governments (although these include recommendations for prosecutions where appropriate). Further, it is constrained to consider issues of human rights abuses, which do not normally include corruption. It is also bogged down by the massive workload imposed on it.

The Central Vigilance Commission (CVC) is a central agency responsible for dealing with corruption amongst senior, federal-level officials. While it has extensive investigative powers, they relate only to central government agencies and relatively senior level officers. Similarly, the investigatory arm of the government in relation to corruption, the CBI, can only act in regard to state-level institutions at the express invitation of the concerned state.

The limitations of this architecture on an India-wide basis are patent in the high levels of corruption still pertaining throughout the country. Although India has improved its Transparency International ranking in recent years, its performance still leaves a lot to be desired and in 2008, it was again slipping, with a ranking of 85th and a score of 3.4 on the perception of corruption index.

A NEW INVESTIGATION AND ACCOUNTABILITY FRAMEWORK

Strengthening National Investigations

The powers and jurisdictional cover provided by the combination of the CBI, IB and NIA are now considerable, particularly in relation to problems, such as terrorism, which is covered by an India-wide mandate in respect of intelligence (the IB) and investigations (the NIA). However, there are still weaknesses with this system, as spelt out above. They concern, inter alia: the cut-off between intelligence and investigations still in evidence between the state police and central authorities; and the fact that the mechanisms to call in the NIA are cumbersome and that it cannot act until an offence has been committed, thus further alienating the intelligence from the investigations relationship. As argued in this chapter, the connections between the crime problem and the terrorism-insurgency problems in India (and South Asia generally) are close. Serious organised crime needs to be addressed on an India-wide basis, and an arrangement such as Australia's Crime Commission should be seriously considered – or else an amendment of the NIA Act should be made to grant the agency similar powers. Further, policing reform lies at the heart of improvement of the investigations and intelligence effort. The Home Minister's security 'revolution' needs to be further extended to embrace more resolute Union Government action on police reforms.

Strengthening Police and Government Accountability

Given the serious nature of the problems confronting India and the clear incapacity of current institutions to deal with them, the reform process initiated by the Home Minister should go much further in imposing accountability mechanisms than it has so far. Considering India's admirable tradition of judicial activism, one model open for further investigation can be the judicial commission model – that is, the establishment of judicial commissions with investigative and coercive powers. Obviously, however, such powers need to be carefully circumscribed to protect human rights.

Several models have had some success in fighting endemic corruption in policing and government. In general, the following are necessary for successful corruption fighting:

- The anti-corruption body should be independent of government in its operations (although its head will of necessity be appointed by the government, but preferably on a fixed term, tenured contract);
- It should have sufficient investigatory powers to do its job (preferably, these should be 'coercive' Royal Commission-like powers);
- It should be adequately financed to do its job; and
- It should be constituted at the correct jurisdictional level·
- In the Indian case, this would mean units at Union and state-government levels.

The cases of Hong Kong and Singapore come to mind. Of these, Hong Kong is more relevant to India, since the situation in Singapore has been addressed in part by paying police high salaries – a facility obviously not available to India.

The Hong Kong model has been in place in various forms since 1974 when the Independent Commission Against Corruption (ICAC) was established. The essential features of the Hong Kong model are that the ICAC is fully independent (answerable only to the head of government), well resourced and strongly backed by law (although in this case by ordinance rather than an act of the legislature).

In the Indian constitutional context, the CVC Act should be amended to provide the above features. The CVC should be enabled to focus on more junior level officers as well as senior officers, and its resources expanded accordingly. It should be provided its own fully staffed investigations unit, which would include responsibility for investigating the integrity of centrally-raised police and paramilitary forces.

Moreover, a revised agency should be presented by the Union Government as an exemplar for a state-level model to be advocated and funded by the Union Government similar to the various state-level anti-corruption commissions in Australia. Some of these, such as in New South Wales, are divided between the Independent Commission Against Corruption, the Police Integrity Commission and the Crime Commission (which is a crime fighting agency with similar powers to the ACC). Others, such as the Western Australian Corruption and Crime Commission cover both crime and corruption fighting (although the investigation role is sub-contracted by the Commission to the Commissioner of Police rather than being carried in-house). All such bodies have independent structures and substantial powers.

Above all, the Indian culture of internal investigations of complaints against police should not be able to stand alone as the only means of redress. It has been shown time and again to be inadequate as a means of stamping out endemic corruption. It certainly has a place, in so far as it will be impossible to investigate all complaints against the police by means of an independent commission. But it should be only part of the menu of remedies available.

REVIEWING INTERNAL ARMED CONFLICT IN INDIA

Rostum Nanavatty has been a reluctant scholar and a committed soldier's General with his feet on the ground. Iconised by his juniors, adored by his peers, feared by many of his seniors, and grudgingly respected by the political elites for expressing directly his views on the civil-military relationship, including issues related to good governance. Perhaps, on record, he will be the only Army Commander who, while holding office and operating in the most geo-strategic state of India, could caution the highest political authority in charge of the internal security of the country about the essential need to pay attention to the role of good governance— an observation which made headlines in the international system and drew the attention and respect of the most powerful nation in the world. The political class could not find fault with his observations, the vociferous press could not sensationalise them, and the bureaucracy refrained from attempting the use of their established methods to malign the character and integrity of this public intellectual in the role of a celebrated soldier.

An undiluted output of the experience and judgment of a soldier that has unwittingly entered the realm of policy relevance rather than being policy oriented. Its utility is, thus, universal and future generations of research scholars introspecting across disciplines and organisational behaviour will find it useful to link theory with practices of public policy formulations related to national security and the civil-military relationship. There is another uniqueness that must be recognised in the writing of this book. It represents a generational legacy of two generations of professional experience percolating down from father to son. The late K J Nanavatty, Imperial Police (IP), Inspector General of Police (IGP), Bombay state and later, of the state of Maharashtra after his retirement in 1964, was appointed as the first IGP of the newly formed state of Nagaland by the Government of India. He definitely would have "scripted a different paradigm for State Police Forces in counter-insurgency in India, had greater Army understanding, cooperation and assistance been forthcoming." Rostum Nanavatty was already a Commissioned Officer in the Indian Army in 1964, and must have been privy to the situation in Nagaland much beyond the experience of young officers. Later, he served as General Officer Commanding 3 Corps responsible for counterinsurgency operations in the states of Nagaland, Manipur and Tripura and in the region of South Assam from 1997-2000.

When the work was in its nascent stage of being formulated as a project, Nanavatty asked for my opinion. Having read the initial proposal, I advised him to introspect on whether he wanted the work to be policy oriented or policy relevant. Thereafter, there was no further input from me or even any comments made by me despite his having given me the draft of the manuscript and reminding me about the same. This was a deliberate attempt on my part to ensure that I did not in any way influence the character of his writing and that I would be in a position to write a review essay on his work in due course of time, which I am doing today with pleasure.

THE NORMATIVE PARADIGM

The present endeavour is not merely to write a review of the book by summarising the content and context of the book and, thus, help the future readers to make up their minds on whether to read it further. Reviews basically are for opinion formation. The present one, firstly, is a piece of research to record the intellectual paradigm within which the work needs to be assessed so that it contributes to the growth of knowledge—as in this case, the relationship between the causal and prescriptive recommendations to manage Internal Armed Conflict in India (IACI) and further the efforts to forge interdependent civil-military cooperation. An intellectual war-game between the conceptualisation of the author's intellectual mind fix against the critical overview by the reviewer to place the work in the larger paradigm of conceptual issues articulated to serve as a permanent reference point.

It is essential at this stage to be explicit since the "must read" universe of this book will largely be the officers of the Indian armed forces who are today in a stage of intellectual transformation to understand and internalise the nuances of professional military education as a part of their professional career in the 21 century modernised Indian Army operating under a democratic system of polity. The author upholds the Constitution of India and pits all actions, thought processes and operationalisation of doctrine and responsibilities of the states and central governments to "counter internal threats to the security of the state" within the framework of the Constitution and makes an important cautionary observation on the suggestion made by some analysts who have gone ahead to prescribe a "joint responsibility of both the union government and the state" and proposing the need of specific mention to be incorporated in the Concurrent List (List III).

It is an abridgement of all the relevant sections of the Constitution of India citing the various Articles to put forth the locus of power and legitimise the action needed by the military for forging joint civil-military cooperation. Nanavatty notes, "The Constitution does not distinguish between law and order and public policy. The responsibility for drawing this distinction devolves on the Supreme Court of India." He, thus, places the role of the bureaucracy to be merely to complement the role of the political executive and the legislators in the Parliament. Therefore, is a significant contribution to understand the role of the armed forces while dealing with IACI. The ten-page Chapter III, with its 56 footnotes, leaves nothing missing to understand the Indian Constitution's various sections related to the use of force to contain IACI. It is recommended that not only the younger generation of the Indian armed forces but the senior formation commanders alike take pains to memorise these ten pages with all the footnotes. This will ensure that the conceptualisation of the role and exercise of power is no longer ambiguous in the minds of those who are asked to act to contain IACI. Nanavatty's incisive interpretation of the Constitution, leading to the flow of recommendations has been seen in certain quarters as a military bias in his approach, which is uncalled for.

The framework of research is straightforward. A comprehensive survey of the literature written, published or discussed on internal armed conflict leading to insurgency, and the prescriptions for counter-insurgency operations have been quantified as empirical facts corroborated for cross-references and applicability. This rich text of primary, secondary and treasury source material has allowed the author to escape the otherwise methodological rigours required to formulate hypotheses essential for universal generalisation to cull out possible rule formation in the vast, volatile and shifting landscape of the paradigmic conflict analysis model in which internal armed conflict would have become a subset of conflict resolution alone. This is where the inherent innovativeness of the author becomes apparent to side-step the discipline narrowness and operate outside the box in a multi-disciplinary format.

The book, as noted by the author in the very first page of the preface, is "India-centric". Nanavatty has juxtaposed the empirical evidence culled out of the vast literature that he has surveyed with observations related to an "India case study" as an analysis, enriching it with his own experience in the field, the operating principles and doctrines that he kept in his subconscious mind as a field commander. Thus, creating a total "Indocentric" and not merely an "India-centric" version of analysis to enable the serious readers understand the causal relationship responsible for the emergence of IACI by those actors and subset of actors whom the political, bureaucratic and social entities in India failed to recognise, and to negotiate a process leading to an integration of the then disruptive forces with the mainstream politics so that they are forced to accept, and operate within, the framework of the Indian federal Constitution. Inherent and implicit in Nanavatty's deliberation is the indication that while the Indian Constitution is common to all the states of the Indian nation-state—even though Jammu and Kashmir (J&K) was granted a special status under Article 370 at the time of India gaining independence in 1947—all the internal armed conflicts and insurgencies are not similar to each other. There is hardly any commonality in each of their occurrences. Hence, the creative part of finding solutions or leadership strategies to each situation will depend on the exercise of the intellectual understanding of the complex cultural matrix of the state where it is occurring and the flexibility to apply the provisions of the Constitution without compromising on its basic tenets, especially where cross-border terrorism vitiates the atmosphere.

Not being trained in the methodology of theoretical research falling within the vast domain of social science research has been, in Nanavatty's case, an advantage. He has not been hindered by a strict paradigm approach of any social science discipline which would have forced him to adopt a methodology of a single discipline conceptual lens of history, sociology, anthropology or political philosophy. Therefore, his non-training in pure theory has permitted him to overlap disciplines, cut across narrow confines and create unmanageable hypotheses required to be proved to arrive at any form of a general theory for application in IACI. Hence, in the strict sense, this "India-centric" book has moved into an "Indo-centric" paradigm in which theory has been inverted on its head to give way to experience and judgment, which is truly trans-disciplinary in nature. The sheer narratives of the ground realities faced, the prescriptive methods recommended and the upholding of the Constitution make it essential for all armchair strategists, policy-makers, political elites and bureaucrats in India to read this book more carefully, to change the mind-fix that they suffer from. It is also essential to indicate that while writing the subaltern history of IACI, the retired armed forces officers must be careful not to indulge in writing or tabulating their views by distorting the rigours of scientific methodology and misusing the freedom of expression.

The Conceptual Construct

In India, ever since independence, the theories related to strategic affairs and national security have rarely been related to the outputs of professional military viewpoints. The role of professional military education has neither been planned, introspected upon nor placed as an essential component of the national education policy. Policies, therefore, of strategic and national security affairs have been the victim of strong opinion rather than being based on a studied approach to safeguard national interests. Nanavatty's work is based on a conceptual analysis supported by observed facts and a studied approach rather than taking recourse to strong opinion. This labour of research undertaken by the author should become an example, especially for every young officer of the Indian armed forces attempting to undertake scholarly work to operationalise concepts by pounding them on the anvil of theory and making outputs of universal and lasting value. Here, I must caution all researchers that while theory can never replace experience and judgment, it always acts as a catalyst to integrate all three.

In the above context, a variety of opinions has emerged, both orally and in print, from a number of experts having long experience and distinguished track records of service in the various organisations of the central government about the content of the work and the context in which it had been undertaken by Nanavatty, The book, thus, becomes marketable amongst the readers who are also serving in government organisations. But the way it is being marketed today shows that it is far from being disseminated to the academic intellectual community or other stakeholders, including those from the corporate sector who now have a vested interest to understand the complex nuances of internal armed conflicts or national security issues that have plagued the Indian nation-state for decades.

These inane opinions appear to be inadequate, pedestrian and unable to project the true nature of the serious deliberations undertaken in the writing of this book. They project a truncated view, lacking depth and insight of the real utility of the work. It will, hence, fail to raise the inquisitiveness of the non-traditional stakeholders at large or the young researchers studying the role of public policy-making in strategic affairs and those in the corporate sector who are slowly but surely becoming the main stakeholders in the affairs of good governance, strategic policy-making and issues related to national interests and national security. Nanavatty's work deserves at the first take the attention of the finest representatives from amongst academia who have international standing in the disciplines covering social psychology, social anthropology, cultural history and public policy-making, and placing such critical opinions in the market place of the knowledge society of the 21 century. Such opinions would then become a catalyst to promote a knowledge-based debate and reaction as was seen after the Council on Foreign Affairs published Samuel Huntington's seminal work on *Clash of Civilizations*.

Further, the opinions written so far, seen after the release of the book on January 16, 2013, range from displaying certain mindsets—all unable to go beyond the box to contribute towards the growth of knowledge. Three distinct categories of opinion can be discerned. The first category represents the fixed mindset of seeing through the conceptual lens of prioritising the utility of coercive force in the civil-military relationship to solve the knotty problems related to application of force to sustain stability. The second category displays the mind fix in a fixed mind and, therefore, identifies biases in the writing that inherently do not exist. This obviously has led such opinion-makers to conceptualisation and seeking an operable control mechanism to all solutions on policy-making by adopting the normative method of suggesting that "administering to govern" rather than "governing to administer" is the real way to achieve good governance. The third category of opinion gives the notion that only accredited, authorised persons can practise good governance. Perhaps the opinion on a work of this dimension would have been better served, if, as I have noted above, it had been made through an interdisciplinary approach in a multi-disciplinary format. The phenomenon of war and the various dimensions of internal armed conflicts, plaguing any nation-state even in the 21 century, comprise a cultural phenomenon having civilisational preconditions. There are no military, bureaucratic or intelligence solutions to cultural problems thriving on inequality, lack of inclusiveness or empowerment. Once these fundamental problematics are understood and the first take opinions are streamlined, the work undertaken by authors like Nanavatty becomes a knowledge enhancer, revealing its inherent worth.

The Content

It is the opinion of the author that IACI will persist, with the military continuing to play a significant role in its management and resolution and that the present work pertains basically to insurgency and counterinsurgency. In the author's note, "The Terminology Trap", Nanavatty observes that there is a propensity on the part of the Indian military to use particularly US military terminology, but the "indiscriminate use of (such) terminologies does little to foster comprehension of a new form of conflict and can actually complicate issues from a legal perspective". The author makes it clear that IACI is an internal issue of the Indian nation-state, the insurgent is not the 'enemy' and counter-insurgency is not war.

"Internal Armed Conflict in General" discusses and also clarifies the definitional aspects related to terrorism, civil disturbances, subversion, insurgency, and civil war. In the 17 pages of exposition with 101 footnotes, the treatment to each term and concept is appropriate with corroborating evidence. It is a reference manual by itself and sets the tonality to place the Indian experience in perspective as contain. A useful pointer is made in differentiating between internal armed conflict and conventional war. There is a table tabulating the Evolution of Fundamental Principles of CounterInsurgency, followed by a comparison of the fundamental principles of counter-insurgency among the British, US and Indian Armies. The inclusion and deliberations on the fundamental principles will be of immense use to the future military leaders in India to understand the political nature of the conflict, the need to isolate the insurgents, mobilise the people, ensure restraint in the use of coercive force, operate within the ambit of the Constitution and the law of the land, and work towards unity of effort/command augmented by real-time intelligence support. Nanavatty warns the readers that despite the terms "unified command" and joint civil-military responsibility finding mention in the Indian doctrine, the government fights shy of taking steps that will ensure the "unity of effort."

The Indian experience related to insurgency with a detailed tabulated analysis of current internal armed conflicts taking place in India. A summary of the Indian Constitution highlighting all the relevant Articles, emergency provisions of the Constitution, empowerment of the government to deploy the "armed forces of the union" is very helpful to understand the role of the Constitution within which the armed forces of the union must function without violation of human rights. It has an interesting observation advocating:

In India, while the severity of the law may well invite criticism, the security forces – state police forces, CRPF and the army – acting in 'good faith' and within the parameters of the Constitution and domestic law must be seen as only doing their duty, by their country, in internal armed conflict.

The role of the Army is exhaustively treated, with the clarity that its function and empowerment to contain internal armed conflict have to be achieved within the framework of the Constitution, though it (Army) views this as its "secondary and less important role" as compared to its primary role "to counter external threats and to defend the country against external forces' aggression and help the civil and state government in time of need". Nanavatty truthfully records his own difference of opinion with Gen N C Vij, then Chief of the Army Staff, on the erection of the man-made obstacle in the form of the 750-km-long permanent wire-based obstacle system along the Line of Control (LoC) in Jammu and Kashmir (J&K) state to contain infiltration, and accepts that "as things turned out, he (Vij) was proved right". The author is equally frank and candid while placing his views on the state's response to insurgency. He records the views of KPS Gill that "the Indian state is sluggish in its response to an emerging internal conflict situation." He further points out that "the absence of joint military doctrine impacts every aspect of the government's campaign (against insurgency). He, hence, advises the formulation and articulation of a joint civil-military doctrine for the conduct of counter-insurgency operations.

7

Myths Shattered in India

The Maharashtra government's 'Memo-randum of Action to be Taken (ATR) by government' in response to the report of the Srikrishna Commission of Inquiry, reiterates the familiar Hindutvawaadi version of the factors responsible for the riots:

"Mumbai is the economic and commercial capital of the country and hence inimical forces were at work, both inside (read Muslims) and outside (read Pakistan's ISI) the country, had planned to destroy the economic base of the country by fomenting trouble (December 1992 and January 1993 riots). This line of reasoning is amply borne out by the subsequent events of March 1993". (Pg. 243, para25)

"Anti–national Muslim forces, within and outside the country, instigated these communal riots, continued them for a long period and carried out serial bomb blasts on March 12, 1993". (Pg.242, para 18)

"A series of stabbings (in January 1993) and these two incidents (the killing of Mathadi workers on January and the burning to death of a Hindu family in Radhabai Chawl in Jogeshwari on January 8, 1993) worried the Hindus about their future and a spontaneous reaction for self–protection followed." (Pg. 242, para20)

The ATR has been submitted by a government led by a party several of whose top leaders — including the party chief, Bal Thackeray and Chief Minister, Manohar Joshi — and a large number of whose workers have been indicted for their role in the violence. It is hardly surprising then that the ATR engages in a perversion of discourse that is typical of the Shiv Sena — no evidence to substantiate the prevarications. In keeping with this party's utter contempt and disregard for constitutional authority and the judiciary, there is not even a token attempt to deal with the series of serious cases and instances enumerated in the report. Instead of applying itself to the issue by issue findings of the Judge, the ATR merely reiterates the series of generalisations that the Shiv Sena and Hindutva combine always use to cloud their criminal acts, generalisations for which neither the party nor the state could offer any worthwhile evidence before the Commission of Inquiry.

The ISI bogey

A significant contribution of the Justice Srikrishna Commission report is that it debunks the unsubstantiated theory peddled by the Sena–BJP–RSS combine — and conveniently accepted by the then Congress government and the administration — that the Mumbai riots in December 1992–January 1993 and the serial bomb blasts in March 1993 were part of a common design and were the result of a Pakistan–inspired ISI (Inter Services Intelligence) conspiracy to de–stabilise India.

This argument has been used repeatedly to justify acts of venom and violence unleashed by Sena leaders and their cadres on sections of Bombay's minorities on the ground that they were carried out in self–defence and were "retaliatory" in character. Soon after the violence of December 1992–January 1993, Gopinath Munde, then leader of the Opposition in the state assembly, and presently the deputy chief minister of Maharashtra (BJP) had alleged that it was the areas infested by the 'infiltrators' from Bangladesh and Pakistan (read Muslim–dominated areas) that had provoked the violence in Mumbai. This theory has been conclusively exposed as malicious by the Commission of Inquiry since no witness, including the Shiv Sena Member of Parliament, Madhukar Sarpotdar, was able to provide any evidence to substantiate this spurious version. (Pg. 165, para 21.42). As to how widely prevalent this theory was is evident from the fact that even the then Governor of Maharashtra, C. Subramanium, had made an entirely unsubstantiated statement alleging a foreign hand behind the riots. (Pg. 220, para 1.21 & Pg.222, para 2.13).

In Chapter VI, Volume 1 of the report that deals with this issue, Justice Srikrishna has concluded that a causative link is in evidence between the two riots and the bomb blasts: "Tiger Memon, the key figure in the serial bomb blasts case, and his family had suffered extensively during the riots and therefore can be said to have deep–rooted motives for revenge. It would appear that one of his trusted accomplices, Javed Dawood Tailor alias Javed Chikna, had also suffered a bullet injury during the riots and therefore he also had a motive for revenge".

The Judge adds: "Apart from these two specific cases, there was a large, amorphous body of angry, frustrated and desperate Muslims keen to seek revenge for the perceived injustice done to and atrocities perpetrated on them or to others of their community and it is this sense of revenge which spawned the conspiracy of the serial bomb blasts. This body of angry, frustrated and desperate Muslims provided the material upon which the anti–national and criminal elements succeeded in building up their conspiracy for the serial bomb blasts." (Pg. 45, Term No.VII, para iii).

After the terms of reference of the Srikrishna Commission were expanded to investigate the "common design" between the riots of 1992–1993 and the serial bomb blasts of 1993, the Commission by an order dated January 22, 1997 directed the government of Maharashtra to disclose the material available before it in this context. By an affidavit of the Additional Chief Secretary (Home) dated February 5, 1997, the Commission was informed that all the material in the possession of the government on this issue had already been disclosed in the affidavits of former Mumbai Police Commissioner, Amarjit Singh Samra, former Additional Commi-ssioner, Mumbai, Vasant Narsingrao Deshmukh, head of investigators, CBI, Mahesh Narain Singh, former Mumbai Police Commissioner, Satish Sahney and two other police officers.

The deposition of Srikant Bapat — Police Commissioner of Mumbai during the riots of December 1992–January 1993 who has been directly and indirectly implicated for his inability in firmly putting down the violence — has been systematically examined and dissected by the Judge, especially with relation to his reluctance both in his affidavit and in court to dub the Shiv Sena as a communal organisation. This officer was also specifically examined by the Commission on the issue of an ISI hand in the two riots. According to his affidavit on oath, the ISI was a factor that contributed to the violence.

However, while in the witness box, Bapat could give no evidence to show that the disturbances which took place on December 6, 1992 "was the result of a tactical plan executed by the ISI, nor was there any material to show that the ISI was responsible for the disturbances in January 1993. All that Bapat has been able to say, in the true fashion of a trained intelligence officer, is that the de–stabilising activities of the ISI were going on for quite some time, but there was no material elicited from the interrogation of the accused in the riot–related cases to establish a link between such cases and ISI agents or destabilisers." (Pg. 197, para2.10).

In this context, the evidence of then Additional Commissioner, Mumbai, V.N. Deshmukh bears mention. This officer gave a singularly courageous testimony that has not only exposed the Sena–BJP combine after it came to power but has candidly admitted to a growing anti–Muslim bias in the Mumbai police force. When examined by the Commission on the ISI and its role, Deshmukh stated that there was "no material to suggest that Pakistani elements were supplying arms and ammunition to Muslims in Bombay to engineer communal riots in December 1992 and January 1993, though a general intelligence input was given by the ministry of Home Affairs, Government of India, that a band of commandos were likely to infiltrate into India to avenge the demolition of the Babri Masjid". But, Deshmukh, "had not come across any information from any of the police stations that they had been able to identify such commandos amongst the accused rounded up preventively or in substantive offences, nor had he come across material suggesting that any of the accused had been motivated by Pakistani elements". (Pg. 200, para 4.2).

The Commission also issued a public notice in newspapers calling upon all members of the public to disclose on affidavit any information that they may have in connection with this term of reference. The only affidavit filed in response to this notice was one filed by Prabhakar V. Pradhan dated August 2,1995. No further evidence in support of this "common design" theory, repeatedly peddled by the Sena and its partners, was forwarded before the Commission. Neither the Sena, nor the police, nor any other section of government or the public has been able to convincingly substantiate this theory.

The Judge, while commenting on this affidavit says that the affidavit filed by Prabhakar V. Pradhan "appears to be based on rumours and does not really indicate any concrete material which would be of use to the Commission. All that he says is that he had casually bumped into someone who claimed that the serial bomb blasts were the handiwork of Central Intelligence Agency (CIA) of USA and not the outcome of revenge of Muslims because of the demolition of the Babri Masjid or the riots of December 1992–January 1993".

"The Commission feels that the contents of the affidavit appear to be sheerly speculative."(Pg. 43, Term No.VI, para–i).

No further evidence was led by the proponents of the Pakistan–ISI mega–conspiracy theory to substantiate it. The evidence of senior police officers doesn't provide further insight. Neither the earlier Congress(I) government, nor the Shiv Sena either as a party or as the senior partner in government since March 1995, has been able to offer the Commission any proof of allegations of an ISI–inspired mega–conspiracy. Enough time was provided by the Commission to furnish any evidence that may have existed. The solitary affidavit submitted from advocate Prabhakar Pradhan has been debunked by Justice Srikrishna on the grounds that it is based on hearsay. Yet, in the ATR, the government reiterates the role of the ISI of Pakistan in instigating the riots and cites "increasing fundamentalism" as a cause of the riots. This is in keeping with the sustained policy of communal organisations to peddle theories that cannot be substantiated through either intelligence reports or other evidence. The Judge has clearly ruled against the state's version of a conspiracy theory while remarking on the causative link — embittered Muslims seeking revenge — between the December 1992 and January 1993 violence and the serial bomb blasts. The ATR twists this observation of the Commission to claim that the Judge has accepted the conspiracy theory and common design. (Pg. 247).

Who cast the first stone?

The importance of Justice Srikrishna's report however, goes far beyond debunking the ISI–conspiracy theory. The report details how, nationwide and in Mumbai particularly, the Shiv Sena–RSS–BJP combine kept the atmosphere on the boil through provocative and incendiary speeches from July 1992 onwards in preparation for the demolition in Ayodhya on December 6, 1992. Following these preparations, it was Hindus led by the Shiv Sena who first came out on the streets on December 6, 1992 to celebrate their "victory". During the processions and celebrations, provocative and threatening anti–Muslim slogans were shouted. The Mumbai police allowed this to happen before, on and after December 6, 1992 unchecked.

This is the second element of consistent distortion, surrounding communal discourse in general and the Mumbai riots in particular that the report exposes. The report thoroughly investigates, documents and thereafter passes judicial comment upon the manner in which communal sentiments were kept on the boil by the BJP and its allies in the sangh parivar for six months prior to the demolition of the mosque at Ayodhya on December 6, 1992.

At the national level, BJP leader L.K. Advani, and his rath yatra that left a trail of bloody riots in its wake all over India, is held responsible by the Judge for the divisive and polarised atmosphere. (Pg. 4, para 2.3).

Within Mumbai, it was the local leaders of the saffron combine who from July 1992 to December 1992, systematically held street and community–level meets whose sole aim was to spit venom and ire against the Muslim community while the ostensible campaign was the building of a Ram temple at Ayodhya. (Pg. 4, para 2.4). An indifferent government and an equally callous administration failed to act decisively to prevent these attempts at deliberate and systematic provocation.

The Judge elucidates how particularly from July 1992 onwards these obviously political campaigns were charged by slogans like,

"Is desh me rahana hoga, to Vande Mataram bolna hoga". Frequently, Ram Paduka proces-sions and Ghantanaad ceremonies (mobilisation rallies and victory celebrations) were used by Hindutvawaadi parties to polarise sections of the Hindu community on the issue. In both these sections, the report has also commented in some detail on the communal activities by Muslim organisations in response to the Ramjanmabhoomi movement that vitiated the atmosphere further. In this context the Student's Islamic Movement of India (SIMI) and the Bombay Muslim Action Committee have been mentioned.

V.N. Deshmukh's evidence offers a senior police officer's perspective on the communal tension that surrounded the kar seva. Deshmukh admitted that "from the day kar seva in Ayodhya was announced, though the police were expecting trouble, they had no idea as to the exact nature of the trouble. From July 1992 there was an undercurrent leading to communal tension on account of several activities being organised to propagate the rival views on the Babri Masjid–Ram Janmabhoomi dispute". (Pg. 200, para 4.3).

In several of the religious activities organised by the Bharatiya Janata Party and Shiv Sena, even long before December 6, 1992, slogans like "Garv se kaho hum Hindu hain" and "Hindustan Hinduonka, nahi kisike baap ka" were shouted and saffron and green flags were displayed prominently at different places. Deshmukh also stated that during this period of July to November 1992, "some of the speeches made by the leaders of Shiv Sena in public meetings which were well attended, particularly by young people, were abusive towards Muslims". (Pg. 200, para 4.3).

This understanding of the motives and functioning of communal parties and organisations is particularly critical given the historical specificity and timing of the report. Not only does the party held responsible for igniting the communal cauldron nationwide head a coalition government at the Centre, the Union Home Minister, L.K. Advani, has been named as an agent provocateur by the Judge (Pg 4, para 2.3). Locally, units of the Sena, BJP, VHP and Bajrang Dal do not escape the Judge's censure. Sena chief, Bal Thackeray, and MP Madhukar Sarpotdar, apart from middle–rung Sena leaders stand similarly indicted. The image of angry and violent Muslims inviting state wrath after December 6, 1992 has been fairly deeply ingrained in the psyche of a section of Mumbaiites. In the section that deals with the causes behind the two phases of riots, the report says that as far as the first phase in December is concerned, the immediate causes were, "the demolition of the Babri Masjid", "the aggravation of Muslim sentiments by the Hindus with their celebration rallies" and, "the insensitive and harsh approach of the police while handling the protesting mobs which initially were not violent". (Pg. 20, para 1.26)

But at 2.30 p.m. on December 6, 1992, the first communal incident that took place in Mumbai after the demolition of the mosque at Ayodhya was in Dharavi, where it was not angry Muslims but rampaging Shiv Sainiks led by Sena leaders Baburao Mane and Ramkrishna Keni who caused the first provocation. The local police allowed Shiv Sainiks to conduct a cycle rally of 200–300 persons. The rally passed through several communally–sensitive, Muslim–dominated areas in Dharavi and terminated at Kala Killa, where a meeting was held and addressed by the local activists of the Shiv Sena. Provocative speeches were made at this meeting. (Pgs. 7, 94 & 197)

Besides, Dharavi was kept simmering by the local wings of both the Bharatiya Janata Party and the Shiv Sena through Ram Paduka Poojan Karyakrams and chowk sabhas between July and December 1992. Two Muslim organisations, the Tanzeem–Allah–o–Akbar and the Dalit–Muslim Suraksha Sangh, also organised meetings in the period of the run–up to the kar seva.

The speeches made by Hindutvawaadi speakers at one particular meeting held in Dharavi on October 18, 1992 have been held by the Judge to be "communally provocative in their militant exhortation to Hindus that they were insecure at the hands of outsiders (Muslims). The police appear to have condoned it on the ground that there was nothing objectionable in those speeches per se as no problem of law and order entailed".

"A pamphlet was circulated in Tamil on October 12, 1992 in which it was emphasised that Muslims had an ancestry of invaders who had come to this country with the sole purpose of plundering it and expanding their religious interests. Neither the local police nor the SB–I, CID seems to have taken such things seriously". (Pg 92, para 10.5)

The ATR has dismissed the first communal incident that took place in Dharavi saying that "the said rally was not to celebrate the demolition of the Babri mosque but a pre–scheduled rally for construction of Ram temple" without addressing the findings in the report of the criminal actions undertaken during this rally. The fact that such mobilisations were used as occasions to spit venom and raise provocative slogans against the Muslim minority as documented by the report in the sections referred to above, in which the Shiv Sena, BJP, RSS, VHP and Bajrang Dal actively participated, have escaped any comment by the state government. (Pg. 240)

A detailed reading of Volume II of the report reveals important instances about similarly provocative rallies, meets and processions held in various parts of Mumbai on December 6, 1992 by the saffron combine after the demolition at Ayodhya. Given the surcharged atmosphere, these were nothing short of provocative. The police administration and the state government committed a fatal error by failing to act decisively against the organisers even at this late stage.

To cite a few of these instances:

Byculla: Between August and December 1992, constant programmes of Ram Paduka Poojans and Ghantanaad ceremonies were organised by the BJP and the VHP to focus attention of Hindus on the Ramjanma-bhoomi issue. (Pg. 67, para 5.33).

Dongri : Not just a communally sensitive area but also a part of south Mumbai, notorious for housing sections of the underworld. Dongri saw a Lalkar Ghantanaad Karyakaram organised by the VHP on December 6, 1992. Preceded by a chowk sabha organised by the VHP a day earlier. This "victory celebration" was also not dispersed by the Senior Inspector of Police. The reason he gave the Commission for his conduct was that it was a religious procession exempted from the order banning assembly and processions. (Pgs. 106–107).

Jogeshwari: A communally–sensitive zone in north Mumbai. The period between October to December 1992 saw hectic activities on the part of both communally–mobilised Hindus and Muslims, extolling their respective points of view on the Ramjanmabhoomi movement. Many activities like Ram Paduka processions and corner meetings, organised by the BJP, VHP and the Bajrang Dal, were held appealing to Hindus to participate in the kar seva at Ayodhya. A victory ghantanaad ceremony was also held here on December 6, 1992. (Pg. 125, para 14.4).

Pydhonie: A section of south Mumbai that has a strong element of the both Hindu communal parties and the Muslim League. Between July–December 1992, Hindutva-waadi parties like the Bharatiya Janata Party, Vishwa Hindu Parishad (VHP), Bajrang Dal and Shiv Sena stepped up their campaign in support of the construction of a Ram temple at the spot where the Babri Masjid stood. Though the police maintained that the peace in the area was very fragile, it appeared to have moved no muscle to prevent such activities on the facile ground that these were harmless "religious activities". In one such activitiy, organised on 23rd October 1992, a Shri Ram Paduka procession was taken out by the VHP. Dnyaneshwar Thorat of VHP and the local Shiv Sena Shakha Pramukh Hemant Koli and others accompanied the procession which wended its way through Muslim–dominated areas. At its termination a speech was given by one Praful Desai during the course of which he emphasised that the procession was not "a shobha yatra" but was intended to bring out the Ram which was concealed in the minds of the people and Ramdrohis should not be allowed to go alive. "No action appears to have been taken by the police in respect of the speech delivered by Praful Desai. There cannot be any doubt that the said speech was communally provocative, the implication being that people who obstructed the construction of a Ram temple at Ayodhya were Ramdrohis and, therefore, they should not be allowed to live. (Pg. 171, para 23.5).

The ATR is completely silent on this incident and similar actions of certain sections that include the Shiv Sena, BJP, Bajrang Dal and VHP in leading provocative mobilisations prior to December 6, 1992 that contributed to a heightening of communal temper all over Mumbai.

"The police appear to be either naive, gullible or partisan in ignoring the dangerous implications of speeches of this kind. That this kind of propaganda was carried out from July to October 1992 is not in dispute. It is obvious that the atmosphere in the Pydhonie area became communally charged on account of the continuous barrage of propagandist processions, meetings, speeches and other activities of the Hindutvawaadi parties. This resulted in the atmosphere being so charged that it needed but a spark to ignite and explode". (Pg.171–172, para 23.5).

R.A.K. Marg: In central Mumbai, this area that experienced brutal violence in both December 1992 and January 1993 had also been held to ransom by communally proactive elements led by the BJP and VHP. Right from July that year they held repeated Ram Paduka programmes, corner sabhas, cycle rallies. Even on December 6, 1992 a ghantanaad ceremony was held to celebrate the demolition of the mosque. (Pg. 177, para 24.7).

Myth of the Hindu backlash

The third malicious element of commu-nal propaganda visible in Mumbai during the relevant period has been the theory of "a Hindu backlash in retaliation" in response to heinous acts against Hindus, like the burning alive of a family in a Jogeshwari slum (Radhabai Chawl incident) preceded by the murder of Mathadi workers. This theory of "Hindu retaliation", led by "Hinduhriday-samrat" Bal Thackeray, that gained wide sway and currency during and after the violence in Mumbai is rooted in Hindu communal discourse of yore. An examination of all judicial Commission reports in post–Independence India since the first major riot in Jabalpur in 1961, shows that the perverted discourse around "Who cast the first stone?" has been maliciously used by Hindu communal organisations — be it the RSS, Jana Sangh, the Sena or the BJP — to justify their blatantly aggressive acts. In every communal riot situation, this discourse points to violent acts of Muslims as being the flashpoint for that violence. This selective discourse conceals the systematic and deliberate provocation of the minority community — through hate–writing, provocative slogans and incendiary and insulting allegations for weeks and sometimes even months preceding the outbreak of violence.

The reason why the spurious theory of a "backlash" gained such wide currency during Mumbai riots was simply because even a Congress(I) Chief Minister, Sudhakarrao Naik and Mumbai Police Commissioner, Srikant Bapat, bought this theory and responded to the violence based not on an appreciation of the ground reality but on a deliberately misinterpreted representation of events.

Justice Srikrishna, commenting on the second phase of riots in January 1993, categorically rejects that it was merely a backlash of the Hindus because of the cases of stabbing, the murder of Mathadi workers and the Radhabai Chawl incident. He observes: "The events which took place between the period 12th December 1992 and 5th January 1993 indicate that there were attacks going on against the Muslims and their properties in different areas". (Pg. 20, para 1.27–ii).

On December 20, 1993, two Muslims were locked in a room and the room set alight within the Goregaon jurisdiction; due to the severe burns suffered one of the victims died.

On the night of December 24–25, 1992 one Mathadi worker was killed; though subsequent police investigations revealed the identity of the criminal to be an alchoholic, the communal atmosphere and communal outfits interpreted that the killing was done by a Muslim.

The Mahaartis launched by the Sena-BJP combine from December 26, 1992 added to the communal tension, endangering the fragile peace which had been established. Some of the Mahaartis were later used as occasions for delivering communally–inciting speeches; the crowds dispersing from the Mahaartis indulging in damage, looting and arson of Muslim establishments on the way. The Mahaartis continued unabated with no restriction on them being imposed by the police throughout January 1993 and came to an end only by the first week of February 1993.

There were also several stabbing incidents carried out by professional criminals in different areas of the city, with the intention of whipping up communal frenzy, in which the majority of the victims happened to be Hindus The stabbings appeared to be executed with professional accuracy intended to kill the victims.

The killers had not been then identified in several cases, though it was presumed, at least in the cases where the Hindus were victims, that the killers were Muslims. The motive for the stabbings appears to have been to whip up communal frenzy between Hindus and Muslims. Some of the Muslim criminal elements operating in South Bombay, like Salim Rampuri and Firoz Konkani, have been identified as the brains behind the stabbing incidents. That they were criminals was underplayed by Hindus; that they were Muslims was all that mattered, and a cry went up that the Muslims were bent upon a second round of riots.

On January 1, 1993, an article appeared in the Shiv Sena organ edited by Bal Thackeray, Saamna, under the heading "Hindunni Akramak Vhayala Have" (Hindus must become aggressors), openly inciting Hindus to violence.

On January 2, 1993 a number of Muslim hutments in M.P. Mill compound within the Tardeo jurisdiction of south Mumbai were set on fire. On the same day, there was an incident in Dharavi where two Muslims were assaulted with iron rods.

On January 3, 1993 there was an attack on a Muslim in Dharavi jurisdiction with a knife. On the same day, several persons claiming to be officials of MHADA, and alleged to be Shiv Sainiks, went around Pratiksha Nagar in Antop Hill jurisdiction surveying the residences of Muslims there.

On January 4, 1993 a big mob of Hindus, led by Shri Gajanan Kirtikar, Shri Ramesh More and other Shiv Sena activists, took a morcha to the Jogeshwari Police Station complaining of lack of security for Hindus. Some of the people in the morcha attacked Chacha Nagar Masjid and the Muslims in the vicinity and injured them. Several Muslim huts in Magdum Nagar in Mahim jurisdiction were set on fire by Hindus.

On the night of January 5, 1993 a Mathadi worker employed in the godown of Vijay Transport Company who was sleeping in the godown went to the street to relieve himself. Suddenly, he was set upon by miscreants who stabbed him to death. Three more Mathadi workers who came out of the godown to help him were also stabbed to death. The murders of the Mathadi workers created tremendous tension in the area. The Mathadi Workers' Union called for a bandh. Huge meetings were held which were addressed by leaders of Mathadi Unions. Speeches were made during this meeting to condemn the police and Government for their ineffectiveness with exhortations that Hindus might have to pick up swords to defend themselves if the police failed to protect them. At the time when these murders of Mathadi workers took place, neither the police, nor the public, had a clue as to the identity of the killers, which came to be established much later. Nonetheless, the Hindus spearheaded by the Shiv Sena kicked up a furore that the murders had been committed by Muslims, virtually giving a call for arms. On January 5 –6, 1993 the Mathadi workers gave a call for bandh of wholesale markets, which also gave immense publicity to the murders of the Mathadis, allegedly by Muslims.

On January 6, 1993, the situation in Mahim went out of control at 9 p.m. Hindus attacked Muslims in Muslim pockets in Mahim area led by Shiv Sena Corporator, Milind Vaidya, and a police constable, Sanjay Gawade, openly carrying a sword. There were serious riots in which frenzied mobs of Hindus and Muslims attacked each other.

Which incident among the list of horrors listed above was worse than the other? Should the Radhabai Chawl incident be elevated to a special category? The only thing that can be said for such selective projections that elevate one tragedy above others and relegate others to mere statistic is that it is poor comment indeed on the times that we live in. When the injury to a victim is measured by whether he/she is Hindu or Muslim and the veracities of testimonies are similarly upheld or dismissed.

Commenting on Bapat's affidavit and testimony, the Judge remarks: "Even the state government and the police were sold on the theory that the Hindu backlash came on account of the said gruesome incidents. Though Bapat has been quick to point out these incidents in his affidavit, he claimed total ignorance with regard to several equally gruesome incidents in which Muslims were victims, which were put to him in his cross–examination." (Pg. 197, Para 2.14).

"For example, he seemed either not to recollect, or be unaware, of the arson of a timber mart in Ghatkopar jurisdiction on December 15, 1992 resulting in four Muslims being burnt alive, an arson in Goregaon jurisdiction on December 20, 1992 in which one of the Muslims was burnt and killed, of the attack on Muslim hutments in M.P. Mill compound on January 2,1993 and large–scale arson of Muslim hutments on January 4, 1993 in Mahim jurisdiction and the morcha led by Shiv Sena leaders Shri Ramesh More and Shri Gajanan Kirtikar to Jogeshwari police station, en route causing havoc in Chacha Nagar and damaging the Chacha Nagar Masjid, of the arson of a taxi carrying two Muslims which was burnt causing their death on January 7,1993 in Antop Hill jurisdiction and the Devipada incident of January 12, 1994 in which two Muslim ladies were stripped naked and attacked by a mob and one lady and her uncle were murdered and burnt." (Pg. 197, para 2.14).

The Judge further observes: "There is legitimate grievance made by the Muslims that the memory and information of Shri Bapat is either selective or that he had been selectively fed with only such material to be placed before the Commission as would suit a particular theory being advanced by the State Government and the police. Bapat also claimed not to know that Shiv Sainiks under the leadership of local Shiv Sena leaders Baburao Mane and Ramkrishna Keni had taken out a celebration cycle rally in Dharavi jurisdictional area (on December 6, 1992) which went around the Muslim areas shouting abusive and provoking slogans during which a stone was thrown at a local Mosque, though he claimed that, if such an incident had happened and reported to him, he would have certainly shown it as the first in the series of incidents referred to in paragraph 42 of his affidavit. Despite the material on record in the concerned case (C.R.No.718 of 1992) showing clearly that the celebration rally/procession had been organised by Shiv Sena, to deny, as Bapat did, the role of Shiv Sena in the riots, is ignoring the obvious." (Pg. 197, para 2.15).

Shiv Sena MP, Madhukar Sarpotdar had in his deposition before the Commission defended his party's philosophy of retaliation even saying that "when incidents against Hindus took place in one part of Mumbai, acts of retaliation against innocent Muslims in other parts was justified." Sarpotdar had also said that as a senior leader of the Shiv Sena he could say that this was the philosophy of his party as well.

A significant section of the ATR is devoted to the murder of the Mathadi workers and the Radhabai Chawl incident. The ATR reiterates the retaliation theory: "when action and reaction are taking place rapidly, it is difficult to investigate as to where they started." The ATR also supports Bal Thackeray's rejection of the interview given to Time magazine but makes no attempt to deal with the provocative and incendiary writings of Thackeray in his mouthpiece, the Saamna, that have been relied upon by the Judge in his indictment of the Sena chief.

No attention has been paid to the incidents listed by the Judge that prove that right from December 20, 1992 till January 5, 1993, stray but gruesome incidents of violence continued unabated where members of both communities were victims. The government is utterly silent on specific instances of brutality that by their very chronology explode the theory that it was the selective targeting of Hindus on January 5–6 and on January 8, 1993 that were responsible for the Hindu backlash. The attitude of the government as reflected in the ATR is uncaring of the enormous loss of life and property that took place during the riots since it merely limits itself to justifying the Shiv Sena's own role in the violence.

Mahaartis

Another misconception surrounds the motives behind the launching of the Mahaarti programme launched by the Sena–BJP combine in the midst of the December 1992 and January 1993 phase of riots. A close look at how this misconception took firm root in the minds of a large section of the people illustrates how communal propaganda plays upon real or assumed aggravations, irritations, and images of the 'Other' and then, at the critical time of a riot, misuses this aggravation by locating it in the current crisis which is an inflamed street atmosphere and again, garners widespread support for that misinterpretation of events.

The issue of Friday prayers, Jumma ki namaaz, taking place on public roads, often blocking road traffic or access of railway commuters to local train stations was here the aggravation. The reason for the spilling over of worshippers into the street was the lack of adequate permission (extra FSI) to build more floors atop mosques. Using this issue as their raison d'etre, the Hindutvawaadis chose a raw and communally–tense Mumbai to launch their programme of Mahaartis that far from being religious incantations were in fact part of the dangerous, Tu-tu, mein-mein ('Us' versus 'Them') syndrome. The Mahaartis were cynically used as launching pads to attack Muslim homes and establishments after violent and provocative slogans against 'laandyas' (an abusive term for a circumcised person) had been raised.

The Shiv Sena–BJP combine chose December 26, 1992, to launch this programme when Mumbai was still tense, still reeling from the ghastly memories of early December.The police remained complacent as the mobs went on the rampage. However, a similar attempt to misuse the programme of Mahaartis was nipped in the bud in Nashik in north Maharashtra (around 200 kms. from Mumbai) where the Police Commissioner banned the programmes outright. (Pgs. 12, para 1.7–iii & Pg. 222, para 2.14).

The Srikrishna Commission report documents in detail this ploy of the Sena–BJP combine in Mumbai aided by an acquiescent state and police administration:

Bhoiwada Police Station: Interrogation of many of the accused Shiv Sainiks from central Mumbai suggests that after the crowd dispersed from the Mahaarti held on January 7, 1993 at Parel T.T, the dispersing crowd indulged in systematic stone–throwing at Muslim establishments along the lane. The Hindu accused stated during interrogation that the crowd returning from Mahaarti held on January 9, 1993 at 7.30 p.m. at Hanuman Mandir on Dadasaheb Phalke Road had attacked the Muslim establishments (C.R.No.34 of 1993). (Pg. 61, para 4.11).

Byculla Police Station: This is another area where the Mahaartis led to violence on January 9, 1993 when participants in the Mahaarti after dispersing indulged in burning and looting Muslim homes and shops. The local police resisted admitting this before the Judge despite evidence that two of the five Mahaartis had been permitted during curfew hours. This is another example of the local police station under the influence and sway of local Shiv Sainiks failing to act against them. (Pg. 70).

D.B. Marg Police Station: Eleven Mahaartis were held within this jurisdiction between December 1992 and January 1993 but the one held at the Kabirwadi Hanuman Mandir on January 9, 1993 has received special mention by the Judge. The Mill Diary of the police for that day records how the crowds dispersing from the Mahaarti turned violent and looted and burnt Muslim shops and establishments but the Senior Inspector Bhakare refused to admit the veracity of police records and record anything that is damaging to the Shiv Sena. (Pgs. 78-79).

Gamdevi Police Station: Nine Mahaartis were held in this area, all organised by the Shiv Sena and the BJP, and all during curfew hours. The Commission has noted first, the extreme reluctance of the Senior Police Inspector, Madhukar Ghorpade, to admit who the organisers were. Communal incidents took place after each Mahaarti, yet no action was taken even after, in one instance, 86 establishments were ransacked and looted. (Pg. 119, para 12.4).

L.T. Marg Police Station: Eighteen Mahaartis were held between January 8 and 18, 1993. After the Radhabai Chawl incident in Jogeshwari, exaggerated and incendiary rumours were spread and after the Mahaartis were launched, there were repeated incidents of Hindu mobs roaming on the streets, looting and ransacking shops and setting goods on fire. (Pg. 145–146).

Mahim Police Station: On January 9, 1993, a Mahaarti was held blocking all road traffic and yet no action was taken by the local police to stop it. Prakash Ayare, the local corporator of the Shiv Sena gave a speech after this Mahaarti. He said that the programme of Mahaartis was being held under the directions of Balasaheb Thackeray and that, because the government was partial to one particular community, Mahaartis would be held to continue to draw attention to the government. The Judge remarks, "Surprisingly, even against the background of acute communal tension prevalent on January 9, 1993, this type of speech was being allowed by the police and not being considered communally provocative. (Pg. 153–154).

Tardeo Police Station: On January 9, 1993, a Mahaarti was held at the Hanuman Mandir organised by the BJP and the Shiv Sena, with the VHP and the Bajrang Dal in the background. It was admitted by all police officers who gave evidence that despite there being tension in the area and the existence of a source report issued by SB–I CID, that the persons returning from the Mahaartis were likely to damage Muslim homes and establishments and homes while dispersing, there was no attempt by the police to stop the Mahaarti from taking place. (Pgs. 189–190).

Senior leaders of the Shiv Sena, including Maharashtra Chief Minister, Manohar Joshi (Pg. 228) and MP, Madhukar Sarpotdar participated in the Mahaartis that were provocative mobilisations. The report also documents the state and police attitude towards Mahaartis as exposed through the evidence recorded of then chief minister Sudhakarrao Naik and then Police Commissioner Bapat:

Naik said on oath before the Judge that he considered the programme of Mahaartis an entirely religious affair and therefore he could not ban them. Subsequently he admitted that the political content of the Mahaartis that started as a religious activity increased as they gained momentum. (Pg. 218, para 1.7).

"Bapat's attempt to equate the problem created during Namaaz on public streets to the problems created by Mahaartis organised by the Hindutva parties, was amusing. It is nobody's case that the practice of Namaaz on the streets was started recently or that Namaaz on the streets was being carried out deliberately with a view to gain political benefits; with the Mahaartis, the avowed and declared object was to pressurise the Government to force the Muslims to stop calling Azaan on the loudspeakers and to stop doing Namaaz on the public streets. That the Mahaartis which started off with such clear political objectives could have been considered to be "per se religious" and exempted from the operation of the ban orders by the Commissioner, strains credulity. Bapat realised that the occasions of Mahaartis were being used for making provocative speeches and shouting provocative slogans and appealed to the Government to solve the problem. However, the Government dilly–dallied till it was too late." (Pg. 198, para 2.18).

Here again, the ATR restricts itself to reiterating the Sena–BJP's official position that the Mahaartis were a "natural and spontaneous response of Hindus who were inconvenienced and irritated by the actions of Muslims in reading the Namaaz on the streets. The ATR has nothing to say to refute the conclusions put out by the Judge in the report that details instances of the Mahaartis leading to abusive and terrorising slogans, followed by acts of arson and the looting of Muslim homes and establishments. All this evidence has been garnered by the Judge through a perusal of the police records, testimonies of policemen and the evidence of ordinary witnesses. Shiv Sena leaders in general, and Prakash Ayare from Mahim in particular, have been named as guilty. Yet, except the general defence of Mahaartis, thegovernment has offered no comment on these indictments. The mala fide intent of the ATR becomes clear when on page after page it offers no explanation for the specific indictments.

Radhabai Chawl tragedy

While referring to the January 1993 phase of the riots, there is a blatant attempt by Hindu communal parties to magnify one incident that took place in a slum in Jogeshwari in north Mumbai in the early hours of January 8, 1993. A family with one male member and five female members were locked inside a chawl and it was set on fire. This one incident has been sensationalised and exaggerated, particularly by the Shiv Sena and Bal Thackeray to justify the "retaliation" of January 1993."

The Judge after detailing, how Mumbai was kept on the boil by targeted acts of violence against the minorities, ably assisted by the Mahaartis to mobilise mobs to go on the rampage, and systematic stabbings of Hindus by Muslim communal elements, concludes that "the communal passions of the Hindus were aroused to fever pitch by the inciting writings in print media, particularly Saamna and Navaakal which gave exaggerated accounts of the Mathadi murders and the Radhabai Chawl incident; rumours were floated that there were imminent attacks by Muslims using sophisticated arms.

These factors impelled some of the irresponsible and hot–headed Hindu elements to take to violence. "From January 8, 1993 at least there is no doubt that the Shiv Sena and Shiv Sainiks took the lead in organising attacks on Muslims and their properties under the guidance of several leaders of the Shiv Sena from the level of Shakha Pramukh to the Shiv Sena Pramukh Bal Thackeray who, like a veteran General, commanded his loyal Shiv Sainiks to retaliate by organized attacks against Muslims. The communal violence and rioting triggered off by the Shiv Sena was hijacked by local criminal elements who saw in it an opportunity to make quick gains. By the time the Shiv Sena realised that enough had been done by way of 'retaliation', the violence and rioting was beyond the control of its leaders who had to issue an appeal to put an end to it." (Pg. 20, para 1.27–ii).

Hundreds of incidents rocked Mumbai in December 1992. These were bestial in that they turned neighbour against neighbour, spurred as they were by hate–driven propaganda. While the systematic target of this venom were members of the Muslim minority, in larger number, both media reports of that period and Justice Srikrishna's report have documented how Muslims and Hindus alike fell victims to the violence. By attempting to magnify either the Radhabai Chawl case of arson and murder or the murder of Mathadi workers, the perpetrators of systematic venom have crudely obliterated the plight of scores of other victims of that period. Just a recount of some of the worst incidents that scarred Mumbai's image that have been documented by the Judge show that when communal violence is allowed to continue unchecked, it spares none in its wake:

December 12: Four dead bodies, all of Hindus, having multiple stab wounds on vital organs and in highly decomposed condition, were recovered from the gutter along A.K. Marg —Nirmal Nagar in Bandra–East. In yet another incident, one Hindu woman by name Shevantabai was found murdered with her throat slit and her body was dumped in the open compound of National Girls' High School adjoining Behrampada. Two more bodies, one of a male Hindu and another identified as that of a uniformed Muslim Police Constable attached to the Nasik Rural Police Head Quarters, were recovered from the septic tank of the public latrine in Behrampada on 20th and 21st December 1992 respectively. These bodies also bore multiple stab injuries. It would appear that there was a systematic attempt to stab and murder Hindus and the policeman, though a Muslim, became a victim of the anger of the Muslims directed against the uniform worn by him. (Pg. 159, para 21.18).

January: Though a hue and cry has been made by the Shiv Sena and the police about recoveries of the bodies of Hindus from the Behrampada area, there is another equally gruesome incident in which five persons from a family of Muslim hawkers were burnt to death by the rioters and their bodies were thrown into the fire to destroy the evidence. In fact, the situation in that incident is graphically described by the witness who says, "the Hindu miscreants were running through lanes and bye–lanes with swords and choppers, etc. and attacking houses of the Muslims and looting and burning the articles on the roads. Police were chasing them. However, the miscreants were taking advantage of lanes and bye–lanes and continuing their destructive activities". A sad commentary on the law and order situation. (Pg. 163, para 21.35).

January 1: "In January 1993, the first incident of communal disturbance occurred on January 1,1993 during which a mob of violent Hindus attacked Muslims behind Jaihind Nagar and Gausiya compound...and threw stones on vehicles plying the Western Express Highway ....probably the immediate target of attack was the Gausiya Masjid and the Muslim residents in close vicinity thereof and the police were attacked because they tried to prevent it.This attack is of some significance as it belies the theory of the Shiv Sena, the state and the police that the Hindus resorted to violence by way of retaliation only after the grisly Radhabai Chawl incident at Jogeshwari. (Pg. 159, para 21.19).

January 7: On January 7, 1993 a taxi in which three Muslims were travelling was set on fire in Pratikshanagar in the Antop Hill jurisdiction resulting in all the inmates being burnt alive. (Pg. 54, para 2.14).

January 9–12: Between January 9–January 12, 1993, a large number of Muslims numbering between 3,000–5,000 had abandoned their homes for fear of attacks from rampaging Shiv Sainiks and congregated on the road without shelter. They were surrounded by 40,000–60,000 Hindus and had to spend almost three days under constant fear of attack till they were rescued by an army column on January 12, 1993. Initially when an attempt was made to supply food to the marooned Muslims, the vehicles containing food were chased away. Finally when the army column was transporting the marooned Muslim families, it was also attacked and had to be dispersed by firing resorted to by army personnel. (Pg. 58, para 2.25).

January 10: There was a serious incident at the Hari Masjid in the RAK Marg jurisdiction on January 10, 1993 in central Mumbai in which six persons, all Muslims, were shot dead by the local police as they offered their Friday prayers and one Hindu died as a result of burns. (Pgs. 178–181).

January 12, 1993: A gruesome incident occurs in Devipada in Kasturba Marg jurisdiction (Borivali, Mumbai North). A Hindu mob surrounds, strips and assaults two Muslim women. The older woman manages to run away. The uncle of the younger woman who comes to rescue the young girl of 19, and that girl, are beaten and burnt alive by the violent mob. The names of the miscreants are disclosed to police by a Hindu lady in the locality. (Though the miscreants were arrested and tried by the Sessions Court at Bombay, later on they were all acquitted on the ground that the panchanamas were defective and that the eye–witnesses were not produced). (Pg. 16, para 1.15).

Once again, the ATR has turned a blind eye to copious details of cases listed in the Commission's report and has restricted itself to an exaggerated dealing with the Radhabai Chawl incident. There appears little stress or concern, as evidenced in the ATR, over a series of other gruesome incidents that occurred and many of which involved Shiv Sainiks.

Acts of Muslim Aggression

The Shiv Sena led by Bal Thackeray, MP, Madhukar Sarpotdar and other leaders like Gajanan Kirtikar and Milind Vaidya have been directly indicted in the Commission's report. The report which is unsparing of acts of Muslim aggression states however that there was no evidence to show that on the side of the minorities there was any single individual or organisation responsible for fomenting trouble.

The specific terms of reference, "whether any individual or group of individuals or any other organisations were responsible for such events and circumstances", the report states categorically: "As far as the December 1992 phase of the rioting by the Muslims is concerned, there is no material to show that it was anything other than a spontaneous reaction of leaderless and incensed Muslim mobs, which commenced as peaceful protest, but soon degenerated into riots. The Hindus must share a part of the blame in provoking the Muslims by their celebration rallies, inciting slogans and rasta rokos which were all organised mostly by Shiv Sainiks, and to a marginal extent by BJP activists.

For the January round of violence, the Shiv Sena has been held squarely to blame. Turning to the events of January 1993, the Commission's view is that though several incidents of violence took place during the period from 15th December 1992 to 5th January 1993, large–scale rioting and violence was commenced from 6th January 1993 by the Hindus, brought to fever pitch by communally inciting propaganda unleashed by Hindu communal organisations and writings in newspapers like Saamna and Navaakal.

It was taken over by Shiv Sena and its leaders who continued to whip up communal frenzy by their statements and acts and writings and directives issued by the Shiv Sena Pramukh Bal Thackeray. The attitude of Shiv Sena as reflected in the Time magazine interview given by Bal Thackeray and its doctrine of 'retaliation', as expounded by Shri Sarpotdar and Shri Manohar Joshi, together with the thinking of Shiv Sainiks that 'Shiv Sena's terror was the true guarantee of the safety of citizens', were responsible for the vigilantism of Shiv Sainiks. Because some criminal Muslims killed innocent Hindus in one corner of the city, the Shiv Sainiks 'retaliated' against innocent Muslims in other corners of the city.

"There is no material on record suggesting that even during this phase (January 1993) any known Muslim individuals or organisations were responsible for the riots, though a number of individual Muslims and Muslim criminal elements appear to have indulged in violence, looting, arson and rioting." (Pg. 22, para 1.2–ii). However, the report is unsparing of several individual acts of Muslim communalism and aggression unlike what the Maharashtra government would have the people believe:

Dharavi: "There were meetings held on October 21 and December 1, 1992 by the Muslims advocating protection of the Babri Masjid and opposing the construction of Ram Mandir at the disputed site at Ayodhya. These meetings were held in Naiknagar on L.B. Shastri Marg… One of the speeches advocated that if the Hindus were to snatch away the Babri Masjid from Muslims, there would be no stopping of disintegration of the country; that if Hindus were to build a Ram Mandir at Ayodhya and usher in Ram Rajya, then the Muslims would, through the Babri Masjid Committee, fly the green flag on the Red Fort at Delhi and rule the country.

Three activists of Tanzeem–Allah–o–Akbar, which organised some of the meetings, Hayatbhai, Sayyedbhai and Shakoorbhai were quite active during the violent incidents which took place on December 7, 1992.

In one of the meetings organized by the Muslims on November 15, 1992, one Maqsood Khan declared that 25 crores of Muslims in India would not remain passive without demanding and getting a partition of the country, as they would not like to remain slaves in this country. Once again, no action ensued, since the police considered that, though objectionable, the speeches were not actionable in law." (Pgs. 92–93, para 10.6).

l Deonar: "This is one police station jurisdiction where, during both phases of riots, the Muslims gave more than they took. During December 1992, police registered 36 cases of communal violence/rioting of which 18 cases were closed by classifying them in "A" summary and charge–sheets were filed in rest of the cases. In one case accused died after the charge–sheet was filed in the Court and the case abated. Out of the 36 cases registered by police, 19 cases were in connection with rioting and mob action and 17 pertained to assaults on individuals. The trouble began in December 1992 at about 9 p.m. on December 6, 1992 when mobs of Muslims started pelting stones at vehicles and BEST buses moving along the link road through Muslim dominated areas. At about 11 p.m. on the same day there was an attack on the house of one Gundeti, a local Bharatiya Janata Party activist and leader of Bharatiya Janata Party from Shivaji Nagar The interrogatory statements of the accused arrested in this case, which included two Hindus, suggest that the reason for the attack was the organising of several meetings in the area by Gundeti. There was also an attack on Shiva temple and Geeta Vikas School and an attack on Hanuman temple at Shivaji Nagar, Plot no.34. There was damage and attempted arson to Shiva temple and Geeta Vikas School. Hanuman temple in Shivaji Nagar was damaged completely and the idol of Hanuman was smashed to pieces. There was heavy stone pelting at the houses around the Hanuman temple. Though the police claimed that the Muslim mob had carried out heavy stone pelting at houses around the Hanuman Mandir in Shivaji Nagar, the panchanama recorded in C.R.No.895 of 1992 does not bear out this fact. Nor is there any reference in the FIR to attack on Hindu houses on Plot No. 34 in Shivaji Nagar." (Pg. 82, para 9.6).

Dongri: Is a predominantly Muslim area with the reputation of being communally–hypersensitive. It is also the haunt of several illegal activities including drug peddling."During the period 8th December 1992 to 31st December 1992, 23 cases of communal incidents were registered by the Dongri police station in which Hindus were aggressors in seven cases and Muslims were aggressors in 16 cases. Contrary to the police perception that during the December 1992 phase of the riots, it was only the Muslims who were aggressors, it appears that the Hindus also contributed their share towards riots and communal incidents during this period. Out of the seven cases in which Hindus were aggressors, four were cases in which Muslims were stabbed; in two cases there was looting and one involved looting and arson of a Muslim establishment. During the same period, out of the 16 cases in which Muslims were aggressors, nine were individual stabbing cases, and seven were cases of looting of different Hindu establishments." (Pg. 108, para 11.21).

Nagpada: "In the period between July–December 1992, there was a lot of activity by the Muslim organisations active in the area.

Students Islamic Movement of India (SIMI) and Bombay Muslim Committee were quite active during this period. On July 24, 1992, an Urdu blackboard was displayed by SIMI which contained extremely provocative writing. During November 15–26, 1992, many Muslim organisations had organised meetings on the Ayodhya–Babri Masjid issue. (Pg. 165, para 22.3).

Nirmal Nagar: "The fury of the Muslims (in December 1992) was directed against the Police Chowky at Behrampada Gate No.18, Police Chowky in Navpada and Ambewadi. Further up in the Golibar locality, against the Shakha of Shiv Sena and the Hindu shops located on the Golibar Road between Ambewadi Chowky and Adarsh Apartments. There was violent confrontation between armed Muslim mobs emerging from the kabrastan shouting anti–Hindu slogans and the police. In an incident of rioting at Indira Nagar the Muslim mobs attacked the Indira Nagar Police Chowky damaged it and set on fire articles inside the Chowky and a scooter of a police officer. There was also an incident of rioting near the Fish Market, Nehru Nagar, Bharani and Dawari Colony during which one Head Constable was assaulted and injured by a chopper wielded by the Muslim in a mob." (Pg. 159).

Mahim: "On December 25, 1992 a pamphlet in the Urdu language was distributed around Jama Masjid area in Mahim. This pamphlet, without doubt, is communally provocative and incites Muslims to fight against the atrocities committed on them by Hindus, starting with the demolition of Babri Masjid and calls upon the Muslims to resolve that, if the Babri Masjid had to be constructed with blood, they should be prepared to do so. The police have registered a case in this connection. Though there was a sizeable Muslim population in this area, the intelligence gathering machinery of police with regard to Muslim activities in this area was totally ineffective. There was only one Muslim police person attached to this police station, even he could not read Urdu and keep tabs on the activities of the Muslims in this area." (Pg. 151, para 19.13).

Pydhonie: Once the riots erupted in January 1993, several known criminals from the area, though undoubtedly Muslims, took advantage of the situation and fanned the fires of communal hatred. Groups led by Salim Rampuri, Abdul Rauf alias Rauf Chacha and others moved around the locality instigating the Muslim youths to come out and help in looting the godowns of Hindus. This area saw the circulation of pamphlets containing incendiary communal material urging Muslims to communal violence and also calls given on loudspeakers fixed on Masjids urging Muslims to come out in large numbers with arms and attack 'Kafirs'. The police has been remiss in not keeping tabs of the activities of known Muslim organistions, Jamait–E–Islam–E–Hind, Muslim League and SIMI (Students Islamic Movement of India), who were known to have participated in some of the previous protests. Similarly, no watch appears to have been kept nor intelligence gathered about the activity of Raza Academy. The slogans shouted by the mobs invariably indicated their anger at the police."

"During the first week of January 1993 there were several cases of stabbing incidents in which Hindus were stabbed after ascertaining their Hindu identity. Most of them have remained unsolved and classified in "A" summary by the Police. The Commission is inclined to think that these were deliberate attempts by professional killers with a view to whip up communal passions." (Pg. 175).

Once again the ATR has nothing to say on individual cases that illustrate/uphold the Commission's findings. Despite the fact that the Commission's report does not spare individual and sporadic acts of Muslim aggression and communal provocation, the ATR comments critically on the findings of the Judge wherein he says that no Muslim organisation was involved in both phases of riots. The only alternative that the ATR can offer is once again, the Pakistan–inspired ISI theory that has been rejected for lack of evidence already.

Police bias

A detailed reading of both volumes of the Justice Srikrishna Commission report is imperative to understand both the rank inefficiency and in–built anti–minority bias that has come to dictate the actions of a large section of our policemen. Erstwhile Police Commissioner of Mumbai, Srikant Bapat's testimony put to severe scrutiny and cross–examination by the Judge is extremely important in this regard. He states on oath not only that he believed January's violence to be the result of a "Hindu backlash", but compounds this unsubstantiated version with complete ignorance of incidents of brutality from December 1992 until January 1993 that were directed against the minorities.

The situation in Mumbai under a Congress(I) administration in December 1992–January 1993 smacked of utter anarchy as police station after police station remained impotent and in no sign of control, while large sections of the police personnel revealed a callous indifference to the plight of the city's minorities, in many cases even participating in blatant acts of criminal violence. In several areas it also appeared that local Shiv Sainiks were guiding the actions of policemen. In the few cases where local Shiv Sena shakha pramukhs were arrested, evidence from police records and the testimonies of policemen shows that, bowing to over political pressure, the police has subsequently released the offenders with no punitive action.

One of the most glaring incidents, though there are several others, has been the Mumbai police's treatment of Sena MP, Madhukar Sarpotdar, who was arrested by Major Goswami of the Indian army for possession of illegal arms during the riots and let off the same evening by Police Commissioner, Bapat. His conduct even within the jurisdiction of his parliamentary constituency, within both the Kherwadi and Nirmal Nagar areas, was incendiary and provocative, spreading canards and rumours rather than assisting the police in dousing the fires of communal hatred and even leading mobs to attack. (Pg. 162–163).

"Communal trouble started on December 6, 1992 in the Nirmal Nagar area with the desecration of a Ganesh idol in the Ganesh Mandir on A.K.Marg.....It appears to the Commission that this incident was a deliberate attempt on the part of some mischievous elements to whip up communal passions and stir up communal riots. Unfortunately the Hindu community in this area appears to have fallen prey to this game–plan, brainwashed by the local leaders of the Shiv Sena, including Madhukar Sarpotdar, who unleashed a barrage of propaganda that Muslims were responsible for the outrage. Though Shri Sarpotdar claimed to have some inside information that the miscreants were Gullu, Ilias and Dilawar, all Muslims, he did not bother to pass on the information to the police, nor did he inform the police as to the source of his information so that the police could carry on an effective investigation. Had the local MP Shri Sarpotdar displayed the same zeal in co–operating with the police, which he showed in making speculative and unfounded allegations, probably the miscreants could have been nailed. For unfathomable reasons, no such efforts were made by Shri Sarpotdar. (Pg. 157-158).

"While the police were prompt in arresting Muslim miscreants at all levels, they showed a marked reluctance to arrest any of the miscreants connected with the Shiv Sena. In fact, the assessments in the Crime Reports suggest that if accused belonging to the Shiv Sena were arrested, there was a likelihood of a flare–up in the communal situation and therefore it was decided that no Shiv Sainik should be arrested. This view was taken not only by the lower police echelons, but also had the approval of the Assistant Commissioner of Police and the zonal Deputy Commissioner of Police. Thus there have been cases where the accused Shiv Sainiks were charge–sheeted even without arrest and interrogations, apparently under the orders of DCP, Pande. It appears to the Commission, that repeated morchas and flexing of muscles by the Shiv Sena hierarchy and the crowds led by them, affected the police morale and psyche. (Pg.162, para 21.27).

There were several other incidents where police conduct was blatantly determined by the strong–arm tactics of the local Shiv Sena Shakha or Vibhag Pramukhs.

In the Agripada jurisdiction, within the BIT chawls with a preponderance of Hindu residents, the few Muslim residents were refused local police assistance when their homes were attacked with men (local Shiv Sainiks) throwing stones and carrying choppers. When one woman resident called the local police station, an unidentified person slammed down the phone saying, "Landyabai chup baitho, Abhi kuch nahin huva." Later, policemen assisted the mob trying to attack residents and loot their homes and it was the arrival of an army picket that saved them a day later.

(Pgs. 48–49). Two police constables were actually arrested in connection with rioting and causing damage to Muslim property along with local Shiv Sainiks. (Pg. 52, para 1.18).

Within the Antop Hill jurisdiction, after three Muslims were burnt alive in a taxi within barely 150 feet of the police picket on January 12, 1993. (Pg. 54, para 2.14). On January 15, 1993 the police arrested two persons in connection with this incident and on the same day a morcha of about 3,000–4,000 men and women led by Sena Shakha Pramukh, Prahlad Thombre, Sena MLA, Kalidas Kolamkar, Congress MLA, Eknath Gaikwad, Sena corporator, Krishna Vishwasrao, Congress corporator, Karuna Mhatre and others came to the police station and to secure the release of one of the accused, Bal Thombre.

The ATR is utterly silent on the role of Shiv Sainiks during the violence that have been referred to in Volume I of the report, particularly of one of the party's leader, Milind Vaidya, in leading attacks on mobs with the help of a policeman, also brandishing a naked sword.

The testimonies of former Mumbai Police Commissioner, Srikant Bapat and the then Additional Commissioner of Police, Mumbai, V.N. Deshmukh bear mention here. The former was indicted for his personal failure in guiding the Mumbai police with adequate authority during the December 1992–January 1993 riots. In his affidavit, Bapat failed to mention the Shiv Sena by name, a fact for which he had been pulled up by the Judge in open court. "Ergo, Commissioner of Police, Bapat, was able to assert boldly that he was not in any possession of any material to indicate that any party or organisation had a hand in the riots. Diplomacy is a quality appreciated in a diplomat; not in police officers. In fact, Bapat's argument that he would be unwilling to name the Shiv Sena as a communal party because it had been registered with the Election Commissioner flies in the face of the "Guidelines" issued by the government which were binding on him and which he was expected to implement." (Pg. 196, para 2.8).

Despite the existence of a state government guideline for "Dealing with communal disturbances", April 30, 1986 in which the RSS, the Shiv Sena and the names of some Muslim organisations are also cited, this instruction did not percolate down to the police station level for effective action. (Pg. 195–196).

Deshmukh's testimony was significant in that it has revealed how during the in the six–month period between January 1996 and June 1996, when the Sena–BJP combine had disbanded the Justice Srikrishna Commission, the state government and the police, for no explicable reason, had destroyed all police records pertaining to the riot period that were not in the possession of the Judge. This revelation was made by Deshmukh in court during his testimony and reveals, more than anything else, the mala fide intent of the alliance government in power. This detail has surprisingly escaped public debate and scrutiny.

"A significant fact admitted by Deshmukh is his assessment of the deep–rooted and biased belief among 80 percent of the lower echelons of the Mumbai police that Muslim youths were more prone to crime though he was quick to add that there was no such impression among senior officers." (Pg. 201, para 4.7). Following manifestations of this bias in 1992–93, some training measures have been initiated by the force. "Mr. Deshmukh was fair enough to accept that, possibly, this in–built impression amongst the members of the police force might have affected their handling the riot situations in December 1992 and January 1993. In any event, it was evident from the manner in which the members of the police force used to act and behave towards members of the Muslim community." (Pg. 201, para 4.7).

The ATR rejects this finding outright saying that the Mumbai police is by and large very secular. No comments are offered on the glaring individual lapses in police conduct used as substantive evidence to back its finding, by the Commission. In the stray cases of lapses, says the ATR without specification, "efforts would be made to enhance the secular character of the police." (Pg. 238, para 1.28–i).

The malaise which affected the functioning of the Mumbai police to such a degree that they failed to anticipate the outbreak of violence and therefore took no action against the provocative posturings of large and influential sections of Hindu communal organisations and, even after the demolition of the Babri Masjid took place, allowed provocative "victory celebrations" that spiralled, not contained, the violence. This laxity was also observed in allowing provocative speeches from sections of the Muslim minority at the outset of the violence.

The ATR is silent on administrative inaction in response to the provocative build–up of communal tension. In the initial stages it was a complete failure of intelligence in gauging the impact, on different sections of the population, of the demolition of the Babri Masjid at Ayodhya (Pg. 23, para 1.1), because of a complete absence of initiative and conviction in applying the "Guidelines for Communal Disturbances" that makes it incumbent on every police station to maintain the "list of communal goondas". (Pg. 34, para 1.7). Consequently, when the then Commissioner of Police instructed the police stations to round up these "communal goondas", there was wholesale confusion in understanding the import of the message, each Senior Police Inspector interpreting it in his own fashion.

The preventive rounding up was, therefore, confined only to known criminals and bad characters on the list of available police stations. (Pg. 196, para 2.8).

While rejecting the Commission's findings that a failure of intelligence about the impact of the kar seva in Ayodhya created further laxity and confusion in the Mumbai police, it has accepted administrative recommendations for a professionally better equipped force. Many of the Commission's recommendations deal with the urgent question of professionalism of the police force, better working conditions, both a dire need of the day. But within the scope of these findings, there are severe indictments for a force that once prided itself on being the best in the country. These observations deal with the growing evidence of communal bias in police conduct, a bias that has meant scant regard for the preservation of law and order among the men in uniform.

"Even after it became apparent that the leaders of the Shiv Sena were active in stoking the fire of the communal riots, the police dragged their feet on the facile and exaggerated assumption that if such leaders were arrested the communal situation would further flare up, or to put it in the words of then Chief Minister,

Sudhakarrao Naik, "Bombay would burn"; not that Bombay did not even burn otherwise. (Pg. 25, para 1.20).

Commission has directly implicated in the violence that offer a glimpse of the Mumbai of December 1992–January 1993, when it appeared that police station after police station had been virtually hijacked by the Shiv Sena and the spurious ideology of its allies. The more detailed Volume II examines 26 police station areas and documents for posterity the evidence of senior police officers that stand out either as shining examples of impartial and courageous action or as shameful instances of dereliction of duty sought to be subsequently covered by evasive testimonies.

On the question of wilful inaction against the incendiary Mahaartis, the report states that instead of firmly dealing with the law and order situation arising out of such provocative programmes, the police merely "left it to the political Judgement of the then Chief Minister who failed to act promptly and effectively by giving clear directives. (Pg. 23, para 1.1).

The Judge observes: "The response of police to appeals from desperate victims, particularly Muslims, was cynical and utterly indifferent. On occasions, the response was that they were unable to leave the appointed post; on others, the attitude was that one Muslim killed, was one Muslim less. The alertness of police pickets left much to be desired. Several arson incidents, stabbing and violence occurred within the eye–sight and earshot of the police pickets without any action by them. In one case, a bakery situated within the very compound in which the police station (Jogeshwari) is located was attacked, looted and burnt in broad daylight without the police lifting a finger. (Pg. 24, para 1.12).

The ATR is utterly silent on these lapses commented upon in the commission's report.That police officers and men, particularly at the junior level, appeared to have an in–built bias against Muslims was evident in their treatment of Muslims suspected of violent acts and Muslim victims of riots. The treatment given was harsh and brutal and, on occasions, bordering on inhuman, hardly doing credit to the police. "The bias of policemen was seen in the active connivance of police constables with the rioting Hindu mobs on occasions, with their adopting the role of passive on–lookers on occasions, and finally, in their lack of enthusiasm in registering offences against Hindus even when the accused were clearly identified, and post–haste classifying the cases in "A" summary." (Pages 12, 24).

The second volume of the report details numerous instances where the Mumbai police closed hundreds of cases thus, leaving the guilty unpunished. The ATR accepts the mala fide reasons for closing the cases but states that these will be re–opened only after a state government committee has examined each case thus closed. Only if found to be a valid case for re–examination, will such a re–examination take place. This in effect means that the prima facie findings of the Judicial Commission of inquiry are not being accepted outright but will be subject to executive scrutiny that, it is reasonable to suspect, given the guilt–ridden role of the current political regime, will be governed by a partisan pressure

"Even the registered riot–related offences were most unsatisfactorily investigated. The investigations showed lack of enthusiasm, lackadaisical approach and utter cynicism. Despite clear clues, the miscreants were not pursued, arrested and interrogated, particularly when the suspected accused happened to be Hindus with connections to Shiv Sena or were Shiv Sainiks. This general apathy appears to be the outcome of the built–in prejudice in the mind of an average policeman that every Muslim is prone to crime."

"The degeneration of the protests, which were initially not violent, in Minara Masjid area on 6th December 992 and Dharavi area on 7th December 1992 into violent riots was partly on account of insensitive handling of the rioters by police. The police should have realised that the Muslim community felt betrayed, hurt, humiliated and distrustful of the authorities on account of the demolition of the Babri Masjid in spite of the assurances and promises at the highest level and that too in the presence of armed police and para–military forces. Though there was some violence like stone–throwing, it should have been controlled by use of persuasion and minimal force."

The section entitled 'Delinquency of Police Personnel' bears mention. It is hear that justice Srikrishna lists the names of 15 police officials found guilty of gross prejudicial conduct. "The evidence before the Commission indicates that the police personnel were found actively participating in riots, communal incidents or incidents of looting arson and so on. The Commission strongly recommends that Government take strict action against the following persons:

Colaba: "S.I. Vasant Madhukar More, A.P.I. Sahebrao Hari Jadhav, PC–3181 Suresh Pandurang Ithape, PN–985 Shivaji Govindrao Kashid, PN–2238 Hanumant Pandurang Chavan and HC–3649 Gopichand Shaitram Borase. These police personnel were responsible for allowing the violent mob to hack to death one Abdul Razak alias Aba Kalshekar (C.R.No.13 of 1993)".

Agripada: "PC–23960 of LA–IV Ashok Naik and Rajaram K. Bhoir were arrested while indulging in rioting and violent activities (C.R.No.98 of 1993). Ashok Naik was arrested by N.M. Joshi Marg Police. No subsequent action was taken".

Byculla: "Sr. P.I. Patankar, P.I. Wahule and S.I. Ramdesai. Their conduct during the riots was extremely communal. They refused to record complaints in which Hindus were the accused and harassed and ill–treated Muslims. Their conduct indicated attempt to shield miscreants belonging to Shiv Sena (C.R. No. 591 of 1992). The Government should also institute an impartial inquiry into the cold–blooded murder of one young boy, Shahnawaz Hassanmiya Wagle. The inquiry conducted by Deputy Commissioner of Police Surinder Kumar is just an eyewash". (Pg. 71–72).

Dongri: "Joint Commissioner of Police R.D. Tyagi, Assistant Police Inspector, Deshmukh and Police Inspector Lahane of the Special Operation Squad are guilty of excessive and unnecessary firing resulting in the death of nine Muslims in the Suleman Bakery incident (C.R.No.46 of 1993). The ostensible reasons for this firing was that the police were "flushing out Kashmiri terrorists".

(Tyagi was rewarded for his conduct by being made police Commissioner in October 1995 by the Sena–BJP government. On retirement in early 1998, prior to the Lok Sabha elections, he declared, "I am a loyal soldier of Balasaheb.")

Mahim: "Police Constable Sanjay Laxman Gawade was openly indulging in riots and violent activities while carrying a naked sword along with Shiv Sena activist Milind Vaidya. Though the constable was placed under suspension and the sanction of the government was sought for his prosecution, the sanction had not yet been granted. The Commission recommends that such sanction should be granted".

L.T. Marg: "Assistant Police Inspector Kamath, for utter dereliction of duty by not acting against the miscreants in the Diamond Jubilee Compound incident (C.R.No.25 of 1993). They burnt down several Muslim hutments in that incident".

M.R.A. Marg: "PC–24242 Vidya-dhar Raghunath Shelar, Police Inspector Salvi, Police Sub–Inspector More. Babu Abdul Shaikh had been taken into custody by them. But because of their conduct, he was attacked and murdered by Hindu miscreants (C.R.No.579 of 1992). Though the accused, all active Shiv Sainiks, have been arrested, the conduct of the police personnel is not beyond reproof".

Nagpada: "Police Inspector Dhavale over–reacted by firing at a mob of 10–12 miscreants throwing stones, resulting in injury to a two–year–old child. Constable Sanjay Bhosale was part of the miscreant mob which broke open and looted articles from the shop 'Cat's Collections'".

Tardeo: "PC–7783 Shrirang Pathade, popularly known as "Richard Hawaldar", was openly collaborating with the Shiv Sainiks in looting and violent activities. These incidents took place over a period of several days and yet the officer was not restrained".

R.A.K. Marg: "Police Sub–Inspec-tor N.K. Kapse's act of unprovoked firing at Hilal Masjid killed seven Muslims (C.R.No.17 of 1993). The police prevaricated while recording evidence on this incident".

Antop Hill: "Inspector B.B. Shinge, Sub–Inspector Shivgonda Patil and Constables A.M. Ghadi, A.Y. Kamble, P.S. Dukare, D.R. Phadtare, S.P. Patil and B.K. Gaikwad failed to protect the lives and properties of the Muslim victims. Only one police officer, Senior Police Inspector, Vinayakrao Raosaheb Patil of the Antop Hill police station was removed from service with effect from

April 30, 1993 for reasons of developing a relationship with "criminals" and "communal elements' in Antop Hill Police station and thereby shielding them from government action. The communal elements in question are Shiv Sena MLA, Kalidas Kolamkar and Sena Shakha Pramukh, Bal Thombre. It was due to this connivance that a massive operation was launched by the Hindu miscreants in Pratikshanagar, some of whom openly professed their connections with the Shiv Sena. This massive operation is the combing and marking of Muslim homes for attack and holding to ransom 3,000–5,000 Muslims for three days and nights on the streets outside their homes without food or water". (Pgs. 53–59).

In each of these instances, the Commission has recommended that government take appropriate action. This means that criminal cases be launched against the guilty police officers immediately. Instead of accepting the Judge's findings as prima facie valid, the ATR says, "a committee under the Director General of Police and consisting of representatives of the Home, Law and Judiciary departments and the Director of Prosecution will further examine the cases for taking appropriate action.

This amounts to nothing short of delaying action, if not rejecting outright the Commission's findings on blatantly criminal, communal behaviour on the part of policemen.

This attitude as reflected in the ATR also amounts to a rejection of the prima facie findings of a Commission of inquiry. The mala fide motives behind this rejection are not far to find, given that in most of the cases the policemen are guilty of actions in collusion with Shiv Sainiks or at their behest. It is unlikely that the examination by this committee will not be similarly subject to partisan considerations.

The report also comments adversely on the abject failure of the Mumbai police in garnering the support of the army despite the fact that army patrols were holding flag marches and the army had been summoned into the metro due to the complete collapse of the state police administration. (Pg. 39, para 1.26). This reluctance to hand over charge to the army despite a fast deteriorating situation led to an avoidable loss of lives, limb and property.

The government rejects the observations of the Commission on the lack of co–ordination with the army but adds, "however steps would be taken to better such co-ordination." Some serious observations have been made by the Judge in his recommendations for avoiding such a collapse of the law and order machinery in future in the report. These pertain to the singular failure of the administration in "Maintaining Records with Reference to Communal Riots" (Pg. 34, para 1.17). Investigations with regard to Communal Offences and Investigations with regard to Riot–Related Offences that get classified into the 'A' category (True but undetected) letting communal riot–related crime go scot–free.

The ATR merely "notes" these recommendations and promises no action.

Sections 153(a) and (b) of the Indian Penal code that deal with "inciting hatred and violence against a particular religious community" have been used too sparingly by the police and the state government in this riot. Even in instances where the police did file cases, against Bal Thackeray particularly, these were delayed for lack of sanction by the earlier Congress(I) government and finally withdrawn by the current Shiv Sena–BJP combine. The then Additional Commissioner, V.N. Deshmukh's evidence reveals how out of the total of 24 cases filed against Thackeray, 16 could not proceed as the government did not grant sanction for prosecution; in six cases sanction had been granted and charge–sheets filed, but the Sena–BJP government decided to withdraw the cases and did so on August 28, 1996 and October 18, 1996. Two cases are still pending in the criminal courts. (Pg. 202, para 4.16).

There is no comment or explanation in the ATR of communally incendiary writings in the Saamna and Navaakal. Worse still, despite this conclusive evidence related to these 15 officers, the ATR rejects the conclusion of the judge on the widespread communal bias governing the acts of our policemen.

Justifying its assertion that the police force is efficient and completely unbiased, the ATR says:"The Commission blames the police for not having been able to control the riots effectively. However, the Government feels that although the police suffered from the paucity of number and resources, they brought the riots under control in minimum time and handled the riots effectively. The police opened fire 153 times in the first phase of riots during the December, 1992. In this, 30 Hindus 133 Muslims and 11 others died; and 93 Hindus, 189 Muslims and 10 others were injured. In the second phase police opened fire 308 times, i.e., double the number of the first phase. In this, 80 Hindus, 90 Muslims and one other died and 326 Hindus, 146 Muslims and 5 others were injured. If the number of dead and injured from both the communities is seen and the leadership and the role of the two communities in the riots is considered, the actions taken by the police does not show any bias against any community. Barring some exceptions, the Government cannot agree with the conclusion of the Commission that police assumed the role of mute spectators during the riots or that they even took part in the riots or that they had lost moral authority to control the riots. On the contrary, while controlling the riots, two police officers and 5 policemen were killed and 184 police officers and 312 policemen were injured. This shows that police sincerely tried to control the mobs firmly and impartially with complete disregard to the grave dangers to their lives.

"The Government feels that barring some stray exceptions, the police force is, by and large, secular, impartial and free from bias. The Government cannot accept the conclusion of the Commission based on stray evidence of one or two officers that the entire police force of Mumbai was communalised or polarised. The Government feels that such a statement could be the personal opinion of that police officer. The impartial way in which Mumbai police have handled these or other communal riots for the last many years, have adequately proved their secular and impartial character". (Pg. 245, para 35).

The history of the Mumbai of December 1992 and January 1993 is a sorry tale of a pathetic paralysis in the administration, compounded by instances of apathy or bias that governed the action of several policemen. Fifteen such cases have been documented in detail. One Police Inspector already dismissed from service for his shameful conduct. The ATR is utterly silent on refuting these specific allegations, resorting to the time–tested technique of the Sena–BJP combine in particular, and Hindutvawaadi forces in general, of resorting to unsubstantiated generalities. Instead of replying case–by–case to 15 cases of blatant communal bias that have been detailed, the ATR attempts to brush off these prima facie findings as the "opinions of individual police officers."

It has been no one's case that the victims of the riots were only Muslims, though the loss of property and business reveals a distinct pattern where the minority has been the target. Neither do the substantiated allegations of increasing anti–minority bias within the force ever suggest that the entire force is so communal. But again, left with no moral authority to refute the direct findings and prima facie conclusions drawn by the Commission, attempts to take shelter behind half–baked truths. A careful reading of the report and the ATR exposes this motivation of the Maharashtra government.

Significant observations have been made by thc Judge under the section, "Religious processions, meetings and use of loudspeakers" (Pg. 38, para 1.23). Since many such processions flare up into communal riots, particularly in congested areas where communities live side–by–side, the Judge has recommended that there should be a stricter control enforced in the matter of religious processions. Similarly, announcements on loudspeakers and religious observances in public places have also led to avoidable friction amongst different communities which have the potential for communal disturbances.

For example, the Commission has recommended that:

"It is recommended that there should be stricter control enforced in the matter of religious processions and a security deposit of not less than Rs. 5,000 should be taken from the organisers of religious processions who should also be called upon to execute a guarantee for the peaceful conduct of procession. If there is any disturbance by the processionists, the deposit should be forfeited and action taken against the organisers of the processions".

"Every religious procession is required to be accompanied by police to ensure that there is no disturbance or attacks upon the processionists or by them. It is suggested that the organisers should be made to pay the charges for deployment of police leaving the number of policemen to be determined by the Senior Police Inspector of the respective police station".

"Religious observances, whether by Hindus or Muslims or any other, in open public places so as to cause obstruction, annoyance or inconvenience to the citizens at large, must be strictly discouraged and action taken against those who defy the instructions of police".

The ATR merely "notes" these recommendations offering no comment nor promising any action. It is highly unlikely that a government headed by the Shiv Sena, a party who's political philosophy and method of mobilisation centres around the appropriation of religious and ostensibly religious festivals would be in any hurry to even accept, let alone implement, these recommendations.

Equally significant observations have been made by the Judge under the section, 'Political interference in police work') where he firmly recommends: "Once a prosecution has been launched against a person for rioting, it should under no circumstances be withdrawn. Not even the repeated ground of 'public interest' should permit prosecutions of communal offences to be withdrawn. It is not only demoralising to the police, but also sends wrong signals to the offenders that they can somehow get away with it." The ATR "notes" this, offering no comment or assurances. (Pg. 38, para 1.25).

8

Terrorism : A Burning Issue for India

India is reckoned as one of the most resourceful nations of the world having enviable potential to grow large and sit among the leading countries. Its journey of growth since its independence has been greatly remarkable, so much so that it was once looked upon as the emerging super power of the world. However, equal is the fact that today it is seen as one of the most terrorism-inflicted nations. Despite of its efforts to curb terrorist attacks in the country, India continues to be the easy target for various terrorist groups making it more and more vulnerable to their malice. There is no exaggeration in saying that India sits on the volcano of terrorism which can erupt anytime and anywhere making the country and its people suffer.

The rise of terrorism in India dates decades back to late 80s. The nation was first struck down with terror in March, 1993 when a series of 13 fatal bomb explosions shook the city of Mumbai killing more than 250 people. Mumbai – the financial capital of the country, since then, has been the most preferred target of the terrorist groups which have proven connections with Pakistan. The city has been attacked several times till date and the major terrorist attacks of July 2006 (explosions in local train killing more than 200) and the unprecedented attack of 26/11 in 2008 (taking toll of over 170 lives in co-ordinated series of attacks on a landmark train station and two of the prime hotels of Mumbai) are still fresh in the memory of the citizens of Mumbai and the entire nation.

Terrorism inspired by Islamic extremists and separatist forces, over years, has loomed large enough in India to caste its vicious shadow on the entire nation. From the very sensitive state Jammu and Kashmir to major cities like Delhi, Bangalore, Hyderabad, Coimbatore, Ahmedabad, Jaipur etc. and several small towns/ suburbs/cities have been affected by terrorist attacks at some point of time in the last two decades.

The country fell prey to few more explosions from relentless terrorist groups this year (two blasts in Hyderabad, one in Bangalore, a terrorist attack on army jawans in Srinagar and a series of bomb blasts in Mahabodhi Temple – a world heritage site in Bihar).

It has been long known and proven that terrorism in India is largely evoked by Pakistan-bred and Pakistan-supported international terrorist groups like Lashkar-e-Taiba (LeT), Jaish-e-Muhammad, Harkat-ul-Mujahadeen (HuM), Students Islamic Group of India (SIMI), Indian Mujahideen, etc. Nothing has changed in all these years, the feeling of insecurity and uncertainty still pervades as these terrorist groups have grown larger, stronger and fearless.

Adding fuel to the fire, India is hit with growing concern about domestic or internal terrorism creating atmosphere of violent unrest in some parts of the nation, especially the north-eastern states of India. The infamous insurgent communist groups like Naxalites, Maoists and ULFA (The United Liberation Front of Assam) are particularly active in rural central and eastern India with an aim to overthrow government.

Why India is a soft target for terrorists?

Terrorism, in last decade, has become a global phenomenon with its widespread outreach across nations including the super power United States of America. After the devastating attack of 9/11 on The World Trade Centre of USA, terrorism and terrorist organizations have globally come to be considered as the greatest threat to peace, prosperity, humanity and safety of the world. Post 9/11 terrorist attack, the issue of terrorism, which had hardly shown its face to the developed world earlier, grew as a matter of serious concern for the entire world. The US, in collaboration with UN, immediately declared their 'War against Terrorism' giving out the message that such heinous anti-human and anti-social acts of terror cannot be tolerated.

For India, the nation of a billion people, the issue is much more challenging as it has been suffering from terrorism eversince. India has been intermittently struck down by a few terrorists taking toll of thousands of lives till date which has raised severe questions on the capability of the nation and its government to deal with this grave issue. One has to accept and government need to admit that India has been and continues to remain as a vulnerable nation in face of terrorism. While the issue needs to be addressed with stringent and firm measures, India has considerably failed in curtailing acts of both internal and external terrorism.

One of the major reasons why India is an easy and soft target for terrorist organizations is the complacent attitude of the government. While government is expected to take bold actions against terrorists, UPA government's liberal attitude in controlling the terrorist activities has exacerbated the problem during its reign. The government guises its cold approach towards eliminating terrorism under the mask of Gandhian philosophy of peace and has always been inclined to resolve the issue through compromise. This certainly has not done any good to the citizens of the country who actually go through all the torment and suffer each time the explosions and violence disrupt their lives.

To have a strong counter-terrorism mechanism, a nation requires 1. strong political will and determination to end terrorism regardless of electoral consequences, 2. stringent policies and laws with equally stringent implementation independent of government interference and 3. high end intelligence. It is the need of the hour that India get a sound counter-terrorism mechanism in order to combat the issue of both internal and external terrorism with outcome oriented approach instead of doing away with 'compromise' and leaving the citizens to suffer.

Zero Tolerance is the only way out

People of India have tolerated enough since ages. It's high time for the authorities to rise up and take a bold stand against terrorism in order to safeguard its people, its resources and above all its pride.

The United States of America, the biggest advocate of human rights in the world, has made rigorous anti-terrorism laws like The Patriot Act 2001. Many other countries (which were not or minimally affected by terrorism before) like France, Japan, Bangladesh, Indonesia, Malaysia, China, Hongkong etc. also became alert after 9/11 and took proactive steps by making special laws against terrorism. This shows that governments of these nations are concerned and serious about the safety and security of its people. Where do we stand? Indian UPA government did pass a Prevention of Terrorism Act (POTA) in 2002 expanding its powers in fighting out terrorism. But surprisingly and unreasonably enough, it repealed POTA in 2004 on the grounds of protection of human rights advocated by a handful of 'five star human rights activists'! The question here arises, is government more concerned about the rights of the brutal anti-national, anti-human extremists than the rights of a billion of its innocent people to live free and safe in their land?

The government is overlooking some serious adverse effects which conspire to handicap the nation in multiple ways. A nation can grow and prosper only when peace and harmony prevails all over the country, not when it constantly lives under the shadow of terror. The never ending story of bombings and attacks in India not only suffocates its progress but it pushes back the nation in fast growing world despite of having maximum population of promising and talented youth. It has left people in state of fear and despair in their own homeland. Moreover, the moment an outsider intrudes on our land to ruin the peace and harmony and succeeds in his mal-intentions; it is a hard blow on our face, our pride and dignity. How long can we, as a nation, tolerate that? Should a government tolerate that? The only answer is NO.

Fighting against terrorism is a fight for humanity. And it has to be fought with strictest of laws and action. It calls for zero tolerance to such evil forces and giving them a 'tit for tat', as it is said "Eet ka jawab patthar se". The people of India are frustrated out of government's dormancy. They now seek a bold and fearless leadership that can release the nation from the strangles of violence and destruction inflicted by internal and external forces.

India can defeat terrorism

US, which commendably made the first terrorist attack on its land the last one with its grit and gumption, is an example for us to look upon. India has the resources and courage to fight any situation that poses a threat to the nation. All we need is an able leadership, strong political will, better policing, strong legal tools and stringent implementation of laws in an unbiased manner. Together they will play a vital role in defeating terrorism and establishing atmosphere of peace all over the nation.

THE TERROR, THE THREAT AND THE TWIST

THE INDIAN Mujahideen are both a grave threat and a complex puzzle for this country. As recently as June-end, the Gujarat Police released the interrogation report of one of IM's key operatives, Danish Riyaz, 29, a software engineer from Ranchi. The Crime Branch had arrested him on 22 June at Vadodara railway station aboard the Secunderabad-Rajkot Express after a tip-off. He was accused of sheltering Abdul Subhan Qureshi in Ranchi, allegedly a mastermind of the Delhi and Ahmedabad blasts of 2008. Under interrogation, (TEHELKA has a copy of this report) Riyaz said that at the moment, the organisation was lying low as most of its operatives were in jails across various parts of the country. He also maintained that with the few number of operatives left, it was a difficult task for the IM to operate in the country and generate any FUNDS. However if news reports appearing on TV channels are to be believed, then Riyaz has now told investigators post the Mumbai blasts that many key IM members who had managed to flee India after the 2008 Batla House encounter were now in touch with the Taliban and were receiving training in Saudi Arabia and across Pakistan. A surprising variation from his earlier statement of the IM being on a backfoot.

"At this point, Riyaz has not said anything with which we can link him to the Mumbai blasts. But yes, what we found during interrogation gives a sense of how people are recruited and the modus operandi. I don't think that he can be directly blamed at this time," Ahmedabad Police Commissioner Sudhir Sinha told TEHELKA.

Mansoor, Subhan, most of the IM operatives are intelligent, suave, articulate, the kind of executive one sees in MNCs. In fact, Hemant Karkare, the slain ATS chief who made the first arrests of IM operatives after a string of bomb blasts across the country in 2008, was so perplexed by their profile that he had told this reporter, "What does one make of these men? Look at their backgrounds. Their academic excellence can put one to shame."

The story of the Indian Mujahideen is both a riddle and a demystifier for the security establishment. Riddle because most of its recruits don't fit the description of a typical madrassa-educated jihadi who subscribes to the obscurantist Wahabi or Salafi school of Islamic thought. Nor do they come from extremely impoverished and socially backward backgrounds, one in which the unemployed Muslim youth, often brought up in large and poor families, get lured by the quick bucks of the ISI agents looking for easy recruits.

Most of the IM operatives arrested in 2008 were not overtly religious and had been educated at regular public or convent schools. In fact, until they joined the IM, a majority of the suspects had almost no leaning towards Islamic learning and thoughts. Even after joining the IM, the burning desire to avenge the 2002 Gujarat riots and the Babri Masjid demolition, and not the pan global ideology of Jihad, had been their main driving force.

Atif Ameen, the IM operative who was killed in the Batla House encounter and who was one of the founding members of the outfit, had a girlfriend. A day before the encounter, 12 IM operatives had assembled at the Batla House apartment and had pizza and Coke for dinner. Almost all of them were active on social networking sites, mainly scouring for new girlfriends. Their Twitter and Facebook accounts later proved to be an important source of information for the sleuths.

A spate of dreadful terror strikes between 2005-08, starting with the 2005 Delhi Diwali blasts and ending with the 2008 Delhi serial blasts, were carried out by a motley crew of college students, software engineers, mechanics, doctors, educationists and small-time criminals. After every blast, all of them used to return to their routine work — students back to colleges, professionals back to their salaried jobs and businessmen back to trading in commodities.

Their only glue was their alienation from the Indian society and disaffection towards government agencies, largely due to some real and some imagined complicity of the State in the anti-Muslim riots.

The counter-terrorism agencies in India had been trained to look for clues of blasts in the chitter-chatter of phone and email communication between Kashmiri militants and their handlers in Pakistan, in the telephone intercepts of ISI agents talking to their operatives in Dhaka and Nepal and in the interrogation reports of Pakistani or Bangladeshi infiltrators arrested from the borders.

Pakistan and the terror outfits operating from there were at the centre of all our counter-terrorism efforts. Though on and off, some of their Indian accomplices were also identified and arrested, the latter mostly performed the role of coolies or couriers for small monetary considerations. Or in the case of the 2006 Mumbai serial blasts, a few old members of the Students Islamic Movement of India (SIMI) were wrongfully arraigned along with seven unidentified and ficticious Pakistani nationals. The SIMI members were accused by the Maharashtra Police of providing logistical support to the unnamed Pakistani terrorists.

But the unravelling of the Indian Mujahideen in 2008 changed the narrative of Islamist terrorism in India. The Batla House encounter came as a rude awakening to the hard reality of homegrown Islamist terrorism for the law enforcement agencies.

The boys who formed the core of this terror outfit did have some financial and logistical support from the ISI in Pakistan, but they were not the handmaiden of any foreign terror outfit or agency, being remote-controlled from across the border. The logistical and theological ties with the Lashkar-e-Toiba (LET) and the ISI were incidental and tactical but not essential to their existence.

And because this new generation of jihadis had no previous criminal records (unlike the 1993 Mumbai serial blasts accused) or known radical Islamic leanings (like the office-bearers of SIMI), they managed to operate under the radar even as Indian agencies kept groping in the dark.

Bangladesh-based HuJI and Pakistan's LeT were the primary suspects after every terror strike in India. And often when there was no Pakistani or Bangladeshi national to catch or kill in an encounter, the local SIMI activists were made the fall guy.

At least three major terror cases – the 2005 Diwali blasts, the 2006 Varanasi blasts and the 7/11 Mumbai train blasts – were wrongly attributed by the Indian agencies. In the Diwali blasts, Kashmiri militants were held accused, in the Varanasi blasts a Muslim cleric with known connection to HuJI was held as the main accused. While in the 7/11 blasts, some former SIMI members were accused by the agencies. Later, investigations revealed that the Indian Mujahideen was behind all these blasts.

GRAPPLING TO make sense of this new phenomenon, at a press conference to announce the arrests of the 2008 Ahmedabad blasts accused, then Gujarat Police Commissioner PC Pande had said rather superficially: "You remove S and I from SIMI and it becomes IM."

But the IM and its foundation, much like its founders, is a product of complex communal configurations. The genesis of the IM dates back roughly to the same time that the Hindu right-wing terror outfit Abhinav Bharat was formed. Hate is the trigger. While Abhinav Bharat wanted a Hindu Rashtra, the IM, going by its mails, wanted to avenge the atrocities against Indian Muslims.

Its founder was Aamir Raza Khan, alleged to be close to the Jaish-e-Mohammed (an organisation known for its operations across PoK and in Nepal). His brother Asif joined hands with Aftab Ansari, a small-time crook, to carry out various kidnappings, including the famous case of businessman Bhaskar Parekh's son and that of Kolkata businessman Partho Roy Burman in 2000. A CBI report mentions that one-fourth of the Rs 4 crore ransom money was given to Mohammad Atta via Mullah Omar to carry out the 9/11 terror attacks and a part of the money was used in the Parliament attacks.

Stress Proves Fatal

Those in the know dismiss this development as being significantly linked to the Mumbai blasts, just as they dismiss the involvement of 42-year-old Faiz Usmani, the elder brother of Afzal Usmani, who is behind bars in Ahmedabad on suspicion of being an IM member.

Interestingly, the Mumbai ATS had just days before the blasts arrested two suspected IM members Mohammed Mobin Abdul Shakoor Khan alias Irfan, 32, and his cousin Ayub Raja Amin Shaikh, 28, for allegedly providing logistical help to Afzal Usmani in the Gujarat blasts of 2006.

Faiz, who was picked up by the Maharashtra ATS after the 13 July Mumbai blasts on grounds of being a conduit for his brothers Afzal and Riyaz Bhatkal, had been making frequent trips to Ahmedabad ever since his brother was arrested. When TEHELKA met him in an Ahmedabad court, Afzal said his brother had only been coming to Ahmedabad to bail him out, quite a plausible explanation.

But the Mumbai Crime Branch arrested Faiz and interrogated him. He was brought to the hospital unconscious and died after attempts to revive him in the ICU failed. The provisional post-mortem report (pending chemical analysis) says that the cause of death appears to be brain haemorrhage.

His family has demanded a investigation, saying that it believes he died due to torture by the police to extract a 'confession' about having played a role in the blasts or some knowledge of the plot.

Ruheda, his wife and mother of six children, believes that her husband died because he was hung upside during interrogation and hence the brain haemorrhage. An inquiry has been initiated by the CID into the death and also to ascertain if whether his arrest was a mistake by the state ATS.

His arrest has created the same kind of furore amongst the community as post the arrest of Samad Bhatkal and earlier Danish Riaz (a journalist, earlier arrested for being an accomplice in the Mumbai 7/11 train blasts). Both were released by the police after it was found that the arrest was a case of mistaken identity.

No wonder, the minority community is watching investigations into the case with great consternation, fearing arbitrary arrests in the wake of the blasts, especially what it considers face-saving exercises by the police to show that it is making progress.

A high-ranking Ahmedabad Police official, who played a key role in the encounter killing of Asif Raza Khan in Rajkot in 2002, feels it is possible that Mullah Omar, Aftab Ansari and Asif knew each other, but the money trail seems dubious.

They were incarcerated in the same cell at Tihar jail during 1996-2000. While Khan was arrested for the possession of RDX, Ansari was held in a murder case and Omar in an abduction case.

It was to avenge his brother's death that Aamir Raza and Aftab Ansari carried out the firing on the American Centre in Kolkata on 22 January 2002, believed to be the first attack carried out by the IM.

Although the organisation did not claim responsibility, two groups rang up newspaper offices – one claiming to be from Bangladesh's Harkat-ul-Jihad al-Islami (HuJI) and the other from the Asif Raza Commandos – a front for the LeT said to have been formed by Aamir Raza before he fled to Pakistan. Aftab Ansari, a law graduate from Benares Hindu University, is married to a Pakistani national and is alleged to have strong links with the underworld. He was arrested after he escaped to Dubai for the shootout at the American Centre and has been in custody in Kolkata since 2002. He had, in fact, boasted about his role in the attack.

He is known to have worked closely for HuJI in India and has been responsible for operations in both India and Nepal. It is from this landmark year, 2002, that Aamir is said to have begun interacting with former SIMI members, as per the confessions of two of the accused, Sadiq Israr and Ansar Ahmed Basha, both residents of Cheeta camp in Turbhe, a Mumbai suburb dominated by Muslims from South India.

But who introduced these SIMI members to Aamir Raza and how did the Indian Mujahideen then come into being? It is here, the agencies say, begins an important link. Intelligence agencies say it was the Shahbandari brothers Riyaz and Iqbal, now infamous as the Bhatkal brothers because they hail from a sleepy town in Karnataka with same name, who introduced Aamir to SIMI, an organisation that many Muslims turned to post the 1993 Mumbai riots. The brothers are being projected as the key faces of the IM.

Riyaz, a charmer, would tell friends that he was ashamed SIMI was so 'spineless', while SIMI office-bearers at Kurla disapproved of what they called his brainwashing of other boys.

Iqbal, a bully who stammered, was unpopular in the Kurla bylanes and in the famous Manish market of Mumbai were he would sell perfumes. The Bhatkal brothers, whose father was in business, were not very pious. "They were your regular jeans-clad boys, no beards, not punctilious with prayers. In fact, they hardly had anything to do with religion," adds one of their friends.

By 2003, the agencies say, the Bhatkal brothers had come in contact with most of the IM operatives. They were angry at the Jamaat-e-Islami, the parent organisation of SIMI, for not being more radical.

They wanted to put up posters across Muslim hubs asking the brotherhood to come together. They were also angry that the perpetrators of the Gujarat riots were allowed to go scot-free. Soon an action plan was chalked out. Sadiq Shaikh (the prime accused in the Mumbai train blasts case of 2006, then behind bars and now absconding) and Abdul Subhan Qureshi alias Tauqeer were asked to identify boys from predominantly Muslim areas in Hyderabad, Azamgarh, Mumbai and Ahmedabad. A desire for revenge for the Babri Masjid demolition and the Gujarat carnage became a common cause.

The year 2007 was when the blasts started, a goal the IM — which no one had heard of before — had been working towards. The chargesheets say Atif Ameen and his Azamgarh module were responsible for providing manpower, Sadiq Shaikh did the liaison work, Iqbal Bhatkal looked after the media cell and Riyaz Bhatkal arranged bomb components and explosives. Brigades were formed: the Sahabuddin brigade to conduct strikes in the south, the Mohd Gaznavi brigade in the north and Shaheed al-Zarqaavi brigade to target VVIPs. Going by the confession statements of the accused and official papers submitted by a collective of Delhi Police Special Cell, Mumbai ATS, Jaipur SIT and the Andhra Pradesh Octopus, these are the statistics: More than 215 people have been killed in the blasts blamed on the IM, including the Lumbini Park and the Gokul Chaat Bhandar blasts in Hyderabad (25 August 2007); the blasts in Uttar Pradesh courts (20 November 2007), Jaipur blasts (13 May 2008); Bengaluru blasts (25 July 2008); Gujarat blasts (26 July 2008) and the Delhi blasts of September 2008. Since then, across the country, close to 65 arrests have been made and the accused chargesheeted.

Absconders still run close to 50, with about 1,000 witnesses testifying. The modus operandi was similar: ammonium nitrate and cellphone alarms were used in all the blasts. This, too, was the case in the recent Mumbai blasts.

But the emails were missing. Right after the other blasts, a mail would be sent by hacking into wi-fi accounts of unsuspecting residents, saying: "We the Indian Mujahideen take responsibility for the attacks. This is our answer to the brutal arrests and injustice by the police in the country."

TWO YEARS ago, TEHELKA's cover story (*Chilling Confession* , 8 August 2009) showed how the star witness in the Gujarat blasts case – on the basis of whose confessions the police arrested 22 people – backtracked. The witness (his name was concealed to protect his identity) said that most of the arrested were innocent, and the blasts were the handiwork of young Muslim boys who had come from outside. TEHELKA had in its investigation also ventured into the Sabarmati Jail and spoken to the accused, including the ever-changing 'masterminds' in the case. It was then that we raised questions on how, if the intelligence agencies were keeping a surveillance on former SIMI members, they could have managed to carry out the blasts.

The same question can be raised now. The Mumbai Police had taken into custody two alleged IM operatives. One of them, Faiz Usmani, died in police custody last week. Agencies interrogating him maintained that he was a conduit for his brother Iqbal Usmani, now behind bars for the Ahmedabad blasts, and Riyaz Bhatkal. If he was indeed part of the conspiracy, why was there no prior intelligence? Sadiq Shaikh too is in custody and his interactions should have led them to others. If Danish Riyaz, touted to be liaising with the Taliban and his Pakistan handlers, was arrested by the Gujarat Police last month, why was no intelligence gathered from him? During 5-18 June, the Madhya Pradesh ATS arrested 18 IM members. So if the activities of all former SIMI members and their regroupings are being monitored, how come no clues were picked up?

When TEHELKA travelled across three states in 2009 to get a perspective on the IM from the agencies and those arrested, it did not seem that there was any SIMI connection. The alleged members were all freshers, religious youngsters in their early 20s and 30s. In Pune, most of those involved were a part of the Quran Foundation; in Surat, it was the Khidmat group. In Delhi, it was Atif Ameen's close-knit friends circle. In Andhra Pradesh, it was a group called Sarani, formed by a group of tech-savvy Muslim boys.

There did not seem to be any money flowing in or any FINANCIAL lure — only a desire to fight atrocities against Muslims. Babri Masjid, Chechnya, Palestine were the touchstones. The youngsters had not personally suffered but empathised with those who had. For instance, the anonymous star witness who spoke to TEHELKA said he was traumatised by the bloodbath at Dani Limda, an area that saw the worst possible communal riots in the 2002 Gujarat carnage. Mansoor Peerbhoy, according to a friend at his company Yahoo, was an art lover, one of the smartest software executives he had ever known.

It does appear that those arrested are either at the bottom rung of the IM hierarchy or have been arrested for merely sheltering the accused. Key players — Riyaz, Yasin and Iqbal Bhatkal, Aamir Raza Khan, Alamzeb Afridi and Subhan Qureshi — are absconding.

So is Atif Ameen, not yet absolved in the Delhi blasts. Qureshi was in fact in Gujarat a month before the blasts in Ahmedabad, a fact that has been proven by the statements of the accused and the witnesses. Yet he was not caught. If the Halol camp near Vadodara was indeed a meeting of former SIMI members and others like Qayamuddin Kapadia, then what was the state

Intelligence Bureau doing? Gujarat Police have named 49 accused as being involved in the blasts in the state. Each police station is investigating the cases in its jurisdiction individually instead of clubbing them together.

The names of five alleged masterminds have been publicised one after the other, but it is not clear on what basis. They are Abu Bashar Siddiqui, Subhan Qureshi, Sajid Mansuri, Yunus Mansuri and Mufti Haleem. Take Abu Bashar Siddiqui, a madrassa teacher from Bina Para town in Azamgarh, who was probably inducted by Subhan Qureshi.

Qureshi's family, including his sister and ailing father, have been tortured, if the family is to be believed. His brother Noman Qureshi, an educated individual working for a respectable firm, says the family has not heard from him since he left home. "Our scars are still fresh... we have endured so much that I do not want to talk about it. My father is ailing," he says.

Siddiqui has been spending time in jails of many states after his arrest, while his family and social justice organisations questioned the way he was arrested. His brother Abu Zafar said, "My brother was picked up… or rather dragged from our village on 14 August 2010. The entire village will vouch for that. But here the offcials are saying that he was arrested on the 16th from Lucknow. They have started the case with a lie."

ANOTHER IM 'mastermind' named in the past, Sadiq Shaikh, 40, was said to be behind the Mumbai train blasts and also acted as recruiter and conspirator in the Delhi and the Gujarat blasts.

Ironically, the Maharashtra ATS, which had till then maintained that the IM was not involved in the train blasts, found itself caught on the wrong foot when a video was released to a news channel in 2009 by the Gujarat Police.

It showed Shaikh saying that he had carried out the train blasts at the instance of the IM. Maharashtra ATS did some damage control by saying that Shaikh was indeed the man responsible for the train blasts but had done so at the behest of HuJI. It was this contradiction that led the Mumbai High Court to acquit Shaikh in the train blasts case. But Shaikh is still behind bars in Ahmedabad, now for the Gujarat and Delhi blasts. In short, the police of these two adjoining states, which have held IM responsible for making their territories prime targets, have been unable to avert attacks allegedly carried out by it, or to name the kingpins.

"It's the investigation and the manner of handling the case, the lack of coordination, that has gone against the agencies. There is no doubt that these men were involved but trying to put them in wrong cases to justify their arrest is what puts the agencies on the wrong foot," says a Maharashtra home department official.

Originally from Azamgarh, UP, Shaikh stayed with his family at Cheeta camp in Mumbai. After having taken a course in refrigeration, Shaikh worked at a Godrej office for five years before moving on to a logistical company called CMS. His company records show that he was present in the city on the day of the Gujarat blasts. His brother Asad, who owns a poultry shop, says their father has been shocked into complete silence. "They tell us that he did the Mumbai blasts, the Gujarat blasts, that he went to Pakistan and Bangladesh... How could he go without a passport? He has always stayed with us or at Azamgarh — people there will vouch for it," he trails off.

His family points out that Shaikh was taken into custody when he left for office on 17 August. When he did not reach, his company called twice asking for him. Later in the day, Shaikh called, saying he would be gone for two days. When he did not return, his sister-in-law called him. Sadiq picked up the phone and said he was busy and would be back in two days. He could not be reached after this.

His family came to know of his arrest only when the Crime Branch called them on the 24th saying that he had been arrested. The Mumbai Police called him the foreign hand responsible for forming the IM with LeT handlers.

Special Cell officials have told TEHELKA that the chargesheet has named al-Qama after Shaikh confessed to his involvement. If that was indeed the truth, then why is it that Shaikh missed out on his name in his confession to the Mumbai Police. The Mumbai Police which had officially stated that the handlers for the 26/11 attacks and that for the Indian Mujahideen were not the same surprisingly submitted a confession of Sadiq Sheikh in the IM chargesheet in which he has named Al-Qama as their operator, the alleged key LeT handler of the 26/11 attacks.

IN HIS confession, a copy of which is with TEHELKA, he has said: "In Bahalwalpur, we were brought to an LeT camp where we met someone called Azam Cheema. From there we were sent to Muzaffarpur where we were given training in Umalpura camp for 25 days. After that we were sent to Bahawalpur where in a desert area we were taught how to make explosives... After that I was sent on a Pakistani passport to Kathmandu in March 2001. After that we reached our village via Patna. I stayed in Para for around two months in Sarai Meer. That's where I met Arif Badar. We both had a SIMI background so we gelled well. We spoke about sending guys to Pakistan for training. I gave Arif Dadar a contact number for Dubai and then returned to Dubai.

"In 2003, Shahnawaz and Rashid (both absconding) reached Dubai. We made Pakistani passports and went to Karachi. We went to a training centre and I stayed in Defence Colony. It's there that I met Colonel Aatif. He gave me two envelopes and asked me to give it to Aamir Raza. I gave it to Aamir in Dubai. Aamir Raza was given a lot of MONEY by the Pakistani Army to create trouble in India."

At the time of going to press, the Maharashtra Home Secretary told TEHELKA: "It would be too early to comment on the involvement of the Indian Mujahideen as far as the current investigation is concerned. We are considering other leads too. But yes, the Indian Mujahideen has been a cause of worry for us. It's a serious threat and we have been working to crack down on the modules."

In conclusion, one can say that it is too early to predict that the Indian Mujahideen is behind the blasts. But investigations into past terror incidents remain shrouded in controversy, with agencies contradicting each other. There do not seem to be any masterminds behind bars, only the operatives who carried out orders from above.

As for those behind bars, they continue to be undertrials for years on end because neither the Maharashtra ATS nor the Gujarat

ATS have built a foolproof case against them. Nor has their being in custody proved fruitful from the point of view of eliciting intelligence and crucial information or to prevent further attacks.

On top of that, there is definite intelligence that fugitives like Yasin and Riyaz Bhatkal have been visiting their home in Karnataka. While the agencies have their handicaps, the practice of arresting easy suspects creates a false complacence and does not help to nab the real perpetrators. And the nation lives with the consequences.

Bibliography

Burki, Shahid Javed: *Pakistan: The Continuing Search for Nationhood,* Westview Press, 1991.

Das. P.K.: *Jihad : Terrorist Strategies Against the West,* Sumit Enterprises, Delhi, 2009.

Dilip H. Mohite : *Rise of Islamic Fundamentalism and the Grand American Strategy* : Kalinga, Delhi, 2002.

Gupta, J.B. Das : *Islamic Fundamentalism and India* : Hope India Publications, Delhi, 2002.

Hiro, Dilip : *Holy Wars: The Rise of Islamic Fundamentalism* New York: Routledge, Chapman and Hall, Inc., 1989.

John O. Voll : *Islam: Continuity and Change in the Modern World,* Syracuse, New York: Syracuse University Press, 1994.

Laquer, Walter, *The New Terrorism: Fanaticism and the Arms of Mass Destruction,* Oxford: Oxford University Press, 1999.

Laquer, Walter: *Terrorism Attack from Computer Hacking,* Oxford: Oxford University Press, 1999.

Multani, R K P : *Islamic Fundamentalism in South Asia* : Sumit Enterprises, Delhi, 2007.

Qureshi, A. Iqbal : *Islam and the Theory of Interest,* Kitab Bhavan, New Delhi, 1994.

Sharma, Rajeev: *Global Jihad : Current Patterns and Future Trends,* Kaveri Books, Delhi, 2006.

Spindlove, J. R.: *Terrorism today: The past, the players, the future,* Upper Saddle Creek, NJ: Prentice Hall, 2000.

Thomas Arnold: *The Spread of Islam in the World, A History of Peaceful Preaching,* Goodword Books, 2001.

Whitaker, D. J.: *The Terrorism Reader,* New York: Routledge, 2001.

Index